Taste *of* Home.
GRANDMA'S FAVORITES

TASTE OF HOME BOOKS • RDA ENTHUSIAST BRANDS, LLC • MILWAUKEE, WI

© 2023 RDA Enthusiast Brands, LLC.
1610 N. 2nd St., Suite 102,
Milwaukee WI 53212-3906
All rights reserved. Taste of Home
is a registered trademark of RDA
Enthusiast Brands, LLC.

Visit us at **tasteofhome.com** for other
Taste of Home books and products.

International Standard Book Number:
D 978-1-62145-993-4
U 978-1-62145-994-1

Component Number:
D 117600116H
U 117600118H

Chief Content Officer, Home & Garden:
Jeanne Sidner
Content Director: Mark Hagen
Creative Director: Raeann Thompson
Senior Editor: Christine Rukavena
Assistant Editor: Sammi DiVito
Senior Art Director: Courtney Lovetere
Deputy Editor, Copy Desk:
Dulcie Shoener
Senior Copy Editor: Ann Walter
Contributing Designer: Jennifer Ruetz

Cover Photography:
Photographer: Mark Derse
Set Stylist: Melissa Franco
Food Stylist: Josh Rink

Pictured on front cover:
Mini Blueberry Bundt Cakes, p. 255

Pattern: Ann_and_Pen/Getty Images

Pictured on back cover:
French Onion Tortellini Soup, p. 181;
Beef Wellington with Madeira Sauce, p. 103;
Favorite Mediterranean Salad, p. 169

Printed in China
1 3 5 7 9 10 8 6 4 2

CONTENTS

W hy not take a seat in Grandma's kitchen, a cozy spot where the welcome is always warm (and so are the cookies), the recipe box is overflowing and the table is never too full for another person to join in the merriment. With *Taste of Home*'s latest edition of *Grandma's Favorites,* you can relive the cherished memories of Grandma's kitchen—one recipe at a time!

Whether you want a slow-cooked supper that simmers for hours or a dish that's done in a dash, this timeless collection containing over 300 of Grandma's beloved recipes has you covered for every occasion.

Bring the family together with:

- **Grandma's Favorite Breakfasts.** Sleepovers at Grandma's were always a special occasion, but the real treat was waking up to a fresh stack of pancakes or a cheesy egg bake.

- **Grandma's Favorite Main Dishes.** There's no shortage of mouthwatering mains to try on Grandma's menu—comforting meals like potpie, chipped beef, roast chicken and pulled pork.

- **Grandma's Favorite Soups & Stews.** Don't even think about going to bed hungry when plenty of bowlfuls of butternut squash, baked potato or beef noodle soup are ready to be enjoyed.

- **Grandma's Favorite Cakes & Pies.** It's nearly impossible to stop at just one serving when Grandma is dishing up slices of her bubbling fruit pies and sky-high cakes.

No matter what time-honored dish your family is clamoring for, we've got you covered. The only hard part will be trying to decide which you like more—the unforgettable entrees, sides, snacks, soups that fill the pages of this cookbook, or the sentiment attached to each tasty bite.

DOUBLE CHOCOLATE
BANANA MUFFINS,
PAGE 88

SUNDAY DINNER MENUS

Whether you're new to meal planning or a longtime pro, consider this handy guide that relies on recipes from this book to create complete meals.

Pot Roast with Gravy, p. 123 • Grandma's Cornbread Dressing, p. 154 • Special Radicchio-Spinach Salad, p. 142 • Lemon & Lime Strawberry Ice, p. 295

Spinach Salmon Bundles, p. 122 • Lentil White Bean Pilaf, p. 159 • Garlic-Roasted Brussels Sprouts with Mustard Sauce, p. 157 • Classic Creme Brulee, p. 273

Prosciutto Phyllo Roll-Ups, p. 46 • Herby Chicken with Apricots & Feta, p. 138 • Royal Broccoli Souffle, p. 145 • Lavender Lemon Bars, p. 210

Sausage-Stuffed Shells, p. 133 • Herbed Cheese Sticks, 78 • Favorite Mediterranean Salad, p. 169 • Surprise Meringues, p. 232

Fried Cheese Ravioli, p. 50 • Chicken Parmesan Burgers, p. 131 • Roasted Peppers & Cauliflower, p. 162 • Caramel Chip Biscotti, p. 230

German-Style Short Ribs, p. 121 • Sauteed Garlic Mushrooms, p. 171 • Herbed Pecan Stuffing, p. 153 • Banana Pudding Parfait, p. 283

Turkey Tenderloin Supreme, p. 134 • Creamy Skillet Noodles with Peas, p. 161 • Honey-Glazed Carrots, p. 158 • Cream Puff Dessert, p. 287

Mom's Roast Chicken, p. 115 • Asparagus & Green Beans with Tarragon Lemon Dip, p. 164 • Creamy Twice-Baked Potatoes, p. 171 • Perfect Rhubarb Pie, p.242

Au Gratin Ham Potpie, p. 99 • Easy Cheesy Biscuits, p. 71 • Pumpkin with Walnuts & Blue Cheese, p. 174 • Salted Nut Squares, p. 227

Quick Watermelon Cooler, p. 43 • Slow-Cooker Barbecue Pulled Pork Sandwiches, p. 104 •Summertime Pasta Salad, p. 165 • Ice Cream Sandwich Cake, p. 284

Roasted Vegetable Dip, p. 57 • Beef Wellington with Madeira Sauce, p. 103 • Buttery Almond Green Beans, p. 153 • Coconut Fudge Cake, p. 246

Lemonade Iced Tea, p. 55 • Coconut Shrimp Chowder, p. 188 • Vegetable Pad Thai, p. 120 • Glazed Fruit Medley, p. 34

APPLE BUTTER
BREAD PUDDING,
PAGE 27

GRANDMA'S FAVORITE

BREAKFASTS

Awaken your family to the aromas of cozy-morning
classics with this collection of spiced bakes,
sizzling meats and sweet brunch bites.

HAM & BISCUIT BREAKFAST BITES

I love using my grandfather's homemade horseradish in dishes. This particular dish is unique because it also calls for rosemary. I enjoy making these on the weekend and often share with my neighbors. These bites freeze nicely too.
—*Danielle Lee, West Palm Beach, FL*

PREP: 20 MIN. • **BAKE:** 20 MIN. • **MAKES:** 1 DOZEN

3½ cups biscuit/baking mix
1 cup 2% milk
⅔ cup shredded cheddar cheese
½ cup chopped green pepper
⅔ cup cubed fully cooked ham or 3½ oz. Canadian bacon, cubed
4 large eggs or 1 cup egg substitute
2 to 3 Tbsp. prepared horseradish
½ tsp. salt
½ tsp. pepper
1½ tsp. minced fresh rosemary or ½ tsp. dried rosemary, crushed

1. Preheat oven to 375°. Stir together biscuit mix and milk to form a soft dough. On a lightly floured surface, pat dough to ¼-in. thickness; cut 12 biscuits using a floured 3½-in. round cutter. Press each onto the bottom and up sides of a greased muffin cup.

2. Divide cheese, green pepper and ham among cups. Whisk together eggs, horseradish, salt and pepper; pour into cups. Sprinkle with rosemary.

3. Bake until eggs are set, 20-25 minutes. Let stand 5 minutes before removing from pan.

1 BREAKFAST BITE: 204 cal., 8g fat (3g sat. fat), 74mg chol., 640mg sod., 26g carb. (2g sugars, 1g fiber), 9g pro.

SHEEPHERDER'S POTATOES

Thyme adds a nice flavor surprise to this hearty casserole. Serve it as a side dish at dinner—or as the main course at breakfast or brunch.
—*Deborah Hill, Coffeyville, KS*

TAKES: 30 MIN. • **MAKES:** 10 SERVINGS

5 to 6 medium potatoes (about 2 lbs.), cooked, peeled and sliced
12 bacon strips, cooked and crumbled
1 large onion, chopped
6 large eggs
¼ cup 2% milk
1 tsp. salt
½ tsp. pepper
2 Tbsp. dried parsley flakes
½ tsp. dried thyme
½ cup shredded cheddar cheese

1. Preheat oven to 350°. In a greased 13x9-in. baking dish, layer potatoes, bacon and onion. In a bowl, beat eggs, milk, salt, pepper, parsley and thyme. Pour over potato mixture.

2. Bake until eggs are almost set, about 15 minutes. Sprinkle with cheese; bake until cheese is melted and the eggs are set, 5-7 minutes longer.

1 SERVING: 388 cal., 9g fat (3g sat. fat), 128mg chol., 503mg sod., 64g carb. (6g sugars, 5g fiber), 14g pro.

HAM & BISCUIT
BREAKFAST BITES

GRANDMA'S SECRET
If you're shredding the cheddar cheese yourself, start by giving your cheese grater a quick spritz with cooking spray to avoid sticking and allow for easier cleanup.

SWEET POTATO PANCAKES WITH CINNAMON CREAM

Topped with a rich cinnamon cream, these pancakes are an ideal dish for celebrating the tastes and aromas of fall.
—*Tammy Rex, New Tripoli, PA*

PREP: 25 MIN. • COOK: 5 MIN./BATCH • MAKES: 12 SERVINGS

- 1 pkg. (8 oz.) cream cheese, softened
- ¼ cup packed brown sugar
- ½ tsp. ground cinnamon
- ½ cup sour cream

PANCAKES
- 6 large eggs
- ¾ cup all-purpose flour
- ½ tsp. ground nutmeg
- ½ tsp. salt
- ¼ tsp. pepper
- 6 cups shredded peeled sweet potatoes (about 3 large)
- 3 cups shredded peeled apples (about 3 large)
- ⅓ cup grated onion
- ½ cup canola oil

1. In a small bowl, beat the cream cheese, brown sugar and cinnamon until blended; beat in sour cream. Set aside.

2. In a large bowl, whisk the eggs, flour, nutmeg, salt and pepper. Add sweet potatoes, apples and onion; toss to coat.

3. In a large nonstick skillet, heat 2 Tbsp. oil over medium heat. Working in batches, drop sweet potato mixture by ⅓ cupfuls into oil; press slightly to flatten. Fry until golden brown, 2-3 minutes on each side, using the remaining oil as needed. Drain on paper towels. Serve with cinnamon topping.

2 PANCAKES WITH 2 TBSP. TOPPING: 325 cal., 21g fat (7g sat. fat), 114mg chol., 203mg sod., 30g carb. (15g sugars, 3g fiber), 6g pro.

SLOW-COOKER FRITTATA PROVENCAL

This recipe means that a delectable dinner is ready when I walk in the door from work.
The meatless slow-cooker meal also makes an elegant brunch for lazy weekend mornings.
—*Connie Eaton, Pittsburgh, PA*

PREP: 30 MIN. • **COOK:** 3 HOURS • **MAKES:** 6 SERVINGS

½ **cup water**
1 **Tbsp. olive oil**
1 **medium Yukon Gold potato, peeled and sliced**
1 **small onion, thinly sliced**
½ **tsp. smoked paprika**
12 **large eggs**
1 **tsp. minced fresh thyme or ¼ tsp. dried thyme**
1 **tsp. hot pepper sauce**
½ **tsp. salt**
¼ **tsp. pepper**
1 **log (4 oz.) fresh goat cheese, coarsely crumbled**
½ **cup chopped soft sun-dried tomatoes (not packed in oil)**

1. Layer two 24-in. pieces of aluminum foil; starting with a long side, fold up foil to create a 1-in.-wide strip. Shape strip into a coil to make a rack for bottom of a 6-qt. oval slow cooker. Add water to slow cooker; set foil rack in water.

2. In a large skillet, heat the oil over medium-high heat. Add potato and onion; cook and stir until potato is lightly browned, 5-7 minutes. Stir in the paprika. Transfer to a greased 1½-qt. baking dish (dish must fit in slow cooker).

3. In a large bowl, whisk eggs, thyme, pepper sauce, salt and pepper; stir in 2 oz. cheese. Pour over potato mixture. Top with tomatoes and remaining goat cheese. Place dish on foil rack.

4. Cook, covered, on low until eggs are set and a knife inserted in center comes out clean, 3-4 hours.

1 SERVING: 245 cal., 14g fat (5g sat. fat), 385mg chol., 338mg sod., 12g carb. (4g sugars, 2g fiber), 15g pro. **DIABETIC EXCHANGES:** 2 medium-fat meat, 1 starch, ½ fat.

FROM GRANDMA'S KITCHEN: When using whole sun-dried tomatoes that are not oil-packed, cover with boiling water and let stand until soft. Drain before chopping.

WAKE-UP CASSEROLE

This dish can be made the night before and kept in the refrigerator.
I frequently make it for church potlucks and for company. Everybody loves it.
—*Iris Frank, Eureka, IL*

PREP: 15 MIN. • BAKE: 1¼ HOURS • MAKES: 8 SERVINGS

8 **frozen hash brown patties**
4 **cups shredded cheddar cheese**
1 **lb. cubed fully cooked ham (2 cups)**
7 **large eggs**
1 **cup 2% milk**
½ **tsp. salt**
½ **tsp. ground mustard**

1. Preheat oven to 350°. Place hash brown patties in a single layer in a greased 13x9-in. baking dish. Sprinkle with cheese and ham. In a large bowl, beat eggs, milk, salt and mustard. Pour over ham.

2. Cover and bake 1 hour. Uncover; bake until edges are golden brown and a knife inserted in the center comes out clean, about 15 minutes longer.

1 SERVING: 437 cal., 26g fat (16g sat. fat), 280mg chol., 1307mg sod., 19g carb. (2g sugars, 2g fiber), 30g pro.

BROCCOLI-MUSHROOM BUBBLE BAKE

I got bored with the same old breakfast casseroles served at our monthly moms' meeting, so I decided to create something new. Judging by the reactions of the other moms, this one's a keeper.
—*Shannon Koene, Blacksburg, VA*

PREP: 20 MIN. • BAKE: 25 MIN. • MAKES: 12 SERVINGS

1 **tsp. canola oil**
½ **lb. fresh mushrooms, finely chopped**
1 **medium onion, finely chopped**
1 **tube (16.3 oz.) large refrigerated flaky biscuits**
1 **pkg. (10 oz.) frozen broccoli with cheese sauce**
3 **large eggs**
1 **can (5 oz.) evaporated milk**
1 **tsp. Italian seasoning**
½ **tsp. garlic powder**
½ **tsp. salt**
¼ **tsp. pepper**
1½ **cups shredded Colby-Monterey Jack cheese**

1. Preheat oven to 350°. In a large skillet, heat oil over medium-high heat. Add mushrooms and onion; cook and stir until tender, 4-6 minutes.

2. Cut each biscuit into 8 pieces; place in a greased 13x9-in. baking dish. Top with mushroom mixture.

3. Cook broccoli with cheese sauce according to package directions. Spoon over mushroom mixture.

4. In a large bowl, whisk eggs, milk and seasonings; pour over top. Sprinkle with cheese. Bake until golden brown, 25-30 minutes.

1 SERVING: 233 cal., 13g fat (6g sat. fat), 64mg chol., 648mg sod., 21g carb. (6g sugars, 1g fiber), 9g pro.

HOT FRUIT & SAUSAGE

Pineapple, brown sugar and cinnamon make plain pork sausage links extra tasty. And the banana slices really complement the sausage. This dish is easy to prepare and makes any breakfast special.
—*Marian Peterson, Wisconsin Rapids, WI*

TAKES: 10 MIN. • MAKES: 6 SERVINGS

1 pkg. (12 oz.) uncooked pork sausage links
¾ cup pineapple tidbits
2 Tbsp. brown sugar
Pinch ground cinnamon
1 medium firm banana, sliced

In a large cast-iron or other heavy skillet, cook sausage according to package directions; drain. Add pineapple, brown sugar and cinnamon; heat through. Stir in banana just before serving.

1 SERVING: 261 cal., 18g fat (6g sat. fat), 47mg chol., 736mg sod., 14g carb. (12g sugars, 1g fiber), 11g pro.

SLOW-COOKER BREAKFAST BURRITOS

Prep these tasty, hearty burritos the night before for a quick breakfast in the morning, or let them cook while you are away on a weekend afternoon for an easy supper.
—*Anna Miller, Churdan, IA*

PREP: 25 MIN. • COOK: 3¾ HOURS + STANDING • MAKES: 12 SERVINGS

1 lb. bulk pork sausage
1 pkg. (28 oz.) frozen O'Brien potatoes, thawed
2 cups shredded sharp cheddar cheese
12 large eggs
½ cup 2% milk
¼ tsp. seasoned salt
⅛ tsp. pepper
12 flour tortillas (8 in.)
Optional toppings: Salsa, sliced jalapenos, chopped tomatoes, sliced green onions and cubed avocado

1. In a large skillet, cook sausage over medium heat until no longer pink, 8-10 minutes, breaking into crumbles; drain.

2. In a greased 4- or 5-qt. slow cooker, layer potatoes, sausage and cheese. In a large bowl, whisk the eggs, milk, seasoned salt and pepper until blended; pour over top.

3. Cook, covered, on low 3¾-4¼ hours or until eggs are set and a thermometer reads 160°. Uncover; let stand 10 minutes. Serve in tortillas with toppings of your choice.

1 BURRITO: 359 cal., 15g fat (6g sat. fat), 205mg chol., 480mg sod., 39g carb. (2g sugars, 3g fiber), 16g pro.

HAM & CHEESE BREAKFAST STRUDELS

These get the morning off to a great start! Sometimes I assemble
the strudels ahead and freeze them individually before baking.

—Jo Groth, Plainfield, IA

PREP: 25 MIN. • **BAKE:** 10 MIN. • **MAKES:** 6 SERVINGS

3 Tbsp. butter, divided
2 Tbsp. all-purpose flour
1 cup 2% milk
⅓ cup shredded Swiss
   cheese
2 Tbsp. grated Parmesan
   cheese
¼ tsp. salt
5 large eggs, lightly beaten
¼ lb. ground fully cooked
   ham (about ¾ cup)
6 sheets phyllo dough
   (14x9-in. size)
½ cup butter, melted
¼ cup dry bread crumbs

TOPPING
2 Tbsp. grated Parmesan
   cheese
2 Tbsp. minced fresh
   parsley

1. In a small saucepan, melt 2 Tbsp. butter. Stir in flour until smooth; gradually add milk. Bring to a boil; cook and stir for 2 minutes or until thickened. Stir in cheeses and salt.

2. In a large nonstick skillet, melt remaining 1 Tbsp. butter over medium heat. Add eggs to pan; cook and stir until almost set. Stir in ham and the cheese sauce; heat through. Remove from heat.

3. Preheat oven to 375°. Place 1 sheet of phyllo dough on a work surface. (Keep remaining phyllo covered with a damp towel to prevent it from drying out.) Brush with melted butter; sprinkle with 2 tsp. bread crumbs. Fold phyllo in half lengthwise; brush again with butter. Spoon ½ cup filling onto phyllo about 2 in. from a short side. Fold side and edges over filling and roll up. Brush with butter. Repeat with remaining phyllo, butter, bread crumbs and filling.

4. Place on a greased baking sheet; sprinkle each with 1 tsp. cheese and 1 tsp. parsley. Bake 10-15 minutes or until golden brown. Serve immediately.

FREEZE OPTION: After topping strudels with cheese and parsley, freeze unbaked on a waxed paper-lined baking sheet until firm. Transfer to a freezer container; return to freezer. To use, bake strudels as directed, increasing time to 30-35 minutes or until heated through and golden brown.

1 STRUDEL: 439 cal., 33g fat (18g sat. fat), 255mg chol., 754mg sod., 20g carb. (4g sugars, 1g fiber), 16g pro.

"I loved these. I made them for my husband's birthday breakfast, and they were a real hit. Delicious."
—MELISFUN, TASTEOFHOME.COM

BAKED CHEDDAR EGGS & POTATOES

I love breakfast, especially when this combo of eggs, potatoes and cheese is on the menu. It starts in a skillet on the stovetop and then I pop it into the oven to bake.
—*Nadine Merheb, Tucson, AZ*

TAKES: 30 MIN. • **MAKES:** 4 SERVINGS

3 Tbsp. butter
1½ lbs. red potatoes, chopped
¼ cup minced fresh parsley
2 garlic cloves, minced
¾ tsp. kosher salt
⅛ tsp. pepper
8 large eggs
½ cup shredded extra-sharp cheddar cheese

1. Preheat oven to 400°. In a 10-in. cast-iron or other ovenproof skillet, heat butter over medium-high heat. Add potatoes; cook and stir until golden brown and tender. Stir in parsley, garlic, salt and pepper. With the back of a spoon, make 4 wells in the potato mixture; break 2 eggs into each well.

2. Bake until egg whites are completely set and yolks begin to thicken but are not hard, 9-11 minutes. Sprinkle with cheese; bake until cheese is melted, about 1 minute.

1 SERVING: 395 cal., 23g fat (12g sat. fat), 461mg chol., 651mg sod., 29g carb. (3g sugars, 3g fiber), 19g pro.

CHEESE & RED PEPPER LATKES

These zesty latkes combine three cheeses with a handful of garlic and a colorful burst of red peppers.
—*Christine Montalvo, Windsor Heights, IA*

PREP: 30 MIN. • **COOK:** 5 MIN./BATCH • **MAKES:** 3 DOZEN

3 large onions, finely chopped
3 medium sweet red peppers, finely chopped
⅓ cup butter, cubed
18 medium garlic cloves, minced, divided
1 Tbsp. celery salt
1 Tbsp. coarsely ground pepper
3 lbs. russet potatoes, peeled and shredded
1½ cups grated Parmesan cheese
1½ cups shredded cheddar cheese
1 cup shredded part-skim mozzarella cheese
1 cup all-purpose flour
¾ cup sour cream
Canola oil for frying
Minced fresh parsley

1. In a large cast-iron or other heavy skillet, saute onions and red peppers in butter until tender. Add ¼ cup garlic, celery salt and pepper; cook 1 minute longer.

2. Transfer to a large bowl. Add the potatoes, cheeses, flour, sour cream and remaining garlic; mix well.

3. Heat ¼ in. of oil in same skillet over medium heat. Working in batches, drop the batter by ¼ cupfuls into hot oil. Press lightly to flatten. Fry until golden brown, carefully turning once. Drain on paper towels. Sprinkle with parsley.

3 LATKES: 437 cal., 29g fat (11g sat. fat), 46mg chol., 677mg sod., 33g carb. (5g sugars, 3g fiber), 12g pro.

FROM GRANDMA'S KITCHEN: Lay shredded potatoes over a layer of paper towels to remove the excess moisture. This will give you crispier latkes.

BAKED CHEDDAR
EGGS & POTATOES

WALNUT GLAZED BACON

Once you taste this bacon, you may never want to go back to the plain kind. It's just right for anyone who loves the salty and sweet flavor combination.
—*Heather Cardeiro, King of Prussia, PA*

PREP: 10 MIN. • **BAKE:** 25 MIN. • **MAKES:** 12 BACON STRIPS

½ **cup finely chopped walnuts**
¼ **cup dark brown sugar**

1 **tsp. all-purpose flour**
12 **thick-sliced bacon strips**

In a small bowl, combine the walnuts, brown sugar and flour. Place bacon on a greased broiler pan; sprinkle with walnut mixture. Bake at 350° until golden brown, 25-30 minutes.

1 BACON STRIP: 110 cal., 8g fat (2g sat. fat), 10mg chol., 251mg sod., 5g carb. (5g sugars, 0 fiber), 5g pro.

TOAD IN THE HOLE

This is one of the first recipes I had my children prepare when they were learning to cook. My little ones are now grown (and have advanced to more difficult recipes), but this continues to be a standby in my home and theirs.
—*Ruth Lechleiter, Breckenridge, MN*

TAKES: 15 MIN. • **MAKES:** 1 SERVING

1 **slice of bread**
1 **tsp. butter**
1 **large egg**
   Salt and pepper to taste

1. Cut a 3-in. hole in the middle of the bread and discard. In a small skillet, melt the butter; place the bread in the skillet.

2. Place egg in the hole. Cook over medium heat until the bread is lightly browned, about 2 minutes. Turn and cook the other side until egg yolk is almost set. Season with salt and pepper.

1 SERVING: 183 cal., 10g fat (4g sat. fat), 196mg chol., 244mg sod., 15g carb. (2g sugars, 1g fiber), 9g pro. **DIABETIC EXCHANGES:** 1 starch, 1 medium-fat meat, 1 fat.

CHOCOLATE CHUNK PANCAKES WITH RASPBERRY SAUCE

Chocolate and raspberries are two of my favorite ingredients, so I pack both into pancakes. I make them for my sister, who adores chocolate too.
—*Katherine Nelson, Centerville, UT*

PREP: 20 MIN. • COOK: 5 MIN./BATCH • MAKES: 12 PANCAKES (1½ CUPS SAUCE)

1 pkg. (10 oz.) frozen sweetened raspberries, thawed
¼ cup orange juice
3 Tbsp. lemon juice
2 Tbsp. sugar

PANCAKES
1½ cups all-purpose flour
3 Tbsp. sugar
1 tsp. baking powder
½ tsp. baking soda
¼ tsp. salt
2 large eggs, room temperature
1 cup 2% milk
¾ cup vanilla yogurt
¼ cup butter, melted
½ cup semisweet chocolate chunks or chips

1. Place raspberries, orange juice, lemon juice and sugar in a blender; cover and process until pureed. Press through a fine-mesh strainer into a bowl; discard seeds.

2. In a large bowl, whisk flour, sugar, baking powder, baking soda and salt. In another bowl, whisk eggs, milk, yogurt and melted butter until blended. Add to dry ingredients, stirring just until moistened. Fold in chocolate chunks.

3. Lightly grease a griddle; heat over medium heat. Pour batter by ¼ cupfuls onto griddle. Cook until bubbles on top begin to pop and bottoms are golden brown. Turn; cook until second side is golden brown. Serve with raspberry sauce.

3 PANCAKES WITH ⅓ CUP SAUCE: 630 cal., 23g fat (13g sat. fat), 131mg chol., 615mg sod., 96g carb. (55g sugars, 6g fiber), 14g pro.

SAVORY APPLE-CHICKEN SAUSAGE

These easy, healthy sausages taste incredible, and they make an elegant brunch dish. The recipe is also very versatile. It can be doubled or tripled for a crowd, and the sausage freezes well either cooked or raw.
—*Angela Buchanan, Longmont, CO*

TAKES: 25 MIN. • MAKES: 8 PATTIES

1 large tart apple, peeled and diced
2 tsp. poultry seasoning
1 tsp. salt
¼ tsp. pepper
1 lb. ground chicken

1. In a large bowl, combine the first 4 ingredients. Crumble chicken over the mixture and mix lightly but thoroughly. Shape into eight 3-in. patties.

2. In a large, greased cast-iron or other heavy skillet, cook patties over medium heat until no longer pink, 5-6 minutes on each side. Drain if necessary.

1 SAUSAGE PATTY: 92 cal., 5g fat (1g sat. fat), 38mg chol., 328mg sod., 4g carb. (3g sugars, 1g fiber), 9g pro. DIABETIC EXCHANGES: 1 medium-fat meat.

PEANUT BUTTER & JELLY FRENCH TOAST

I've always tried to make cooking fun—for myself, my daughters and my grandchildren. Cooking teaches children the importance of following directions and being organized. This recipe is easy to make, and kids really like it.
—*Flo Burtnett, Gage, OK*

TAKES: 20 MIN. • MAKES: 6 SERVINGS

¾ **cup peanut butter**
12 **slices bread**
6 **Tbsp. jelly or jam**
3 **large eggs**
¾ **cup 2% milk**
¼ **tsp. salt**
2 **Tbsp. butter**

1. Spread peanut butter on 6 slices of bread; spread jelly on the remaining 6 slices of bread. Put 1 slice of each together to form sandwiches. In a large bowl, whisk the eggs, milk and salt. Dip both sides of sandwiches in egg mixture.

2. In a large skillet, melt the butter over medium heat. Cook sandwiches for 2-3 minutes on each side or until golden brown.

1 PIECE: 450 cal., 22g fat (5g sat. fat), 96mg chol., 567mg sod., 50g carb. (20g sugars, 3g fiber), 16g pro.

HAM & CHEDDAR BRUNCH RING

It's surprisingly easy to transform ordinary breakfast standbys into next-level brunch centerpieces. This looks and smells so good, you might have to fend off guests en route from oven to table. Dig in!
—*James Schend, Pleasant Prairie, WI*

PREP: 25 MIN. • BAKE: 20 MIN. • MAKES: 8 SERVINGS

1 **tube (8 oz.) refrigerated crescent rolls**
10 **pieces thinly sliced deli ham**
1 **cup shredded cheddar cheese, divided**
11 **large eggs, divided use**
¾ **cup roasted sweet red peppers, drained and chopped**
4 **green onions, thinly sliced**
1 **Tbsp. olive oil**
1 **tsp. minced garlic**
2 **tsp. sesame seeds, optional**
Chopped fresh parsley, optional

1. Preheat oven to 375°. Unroll crescent dough and separate into triangles. On an ungreased 12-in. pizza pan, arrange triangles in a ring with points toward the outside and wide ends overlapping to create a 3-in.-diameter hole in the center. Press overlapping dough to seal. Fold ham slices lengthwise and place on top of the wide end of each triangle. Sprinkle with half the cheese.

2. In a large bowl, beat 10 eggs; add chopped peppers. In a large skillet, cook green onions in oil over medium heat until tender, 2-3 minutes. Add garlic; cook 30 seconds. Pour in egg mixture; cook and stir until eggs are thickened and no liquid egg remains. Spoon egg mixture over cheese on the wide end of the triangles; sprinkle with remaining cheese. Fold pointed ends of triangles over filling, tucking points under to form a ring with a small hole in the center (filling will be visible). Beat remaining egg; brush over pastry. If desired, sprinkle with sesame seeds.

3. Bake until golden brown and heated through, 20-25 minutes. If desired, top with parsley to serve.

1 SERVING: 313 cal., 19g fat (5g sat. fat), 282mg chol., 735mg sod., 15g carb. (5g sugars, 0 fiber), 19g pro.

PEANUT BUTTER
& JELLY
FRENCH TOAST

OVERNIGHT BAKED EGGS BRUSCHETTA

I like to spend as much time as I can with my guests when they stay with me for the holidays,
so I rely on make-ahead recipes to help that happen. Because most overnight brunch
casseroles are so similar, I came up with a breakfast bruschetta for a fun change of pace.

—*Judi Berman-Yamada, Portland, OR*

PREP: 45 MIN. + CHILLING • **BAKE:** 10 MIN. • **MAKES:** 9 SERVINGS

- 1 **tube (13.8 oz.) refrigerated pizza crust**
- 1 **Tbsp. cornmeal**
- 3 **Tbsp. olive oil, divided**
- 1½ **cups shredded part-skim mozzarella cheese, divided**
- ¾ **lb. sliced baby portobello mushrooms**
- ¾ **tsp. garlic powder**
- ¾ **tsp. dried rosemary, crushed**
- ½ **tsp. pepper**
- ¼ **tsp. salt**
- 2 **cups pizza sauce**
- 1 **Tbsp. white vinegar**
- 9 **large eggs**
- 2 **oz. fresh goat cheese, crumbled**
- ½ **cup french-fried onions**
  Minced fresh basil

1. Preheat oven to 400°. Unroll the pizza crust and press onto bottom of a greased 15x10x1-in. baking pan that's been sprinkled with cornmeal. Brush crust with 1 Tbsp. oil; sprinkle with ¾ cup mozzarella cheese. Bake 8 minutes.

2. Meanwhile, in a large skillet, heat remaining 2 Tbsp. oil over medium-high heat. Add mushrooms; cook and stir until tender. Stir in garlic powder, rosemary, pepper and salt. Stir pizza sauce into mushrooms; spread mushroom mixture over crust.

3. In a large skillet with high sides, bring vinegar and 2-3 in. water to a boil. Reduce the heat to maintain a gentle simmer. Break cold eggs, 1 at a time, into a small bowl. Holding bowl close to surface of water, slip eggs into water.

4. Cook eggs, uncovered, for 3-5 minutes or until whites are completely set and yolks begin to thicken but are not hard. Using a slotted spoon, remove eggs; place over mushroom mixture in baking pan. Sprinkle goat cheese and remaining ¾ cup mozzarella over eggs and mushrooms. Refrigerate, covered, overnight.

5. Remove pan from the refrigerator 30 minutes before baking. Preheat oven to 400°. Sprinkle onions over top. Bake, uncovered, until golden brown and heated through, 10-15 minutes. Top with basil just before serving.

1 PIECE: 345 cal., 17g fat (5g sat. fat), 227mg chol., 798mg sod., 29g carb. (6g sugars, 2g fiber), 17g pro.

PRESSURE-COOKER SAUSAGE & WAFFLE BAKE

Here's an easy dish guaranteed to create excitement at the breakfast table!
Nothing is missing from this sweet and savory combination. It's so wrong, it's right!
—*Courtney Lentz, Boston, MA*

PREP: 20 MIN. • **COOK:** 20 MIN. + STANDING • **MAKES:** 6 SERVINGS

1   lb. bulk spicy breakfast
    pork sausage
1½ tsp. rubbed sage
¼   tsp. fennel seed
5   frozen waffles, cut into
    bite-sized pieces
4   large eggs
⅔   cup half-and-half cream
2   Tbsp. maple syrup
⅛   tsp. salt
⅛   tsp. pepper
1   cup shredded cheddar
    cheese

1. Select saute or browning setting on a 6-qt. electric pressure cooker; adjust for medium heat. Cook sausage until no longer pink, 6-8 minutes, breaking into crumbles; drain. Add sage and fennel. Press cancel. Place waffles in a greased 1½-qt. baking dish; top with sausage mixture. In a bowl, mix eggs, cream, syrup and seasonings. Pour over sausage and waffles; top with cheese. Cover baking dish with foil. Wipe pressure cooker clean.

2. Place trivet insert and 1 cup water in pressure cooker. Fold an 18x12-in. piece of foil lengthwise into thirds, making a sling. Use the sling to lower the dish onto the trivet. Lock lid; close pressure-release valve. Adjust to pressure-cook on high for 20 minutes. Let pressure release naturally for 5 minutes; quick-release any remaining pressure.

3. Using the foil sling, carefully remove baking dish. Let stand for 10 minutes. Serve with additional maple syrup.

1 SERVING: 445 cal., 31g fat (12g sat. fat), 201mg chol., 880mg sod., 20g carb. (7g sugars, 1g fiber), 19g pro.

BLUEBERRY FRUIT SMOOTHIE

Transport yourself back to the soda-fountain days with this nutritious
alternative to traditional malts, shakes and sodas! You'll fall for its gorgeous color.
—*Mary LaJoie, Orwell, VT*

TAKES: 5 MIN. • **MAKES:** 3 SERVINGS

1   cup reduced-fat vanilla
    ice cream
1   cup fresh or frozen
    blueberries
½   cup chopped peeled
    fresh peaches or frozen
    unsweetened sliced
    peaches
½   cup pineapple juice
¼   cup vanilla yogurt

1. In a blender, combine all ingredients; cover and process until smooth. Pour into chilled glasses; serve immediately.

¾ CUP: 168 cal., 3g fat (2g sat. fat), 15mg chol., 52mg sod., 33g carb. (25g sugars, 2g fiber), 4g pro. **DIABETIC EXCHANGES:** 1 starch, 1 fruit, ½ fat.

OLD-WORLD PUFF PANCAKE

My grandmother taught my mom how to make this dish, which was popular during the Depression. At that time, cooks measured ingredients in pinches, dashes and dibs, but through the years accurate amounts were noted. My wife and I continue to enjoy this dish today, particularly for brunch.
—*Auton Miller, Piney Flats, TN*

TAKES: 30 MIN. • MAKES: 4 SERVINGS

2 Tbsp. butter
3 large eggs, room temperature
¾ cup 2% milk
¾ cup all-purpose flour
2 tsp. sugar
1 tsp. ground nutmeg
   Confectioners' sugar
   Lemon wedges
   Syrup, optional
   Fresh raspberries, optional

1. Place butter in a 10-in. ovenproof skillet; place in a 425° oven until melted, 2-3 minutes. In a blender, process the eggs, milk, flour, sugar and nutmeg until smooth. Pour into prepared skillet.

2. Bake at 425° until puffed and browned, 16-18 minutes. Dust with confectioners' sugar. Serve with the lemon wedges and, if desired, syrup and raspberries.

1 PIECE: 178 cal., 5g fat (2g sat. fat), 144mg chol., 74mg sod., 23g carb. (5g sugars, 1g fiber), 9g pro.

CHOCOLATE PEANUT BUTTER OVERNIGHT OATS

Soon after I learned about overnight oats I decided to create a recipe with my favorite sugary combination: chocolate and peanut butter. Overnight oats are a perfect breakfast for busy mornings.
—*Anna Bentley, Swanzey, NH*

PREP: 10 MIN. + CHILLING • MAKES: 1 SERVING

½ cup old-fashioned oats
⅓ cup chocolate or plain almond milk
1 Tbsp. baking cocoa
1 Tbsp. creamy peanut butter, warmed
1 Tbsp. maple syrup
   Miniature dairy-free semisweet chocolate chips, optional

In a small container or Mason jar, combine the oats, milk, cocoa, peanut butter and maple syrup. Seal and refrigerate overnight. If desired, top with additional peanut butter and mini chocolate chips.

½ CUP: 346 cal., 13g fat (2g sat. fat), 0 chol., 121mg sod., 53g carb. (21g sugars, 6g fiber), 10g pro.

APPLE BUTTER BREAD PUDDING

This is one of my mother's best recipes! I'm sure your family will be delighted with it too. Serve it as a dessert or a very special breakfast treat.
—Jerri Gradert, Lincoln, NE

PREP: 20 MIN. + STANDING • BAKE: 50 MIN. • MAKES: 12 SERVINGS

⅓ cup raisins
1 cup apple butter
6 croissants, split

CUSTARD
8 large eggs
3 cups 2% milk
1½ cups sugar
2 tsp. vanilla extract
¼ tsp. salt

STREUSEL
½ cup all-purpose flour
½ cup packed brown sugar
¼ tsp. salt
¼ cup cold butter

1. Place raisins in a small bowl. Cover with boiling water; let stand for 5 minutes. Drain and set aside.

2. Combine apple butter and raisins. Spread over croissant bottoms; replace tops. Cut each croissant into 3 pieces; place in a greased 13x9-in. baking dish.

3. In a large bowl, combine the eggs, milk, sugar, vanilla and salt. Pour over croissants; let stand for 30 minutes or until the bread is softened.

4. In a small bowl, combine the flour, brown sugar and salt. Cut in butter until mixture resembles coarse crumbs. Sprinkle over top.

5. Bake, uncovered, at 350° for 50-60 minutes or until a knife inserted in the center comes out clean. Serve warm. Refrigerate the leftovers.

NOTE: This recipe was tested with commercially prepared apple butter.

1 SERVING: 433 cal., 14g fat (7g sat. fat), 175mg chol., 422mg sod., 68g carb. (51g sugars, 1g fiber), 9g pro.

PRESSURE-COOKER POT ROAST HASH

I love to cook a Sunday-style pot roast for weeknights. Make it into pot roast hash for any day of the week.
—*Gina Jackson, Ogdensburg, NY*

PREP: 20 MIN. • COOK: 45 MIN. + RELEASING • MAKES: 10 SERVINGS

1 cup warm water
   (110° to 115°)
1 Tbsp. beef base
½ lb. sliced fresh
   mushrooms
1 large onion, coarsely
   chopped
3 garlic cloves, minced
1 boneless beef chuck
   roast (3 lbs.)
½ tsp. pepper
1 Tbsp. Worcestershire
   sauce
1 pkg. (28 oz.) frozen
   O'Brien potatoes

EGGS
 2 Tbsp. butter, divided
10 large eggs, divided use
½ tsp. salt, divided
½ tsp. pepper, divided
   Minced chives

1. In a 6-qt. electric pressure cooker, whisk water and beef base; add mushrooms, onion and garlic. Sprinkle roast with pepper; transfer to pressure cooker. Drizzle with Worcestershire sauce. Lock lid; close pressure-release valve. Adjust to pressure-cook on high for 45 minutes. Allow pressure to naturally release for 10 minutes, then quick-release any remaining pressure.

2. Remove roast; when cool enough to handle, shred meat with 2 forks. In a large skillet, cook the potatoes according to package directions; stir in shredded beef. Using a slotted spoon, transfer vegetables from pressure cooker to skillet; heat through. Discard cooking juices.

3. For eggs, heat 1 Tbsp. butter over medium-high heat in another large skillet. Break 5 eggs, 1 at a time, into pan. Sprinkle with half the salt and pepper. Reduce heat to low. Cook until the eggs reach desired doneness, turning after whites are set if desired. Repeat with the remaining butter, eggs, salt and pepper. Serve eggs over hash; sprinkle with chives.

1 SERVING: 429 cal., 24g fat (8g sat. fat), 281mg chol., 15mg sod., 15g carb. (2g sugars, 2g fiber), 35g pro.

GOLDEN BUTTERMILK WAFFLES

You'll hear nothing but cheering from family or friends when you stack up these golden waffles for breakfast! My clan regularly requests this morning mainstay.
—*Kim Branges, Grand Canyon, AZ*

TAKES: 25 MIN. • MAKES: 16 WAFFLES (4 IN.)

1¾ cups all-purpose flour
 1 tsp. baking powder
 1 tsp. baking soda
½ tsp. salt
 2 large eggs, room
   temperature
 2 cups buttermilk
⅓ cup canola oil
   Optional: Sliced
   fresh strawberries,
   strawberry syrup and
   whipped cream

1. In a large bowl, combine the flour, baking powder, baking soda and salt. In another bowl, beat the eggs; add buttermilk and oil. Stir into dry ingredients just until combined.

2. Bake in a preheated waffle maker according to manufacturer's directions until golden brown. If desired, serve with sliced fresh strawberries, syrup and whipped cream.

2 WAFFLES: 223 cal., 11g fat (2g sat. fat), 56mg chol., 435mg sod., 24g carb. (4g sugars, 1g fiber), 6g pro.

GRANDMA'S SECRET
Having trouble finding the beef base for this recipe? It should be near the broth and bouillon at your local grocery store.

PRESSURE-COOKER
POT ROAST HASH

CHEDDAR-BUTTERNUT SQUASH CLAFOUTIS

I came up with this savory version of the classic French dessert, clafoutis, and shared it for dinner with a salad. My friends loved it, but in the end I could have eaten the whole pan myself.
— *Joseph A. Sciascia, San Mateo, California*

PREP: 20 MIN. • **COOK:** 50 MIN. + STANDING • **MAKES:** 6 SERVINGS

3 cups cubed peeled butternut squash
2 tsp. olive oil
1 tsp. minced fresh rosemary or ½ tsp. dried rosemary, crushed
1 tsp. minced fresh thyme or ½ tsp. dried thyme
½ tsp. kosher salt
¼ tsp. coarsely ground pepper

4 large eggs
1½ cups 2% milk
½ cup all-purpose flour
¼ tsp. cayenne pepper
2 cups shredded sharp white cheddar cheese
¼ cup grated Parmesan and Romano cheese blend
1 Tbsp. butter
1 Tbsp. minced fresh chives

1. Preheat oven to 400°. Place cubed butternut squash in a 12-in. cast-iron skillet. Drizzle with oil. Sprinkle with rosemary, thyme, salt and pepper; toss to coat. Roast for 15-20 minutes or until just tender. Remove from pan and keep warm.

2. In a large bowl, whisk eggs, milk, flour and cayenne; stir in cheeses. Place butter in same skillet; place skillet in oven until butter is melted, 1-2 minutes. Carefully tilt pan to coat bottom and side with butter. Pour the egg mixture into skillet; top with roasted squash.

3. Bake until puffed and edge is browned, 30-35 minutes. Let stand 15 minutes before cutting. Sprinkle with chives and additional Parmesan and Romano cheese blend.

1 PIECE: 357 cal., 22g fat (11g sat. fat), 176mg chol., 586mg sod., 22g carb. (5g sugars, 2g fiber), 19g pro.

"I've made this a dozen times, and the result is always delicious. I now keep a block of cheddar in the fridge just to be able to make this."
—GUEST1380, TASTEOFHOME.COM

POTATO SAUSAGE FRITTATA

With sausage, bacon, eggs and potatoes, this frittata is one hearty meal! Although I double the recipe for my large family, we never have any leftovers. As good as this dish is, you can experiment to customize it for your family. Try using ham, bell peppers, chorizo—the sky's the limit!
—*Patricia Lee, Eatonton, GA*

TAKES: 30 MIN. • MAKES: 4 SERVINGS

½ **lb. bulk pork sausage**
6 **bacon strips, diced**
1½ **cups finely chopped red potatoes**
1 **medium onion, finely chopped**
8 **large eggs**
2 **tsp. dried parsley flakes**
¾ **tsp. salt**
⅛ **tsp. pepper**

1. In a large cast-iron or other ovenproof skillet, cook sausage over medium heat until no longer pink. Remove and set aside. In the same skillet, cook the bacon over medium heat until crisp. Using a slotted spoon, remove to paper towels; drain, reserving 2 Tbsp. drippings.

2. In the drippings, saute potatoes and onion until tender. In a large bowl, whisk the eggs, parsley, salt and pepper. Return sausage and bacon to the skillet; top with egg mixture.

3. Cover and cook over low heat until eggs are almost set, 8-10 minutes. Uncover; broil 6 in. from the heat until eggs are set, about 2 minutes. Cut into wedges.

1 PIECE: 518 cal., 39g fat (13g sat. fat), 430mg chol., 1213mg sod., 16g carb. (3g sugars, 2g fiber), 25g pro.

CONFETTI SCRAMBLED EGG POCKETS

This sunny specialty is a colorful crowd-pleaser. My eight grandchildren often enjoy these egg-packed pitas for Saturday morning brunch or with a light salad for supper.
—*Dixie Terry, Goreville, IL*

TAKES: 20 MIN. • MAKES: 6 SERVINGS

1 **cup fresh or frozen corn**
¼ **cup chopped green pepper**
2 **Tbsp. chopped onion**
1 **jar (2 oz.) diced pimientos, drained**
1 **Tbsp. butter**
8 **large eggs**
¼ **cup reduced-fat evaporated milk**
½ **tsp. seasoned salt**
1 **medium tomato, seeded and chopped**
1 **green onion, sliced**
6 **whole wheat pita pocket halves**
   Salsa, optional

1. In a large nonstick skillet, saute the corn, green pepper, onion and pimientos in butter for 5-7 minutes or until tender.

2. In a large bowl, combine the eggs, milk and salt; pour into the skillet. Cook and stir over medium heat until eggs are completely set. Stir in the tomato and green onion. Spoon about ⅔ cup into each pita half. Serve with salsa if desired.

1 PITA HALF: 224 cal., 9g fat (3g sat. fat), 255mg chol., 402mg sod., 24g carb. (5g sugars, 3g fiber), 13g pro. **DIABETIC EXCHANGES:** 1½ starch, 1 medium-fat meat, ½ fat.

BANANAS FOSTER BAKED FRENCH TOAST

This yummy baked French toast serves up all the taste of the spectacular dessert in fine fashion.
—*Laurence Nasson, Hingham, MA*

PREP: 20 MIN. + CHILLING • BAKE: 35 MIN. • MAKES: 6 SERVINGS

½ cup butter, cubed
⅔ cup packed brown sugar
½ cup heavy whipping cream
½ tsp. ground cinnamon
½ tsp. ground allspice
¼ cup chopped pecans, optional
3 large bananas, sliced
12 slices egg bread or challah (about ¾ lb.)
1½ cups 2% milk
3 large eggs
1 Tbsp. sugar
1 tsp. vanilla extract

1. Place butter in a microwave-safe bowl; microwave, covered, until melted, 30-45 seconds. Stir in the brown sugar, cream, cinnamon, allspice and, if desired, pecans. Add bananas; toss gently to coat.

2. Transfer to a greased 13x9-in. baking dish. Arrange bread over top, trimming to fit as necessary.

3. Place remaining ingredients in a blender; process just until blended. Pour over bread. Refrigerate, covered, for 8 hours or overnight.

4. Preheat oven to 375°. Remove French toast from refrigerator while oven heats. Bake, uncovered, until a knife inserted in the center comes out clean, 35-40 minutes. Let stand 5-10 minutes. Invert to serve.

1 PIECE: 658 cal., 31g fat (17g sat. fat), 218mg chol., 584mg sod., 84g carb. (39g sugars, 4g fiber), 14g pro.

CHEDDAR BACON GRITS

In the South, grits are served plain with a little butter or loaded with extras, as is my recipe with bacon, cheddar and green chiles.
—*Amanda Reed, Nashville, TN*

TAKES: 30 MIN. • MAKES: 12 SERVINGS

8 cups water
2 cups uncooked old-fashioned grits
1 tsp. salt
¼ tsp. paprika
2 cups shredded white cheddar cheese
5 bacon strips, cooked and crumbled
1 can (4 oz.) chopped green chiles
Sliced green onions, optional

1. In a 6-qt. stockpot, bring water to a boil. Slowly stir in grits, salt and paprika. Reduce heat; cook, covered, 15-20 minutes or until thickened, stirring occasionally.

2. Reduce heat to low. Stir in cheese, bacon and chiles until cheese is melted. If desired, sprinkle with green onions.

¾ CUP: 199 cal., 8g fat (4g sat. fat), 22mg chol., 418mg sod., 24g carb. (0 sugars, 1g fiber), 7g pro.

BANANAS FOSTER
BAKED FRENCH TOAST

OVERNIGHT CHERRY-ALMOND OATMEAL

Would you like breakfast ready for you when the sun comes up? If so, try my hot cereal. It's so simple: Just place the ingredients in the slow cooker and turn it on before you go to bed. In the morning, enjoy a healthy, warm and satisfying dish.
—*Geraldine Saucier, Albuquerque, NM*

PREP: 10 MIN. • **COOK:** 7 HOURS • **MAKES:** 6 SERVINGS

4 cups vanilla almond milk	**⅓ cup packed brown sugar**
1 cup steel-cut oats	**½ tsp. salt**
1 cup dried cherries	**½ tsp. ground cinnamon**

1. In a 3-qt. slow cooker coated with cooking spray, combine all ingredients. Cook, covered, on low until oats are tender, 7-8 hours.

2. Stir before serving. If desired, serve with additional milk.

NOTE: Steel-cut oats are also known as Scotch oats or Irish oatmeal.

¾ CUP: 276 cal., 4g fat (0 sat. fat), 0 chol., 306mg sod., 57g carb. (35g sugars, 4g fiber), 5g pro.

GLAZED FRUIT MEDLEY

The orange dressing on this salad complements the fresh fruit flavors beautifully. It's perfect for a spring or summer brunch.
—*Karen Bourne, Magrath, AB*

PREP: 20 MIN. + CHILLING • **MAKES:** 10 SERVINGS

2 cups orange juice
1 cup sugar
2 Tbsp. cornstarch
3 cups cubed honeydew melon
3 medium firm bananas, sliced
2 cups green grapes
2 cups halved fresh strawberries

1. In a small saucepan, mix orange juice, sugar and cornstarch until smooth. Bring to a boil, stirring constantly; cook and stir for 2 minutes or until thickened. Transfer to a small bowl; cool slightly. Refrigerate, covered, for at least 2 hours.

2. Just before serving, combine the fruit in a large serving bowl. Drizzle with orange juice mixture; toss gently to coat.

¾ CUP: 188 cal., 1g fat (0 sat. fat), 0 chol., 7mg sod., 47g carb. (41g sugars, 2g fiber), 1g pro.

BLUEBERRY-ORANGE BLINTZES

Blintzes are aces for brunch time because I can make the crepes ahead.
They taste so indulgent that guests don't know they're lower in fat and calories.
—Mary Johnson, Coloma, WI

PREP: 25 MIN. + CHILLING • **BAKE:** 10 MIN. • **MAKES:** 6 SERVINGS

1   **large egg**
1   **cup fat-free milk**
¾   **cup all-purpose flour**
1   **carton (15 oz.) part-skim ricotta cheese**
6   **Tbsp. orange marmalade, divided**
1   **Tbsp. sugar**
⅛   **tsp. ground cinnamon**
2   **cups fresh blueberries or raspberries, divided**
⅔   **cup reduced-fat sour cream**

1. In a large bowl, whisk egg, milk and flour until blended. Refrigerate, covered, 1 hour.

2. Preheat oven to 350°. Place a 6-in. skillet coated with cooking spray over medium heat. Stir batter; fill a ¼-cup measure halfway with batter and pour into center of pan. Quickly lift and tilt pan to coat bottom evenly. Cook until top appears dry; turn crepe over and cook 15-20 seconds longer or until bottom is cooked. Remove to a wire rack. Repeat with remaining batter.

3. In a small bowl, mix ricotta cheese, 2 Tbsp. marmalade, sugar and cinnamon. Spoon about 2 Tbsp. mixture onto each crepe; top with about 1 Tbsp. blueberries. Fold opposite sides of crepes over filling, forming a rectangular bundle.

4. Place blintzes on a 15x10x1-in. baking pan coated with cooking spray, seam side down. Bake, uncovered, for 10-15 minutes or until heated through. Serve with sour cream and the remaining marmalade and blueberries.

FREEZE OPTION: Freeze cooled crepes between layers of waxed paper in a freezer container. To use, thaw in refrigerator overnight. Proceed as directed.

2 BLINTZES WITH TOPPINGS: 301 cal., 9g fat (5g sat. fat), 63mg chol., 129mg sod., 42g carb. (23g sugars, 2g fiber), 14g pro.
DIABETIC EXCHANGES: 2 starch, 2 lean meat, ½ fruit.

BAKED EGGS LORRAINE

Super easy and elegant, this is one of my favorite special-occasion dishes. It's absolutely delicious!
—Sandra Woolard, DeLand, FL

PREP: 15 MIN. • COOK: 25 MIN. • MAKES: 2 SERVINGS

4 slices Canadian bacon
2 slices Swiss cheese
4 large eggs
2 Tbsp. sour cream
⅛ tsp. salt
⅛ tsp. pepper
 Minced chives, optional

1. Coat 2 shallow oval 1½-cup baking dishes with cooking spray. Line with Canadian bacon; top with cheese. Carefully break 2 eggs into each dish.

2. In a small bowl, whisk sour cream, salt and pepper until smooth; drop by teaspoonfuls onto eggs.

3. Bake, uncovered, at 350° for 25-30 minutes or until eggs are completely set. Sprinkle with chives if desired.

1 SERVING: 349 cal., 23g fat (11g sat. fat), 485mg chol., 1051mg sod., 2g carb. (2g sugars, 0 fiber), 30g pro.

POTLUCK EGGS BENEDICT

If you're looking for a hearty breakfast or brunch dish, look no further. Folks can't wait to dig in to the combination of eggs, ham, cheese and asparagus in this recipe.
—Pauline Van Breemen, Franklin, IN

TAKES: 30 MIN. • MAKES: 12 SERVINGS

1 lb. fresh asparagus, trimmed
¾ cup butter, cubed
¾ cup all-purpose flour
4 cups whole milk
1 can (14½ oz.) chicken broth
1 lb. cubed fully cooked ham
1 cup shredded cheddar cheese
8 hard-boiled large eggs, quartered
½ tsp. salt
⅛ tsp. cayenne pepper
12 biscuits, warmed

1. Cut asparagus into ½-in. pieces, using only tender parts of spears. Cook in a small amount of boiling water until tender, about 5 minutes; drain. Set aside to cool.

2. Melt butter in a saucepan; stir in flour until smooth. Add milk and broth; bring to a boil. Cook and stir for 2 minutes. Add ham and cheese; stir until cheese is melted. Add eggs, salt, cayenne and asparagus; heat through. Serve over biscuits.

¾ CUP WITH 1 BISCUIT: 491 cal., 31g fat (18g sat. fat), 192mg chol., 1371mg sod., 33g carb. (7g sugars, 1g fiber), 21g pro.

CHEESY HASH BROWN BAKE

Prepare this cheesy dish ahead of time for
less stress on brunch day. You'll love it!
—*Karen Burns, Chandler, TX*

PREP: 10 MIN. • **BAKE:** 40 MIN. • **MAKES:** 10 SERVINGS

1 pkg. (30 oz.) frozen
shredded hash brown
potatoes, thawed
2 cans (10¾ oz. each)
condensed cream of
potato soup, undiluted
2 cups sour cream

2 cups shredded cheddar
cheese, divided
1 cup grated Parmesan
cheese
Sliced green onions,
optional

1. Preheat oven to 350°. In a large bowl, combine potatoes, soup, sour cream, 1¾ cups cheddar cheese and the Parmesan cheese. Place in a greased 3-qt. baking dish. Sprinkle with the remaining cheddar cheese.

2. Bake, uncovered, until bubbly and the cheese is melted, 40-45 minutes. Let stand 5 minutes before serving. If desired, sprinkle with green onions.

½ CUP: 305 cal., 18g fat (12g sat. fat), 65mg chol., 554mg sod., 21g carb. (3g sugars, 1g fiber), 12g pro.

ZIPPY HASH BROWN BAKE: Substitute pepper jack cheese for the cheddar and omit the Parmesan.

NACHO HASH BROWN BAKE: Substitute 1 can (10¾ oz.) condensed cream of celery soup and 1 can (10¾ oz.) condensed nacho cheese soup for the potato soup. Substitute Mexican cheese blend for the cheddar and omit the Parmesan.

FROM GRANDMA'S KITCHEN: Try adding a crunchy topping such as cornflakes, french-fried onions or crushed Ritz crackers tossed with butter.

HAM CROQUETTES WITH
MUSTARD SAUCE, PAGE 61

SNACKS

Turn your typical afternoon snack into a tasty treat
with these small plates and delicious bites. They'll
keep you satisfied all the way to supper.

STICKY MAPLE
PEPPER GLAZED
CHICKEN WINGS

STICKY MAPLE PEPPER GLAZED CHICKEN WINGS

This is one of my favorite appetizers to make over the holidays! The coarse ground
pepper cuts the sweetness of the maple syrup by adding just the right amount of heat.
These chicken wings are best fresh out of the oven (they are nice and crispy),
but they are also delicious if made ahead and kept warm in a slow cooker.
—*Shannon Dobos, Calgary, AB*

PREP: 25 MIN. • BAKE: 40 MIN. • MAKES: ABOUT 40 PIECES

SNACKS

4 lbs. chicken wings
¼ cup all-purpose flour
½ Tbsp. baking powder
1 tsp. coarsely ground pepper
1 tsp. kosher salt
½ tsp. garlic powder

GLAZE
⅔ cup maple syrup
2 tsp. coarsely ground pepper
2 tsp. soy sauce
1 garlic clove, minced
Chopped green onions, optional

1. Preheat oven to 425°. Line two 15x10x1-in. baking pans with foil and coat with cooking spray; set aside.

2. Using a sharp knife, cut through the 2 wing joints; discard wing tips. In a shallow bowl, combine flour, baking powder, pepper, salt and garlic powder. Add wing pieces, a few at a time, and toss to coat; shake off excess.

3. Place on prepared baking sheets. Bake until no longer pink, 40-50 minutes, turning once. Meanwhile, in a small saucepan, combine glaze ingredients. Bring to a boil. Reduce heat; simmer until thickened, 5-7 minutes, stirring frequently. Drizzle over wings; toss to coat. If desired, top with chopped green onions.

1 PIECE: 66 cal., 3g fat (1g sat. fat), 14mg chol., 63mg sod., 4g carb. (3g sugars, 0 fiber), 5g pro.

CARAMEL APPLE FLOAT

Who doesn't love the flavors of caramel, apples and vanilla ice cream together? If I'm feeling fancy,
I drizzle caramel syrup around the inside of my glass before adding the apple cider and ginger ale.
—*Cindy Reams, Philipsburg, PA*

TAKES: 10 MIN. • MAKES: 2 SERVINGS

1 cup chilled apple cider or unsweetened apple juice
1 cup chilled ginger ale or lemon-lime soda
1 cup vanilla ice cream
2 Tbsp. caramel sundae syrup
Finely chopped peeled apple, optional

Divide cider and ginger ale between 2 glasses. Top each with ice cream; drizzle with caramel syrup. Add the chopped apples if desired.

1 SERVING: 220 cal., 4g fat (2g sat. fat), 15mg chol., 102mg sod., 46g carb. (41g sugars, 0 fiber), 2g pro.

41

CREAMY JALAPENO POPPER DIP

This recipe will remind you of a jalapeno popper without all the messiness.
If my husband had his way, he would have me make this for him every weekend.
Serve it with tortilla chips, whole wheat crackers or pita chips.
—*Deborah Peirce, Virginia Beach, VA*

PREP: 15 MIN. • BAKE: 30 MIN. • MAKES: 2 CUPS

4 **bacon strips, chopped**
1 **pkg. (8 oz.) cream cheese, softened**
2 **cups shredded cheddar cheese**
½ **cup sour cream**
¼ **cup 2% milk**
3 **jalapeno peppers, seeded and chopped**
1 **tsp. white wine vinegar**
⅓ **cup panko bread crumbs**
2 **Tbsp. butter**
Tortilla chips

1. Preheat oven to 350°. In a small skillet, cook bacon over medium heat until crisp, stirring occasionally. Remove with a slotted spoon; drain on paper towels. Discard drippings, reserving 1 Tbsp..

2. In a large bowl, mix cream cheese, cheddar cheese, sour cream, milk, jalapenos, vinegar, cooked bacon and reserved drippings. Transfer to a greased 8-in. square baking dish. Sprinkle with bread crumbs; dot with butter.

3. Bake until bubbly and topping is golden brown, 30-35 minutes. Serve with chips.

NOTE: Wear disposable gloves when cutting hot peppers; the oils can burn skin. Avoid touching your face.

¼ CUP: 422 cal., 36g fat (24g sat. fat), 120mg chol., 566mg sod., 6g carb. (1g sugars, 0 fiber), 18g pro.

OLD-FASHIONED EGGNOG

Celebrating the holidays with eggnog is an American tradition that dates to Colonial days. I toast the season with a smooth and creamy concoction that keeps family and friends coming back for more.
—*Pat Waymire, Yellow Springs, OH*

PREP: 40 MIN. + CHILLING • MAKES: 16 SERVINGS (ABOUT 3 QT.)

12 **large eggs**
1½ **cups sugar**
½ **tsp. salt**
2 **qt. whole milk, divided**
2 **Tbsp. vanilla extract**
1 **tsp. ground nutmeg**
2 **cups heavy whipping cream**
Optional: Whipped cream, additional nutmeg and cinnamon sticks

1. In a heavy saucepan, whisk together eggs, sugar and salt. Gradually add 1 qt. milk. Cook and stir over low heat until a thermometer reads 160°, about 25 minutes. Pour into a large bowl; stir in vanilla, nutmeg and remaining milk. Place bowl in an ice-water bath; stir frequently until cool. If mixture separates, process in a blender until smooth. Cover and refrigerate at least 3 hours.

2. When ready to serve, beat cream in a bowl on high until soft peaks form; whisk gently into cooled mixture. Pour eggnog into a chilled 5-qt. punch bowl. If desired, top the eggnog with dollops of whipped cream, sprinkle with additional nutmeg and serve with cinnamon sticks.

¾ CUP: 308 cal., 18g fat (10g sat. fat), 186mg chol., 188mg sod., 26g carb. (26g sugars, 0 fiber), 9g pro.

CHEESE-STUFFED CHERRY TOMATOES

We grow plenty of tomatoes, so my husband and I often handpick enough cherry tomatoes for these easy-to-fix appetizers. This is one of our favorite recipes, and it's impossible to eat just one.

—*Mary Lou Robison, Greensboro, NC*

PREP: 15 MIN. + CHILLING • **MAKES:** 1 DOZEN

1 pint cherry tomatoes
1 pkg. (4 oz.) crumbled feta cheese
½ cup finely chopped red onion
½ cup olive oil
¼ cup red wine vinegar
1 Tbsp. dried oregano
Salt and pepper to taste

1. Cut a thin slice off the top of each tomato. Scoop out and discard pulp. Invert tomatoes onto paper towels to drain. Combine cheese and onion; spoon into tomatoes.

2. In a small bowl, whisk the oil, vinegar, oregano, salt and pepper. Spoon over tomatoes. Cover and refrigerate 30 minutes or until ready to serve.

1 TOMATO: 111 cal., 11g fat (2g sat. fat), 5mg chol., 93mg sod., 2g carb. (1g sugars, 1g fiber), 2g pro.

QUICK WATERMELON COOLER

Summer means cooling off with a slice of watermelon and a glass of cold lemonade. This combines two favorites in one.

—*Darlene Brenden, Salem, OR*

TAKES: 10 MIN. • **MAKES:** 4 SERVINGS

2 cups lemonade
3 cups seedless watermelon, coarsely chopped
1 cup crushed ice

1. In a blender, combine all ingredients; cover and process until smooth. Pour into chilled glasses; serve immediately.

1 CUP: 86 cal., 0 fat (0 sat. fat), 0 chol., 12mg sod., 24g carb. (22g sugars, 1g fiber), 0 pro. **DIABETIC EXCHANGES:** 1 starch, ½ fruit.

"We made a big, punch-bowl–sized batch of this for a bridal shower, and everyone loved it! It's delicious and not too sweet, and it really lives up to the name of 'cooler.'"
—ELIZSETON, TASTEOFHOME.COM

AIR-FRYER PIZZA PUFFS

I love pizza in any form, so it seemed only logical to turn my pizza love into an appetizer. These little bundles can be made ahead of time and chilled until you're ready to pop them into the air fryer.
—*Vivi Taylor, Middleburg, FL*

PREP: 20 MIN. • COOK: 10 MIN./BATCH • MAKES: 20 SERVINGS

1 loaf (1 lb.) frozen pizza
  dough, thawed
20 slices pepperoni
8 oz. part-skim mozzarella
  cheese, cut into 20 cubes
¼ cup butter
2 small garlic cloves,
  minced
  Dash salt
  Marinara sauce, warmed
  Optional: Crushed red
  pepper flakes and grated
  Parmesan cheese

1. Preheat air fryer to 350°. Shape dough into 1½-in. balls; flatten into ⅛-in.-thick circles. Place 1 pepperoni slice and 1 cheese cube in center of each circle; wrap dough around pepperoni and cheese. Pinch the edges to seal; shape into a ball. Repeat with remaining dough, cheese and pepperoni.

2. In batches, place seam side up in a single layer on greased tray in the air-fryer basket; cook until light golden brown, 6-8 minutes. Cool slightly.

3. Meanwhile, in a small saucepan, melt butter over low heat. Add garlic and salt, taking care not to brown butter or garlic; brush over puffs. Serve with the marinara sauce; if desired, sprinkle with red pepper flakes and Parmesan.

FREEZE OPTION: Cover and freeze the unbaked pizza puffs on waxed paper-lined baking sheets until firm. Transfer to a freezer container; seal and return to freezer. To use, preheat air fryer to 350°; cook pizza puffs on greased tray in air-fryer basket as directed, increasing time as necessary until golden brown.

NOTE: In our testing, we find cook times vary dramatically between brands of air fryers. As a result, we give wider than normal ranges on suggested cook times. Begin checking at the first time listed and adjust as needed.

1 PIZZA PUFF: 120 cal., 6g fat (3g sat. fat), 15mg chol., 189mg sod., 11g carb. (1g sugars, 0 fiber), 5g pro.

GRANDMA'S SECRET

If you want to enjoy these pizza puffs with a little more of a spicy hit, try substituting pepper jack for the mozzarella cheese.

PROSCIUTTO PHYLLO ROLL-UPS

These elegant finger foods use delicate phyllo dough. With artichoke sauce on the side, the cheesy rolls make extra-special hors d'oeuvres.

—*Michaela Rosenthal, Indio, CA*

PREP: 30 MIN. • **BAKE:** 10 MIN. • **MAKES:** 2 DOZEN (1 CUP SAUCE)

24 sheets phyllo dough (14x9 in.)
¼ cup butter, melted
8 thin slices prosciutto, cut into 1-in. strips
24 fresh asparagus spears, trimmed
24 fresh green beans, trimmed

ARTICHOKE SAUCE

¼ cup sour cream
½ tsp. lemon juice
1 jar (6 oz.) marinated artichoke hearts, drained
2 oz. cream cheese, softened
¼ cup chopped roasted sweet red peppers, drained
3 Tbsp. grated Parmesan cheese
2 green onions, chopped
1 garlic clove, peeled
¼ tsp. white pepper
¼ tsp. cayenne pepper

1. Preheat oven to 400°. Line baking sheets with parchment; set aside. Place 1 sheet of phyllo dough on a work surface (keep the remaining dough covered with a damp towel to avoid drying out). Brush with butter; fold in half lengthwise. Brush with butter; fold in half widthwise.

2. Brush with the butter; top with a prosciutto strip. Place an asparagus spear and a green bean at a diagonal on bottom right corner; roll up. Repeat with remaining dough, butter, prosciutto and vegetables.

3. Place roll-ups on prepared baking sheets. Bake until golden brown, 6-8 minutes. Meanwhile, in a blender, combine sauce ingredients; cover and process until smooth. Transfer to a small bowl; serve with roll-ups.

1 ROLL-UP WITH 2 TSP. SAUCE: 90 cal., 5g fat (3g sat. fat), 14mg chol., 218mg sod., 8g carb. (1g sugars, 1g fiber), 3g pro.

PEANUT BUTTER, STRAWBERRY & HONEY SANDWICH

Who needs jam when you have fresh strawberries? A drizzle of honey and a bit of mint make this sandwich stand out.
—*James Schend, Pleasant Prairie, WI*

TAKES: 5 MIN. • MAKES: 1 SERVING

1 Tbsp. creamy
  peanut butter
1 slice crusty white bread
¼ cup sliced fresh
  strawberries
1 tsp. thinly sliced
  fresh mint
1 tsp. honey

Spread peanut butter over bread. Top with strawberries and mint; drizzle with honey.

1 OPEN-FACED SANDWICH: 208 cal., 9g fat (2g sat. fat), 0 chol., 211mg sod., 27g carb. (11g sugars, 2g fiber), 6g pro.

FROM GRANDMA'S KITCHEN: If you're in a pinch and don't have mint handy, you could substitute basil or thyme.

MAPLE CRUNCH POPCORN

For a snack that's sure to bring smiles, try this medley of popcorn and pecans covered in a sweet and buttery coating.
—*Elmira Trombetti, Paducah, KY*

TAKES: 25 MIN. • MAKES: 3½ QT.

10 cups popped popcorn
1½ cups pecan halves,
  toasted
1⅓ cups sugar
1 cup butter, cubed
¼ cup maple syrup
¼ cup corn syrup
½ tsp. salt
1 tsp. maple flavoring

1. Place popcorn and pecans in a large bowl; set aside. In a large heavy saucepan, combine the sugar, butter, maple syrup, corn syrup and salt. Cook and stir over medium heat until a candy thermometer reads 300° (hard-crack stage). Remove from heat; stir in maple flavoring. Quickly pour over popcorn mixture and mix well.

2. Transfer to baking sheets lined with waxed paper to cool. Break into clusters. Store in airtight containers.

NOTE: We recommend that you test your candy thermometer before each use by bringing water to a boil; the thermometer should read 212°. Adjust your recipe temperature up or down based on your test.

¾ CUP: 270 cal., 19g fat (7g sat. fat), 27mg chol., 205mg sod., 25g carb. (19g sugars, 1g fiber), 1g pro.

TOMATO-HERB FOCACCIA

With its medley of herbs and tomatoes, this rustic bread will liven up any occasion, whether it's a family dinner or a game-day get-together. It never lasts long!
—*Janet Miller, Indianapolis, IN*

PREP: 30 MIN. + RISING • **BAKE:** 20 MIN. • **MAKES:** 12 SERVINGS

1 pkg. (¼ oz.) active dry yeast
1 cup warm water (110° to 115°)
2 Tbsp. olive oil, divided
1½ tsp. salt
1 tsp. sugar
1 tsp. garlic powder
1 tsp. each dried oregano, thyme and rosemary, crushed
½ tsp. dried basil
Dash pepper
2 to 2½ cups all-purpose flour
2 plum tomatoes, thinly sliced
¼ cup shredded part-skim mozzarella cheese
1 Tbsp. grated Parmesan cheese

1. In a large bowl, dissolve yeast in warm water. Add 1 Tbsp. oil, salt, sugar, garlic powder, herbs, pepper and 1½ cups flour. Beat until smooth. Stir in enough remaining flour to form a soft dough (dough will be sticky).

2. Turn onto a floured surface; knead until smooth and elastic, 6-8 minutes. Place in a greased bowl, turning once to grease the top. Cover and let rise in a warm place until doubled, about 1 hour.

3. Punch dough down. Cover and let rest for 10 minutes. Shape into a 13x9-in. rectangle; place on a greased baking sheet. Cover and let rise until doubled, about 30 minutes. With fingertips, make several dimples over top of dough.

4. Brush dough with remaining oil; arrange tomatoes over the top. Sprinkle with cheeses. Bake at 400° for 20-25 minutes or until golden brown. Remove to a wire rack.

FREEZE OPTION: Freeze cooled focaccia squares in freezer containers, separating layers with waxed paper. To use, reheat the squares on a baking sheet in a preheated 400° oven until heated through.

1 PIECE: 112 cal., 3g fat (1g sat. fat), 2mg chol., 320mg sod., 18g carb. (1g sugars, 1g fiber), 3g pro. **DIABETIC EXCHANGES:** 1 starch, ½ fat.

FROM GRANDMA'S KITCHEN: The best way to tell if your bread dough is properly kneaded is the windowpane test. To do this, tear off a chunk of dough and stretch it between your fingers. If the dough tears, you haven't developed enough gluten and it needs more kneading. If the dough stretches without breaking, making a windowpane of sorts, you're finished and you can let the dough rest.

FRIED CHEESE RAVIOLI

Be sure to make enough of these crispy, coated ravioli. They're bound to be the hit of your party. The golden-brown pillows are easy to pick up and dip in tomato sauce.
—*Kate Dampier, Quail Valley, CA*

PREP: 15 MIN. • COOK: 20 MIN. • MAKES: ABOUT 2½ DOZEN

1 pkg. (9 oz.) refrigerated cheese ravioli
1 large egg, room temperature
1 cup seasoned bread crumbs
¼ cup shredded Parmesan cheese
1½ tsp. dried basil
½ cup canola oil, divided
Additional shredded Parmesan cheese, optional
1 cup marinara sauce or meatless spaghetti sauce, warmed

1. Cook ravioli according to package directions; drain and pat dry. In a shallow bowl, lightly beat the egg. In another shallow bowl, combine the bread crumbs, cheese and basil. Dip ravioli in egg, then in bread crumb mixture.

2. In a large skillet or deep-fat fryer, heat ¼ cup oil over medium heat. Fry the ravioli in batches for 30-60 seconds on each side or until golden brown and crispy; drain on paper towels. Halfway through frying, replace the oil; wipe out skillet with paper towels if necessary.

3. Sprinkle with additional cheese if desired. Serve ravioli with marinara sauce.

1 RAVIOLI: 58 cal., 2g fat (1g sat. fat), 11mg chol., 158mg sod., 7g carb. (1g sugars, 1g fiber), 2g pro.

MOM'S MEATBALLS

These moist meatballs are tender and flavorful. Serve some for dinner and freeze the extras to enjoy on a rainy day.
—*Dorothy Smith, El Dorado, AR*

TAKES: 25 MIN. • MAKES: 7 DOZEN

1½ cups chopped onion
⅓ cup ketchup
3 Tbsp. lemon juice
1 Tbsp. Worcestershire sauce
¾ cup crushed saltines (about 24 crackers)
3 lbs. ground beef

1. In a large bowl, combine the onion, ketchup, lemon juice, Worcestershire sauce and crackers. Crumble the beef over mixture and mix lightly but thoroughly. Shape into 1-in. balls.

2. Place the meatballs on a greased rack in a shallow baking pan. Bake, uncovered, at 400° for 10 minutes or until meat is no longer pink; drain. Serve meatballs immediately, or refrigerate or freeze for use in other recipes.

1 MEATBALL: 36 cal., 2g fat (1g sat. fat), 11mg chol., 28mg sod., 1g carb. (0 sugars, 0 fiber), 3g pro.

"I make these meatballs often. Although there is no sauce, our family loves them—sometimes just by themselves! They're great, however, tossed into spaghetti sauce or on a hoagie roll."
—FAITHFULEA, TASTEOFHOME.COM

FRIED
CHEESE RAVIOLI

GRANDMA'S SECRET
Consider trying this recipe with other types of ravioli, such as beef or sausage ravioli, or specialty ravioli, such as those stuffed with butternut squash, mushroom or lobster.

CHEESY
SUN CRISPS

CHEESY SUN CRISPS

These crisps have a wonderful cheesy flavor that's perfect for snacking.
—*Mary Detweiler, Middlefield, OH*

PREP: 10 MIN. + CHILLING • BAKE: 10 MIN. • MAKES: 32 SERVINGS

- 2 **cups shredded cheddar cheese**
- ½ **cup grated Parmesan cheese**
- ½ **cup butter, softened**
- 3 **Tbsp. water**
- 1 **cup all-purpose flour**
- ¼ **tsp. salt**
- 1 **cup quick-cooking oats**
- ⅔ **cup roasted salted sunflower kernels**

1. In a bowl, combine cheddar and Parmesan cheeses, butter and water until well mixed. Combine the flour and salt; add to cheese mixture. Stir in oats and sunflower kernels. Knead dough until it holds together. Shape into a 12-in. roll.

2. Wrap tightly; chill for 4 hours or overnight. Allow to stand at room temperature for 10 minutes before cutting into ⅛-in. slices. Preheat oven to 400°.

3. Place on greased foil-lined baking sheets. Bake until edges are golden, 8 to 10 minutes. Slide crackers and foil off baking sheets to wire racks to cool.

3 CRISPS: 97 cal., 7g fat (4g sat. fat), 16mg chol., 130mg sod., 5g carb. (0 sugars, 1g fiber), 3g pro.

HOLIDAY HOT DRINK MIX

This is a fantastic mix to have in the cupboard for cold wintry days. Using strawberry drink mix instead of chocolate makes it fun for kids of all ages.
—*Nancy Zimmerman, Cape May Court House, NJ*

PREP: 5 MIN. • MAKES: 15 SERVINGS (5 CUPS MIX)

- 2½ **cups nonfat dry milk powder**
- 2 **cups white or pastel miniature marshmallows**
- 1 **cup strawberry or chocolate drink mix**
- ½ **cup confectioners' sugar**
- ⅓ **cup buttermilk blend powder**
- ⅓ **cup powdered nondairy creamer**

ADDITIONAL INGREDIENT (FOR EACH SERVING)
- ¾ **cup boiling water**

1. In a large bowl, combine the first 6 ingredients. Store in an airtight container in a cool, dry place for up to 6 months.

2. To prepare each serving: Dissolve ⅓ cup mix in ¾ cup boiling water; stir well.

NOTE: This recipe was tested with Nesquik drink mix and Saco brand buttermilk blend powder.

⅓ CUP MIX: 118 cal., 1g fat (1g sat. fat), 4mg chol., 123mg sod., 23g carb. (20g sugars, 0 fiber), 5g pro.

FROM GRANDMA'S KITCHEN: To make these drinks extra festive, try moistening the rim of a glass with honey and dipping it into a bowl of red or green nonpareils to make a sprinkle-coated rim. Serve with the prepared drink mix.

CRAB CAKES WITH CHESAPEAKE BAY MAYO

I placed my personal stamp on my Aunt Ellie's crab cake recipe by changing
up some of her ingredients. They're served with a tart and tangy creamy sauce.
You can serve them on an appetizer spread or as a terrific first course at a formal dinner.
—*Michelle Critchell, Moon, VA*

PREP: 20 MIN. + CHILLING • **COOK:** 10 MIN./BATCH • **MAKES:** 16 APPETIZERS

½ cup sour cream
½ cup mayonnaise
2 Tbsp. sweet pickle relish
1 Tbsp. spicy brown mustard
¼ tsp. seafood seasoning

CRAB CAKES

1 large egg, beaten
¼ cup grated Parmesan cheese
¼ cup seasoned bread crumbs
¼ cup mayonnaise
2 Tbsp. finely chopped onion
1 Tbsp. minced fresh parsley
1 Tbsp. spicy brown mustard
½ tsp. seafood seasoning
⅛ tsp. pepper
3 cans (6 oz. each) lump crabmeat, drained
¼ cup canola oil

1. In a large bowl, combine the first 5 ingredients. Cover and chill until serving. For crab cakes, in a large bowl, combine egg, cheese, bread crumbs, mayonnaise, onion, parsley, mustard, seafood seasoning and pepper. Fold in crab. Refrigerate for at least 30 minutes.

2. With floured hands, shape the mixture by 2 tablespoonfuls into ½-in.-thick patties. In a large skillet over medium heat, cook crab cakes in oil in batches for 3-4 minutes on each side or until golden brown. Serve with sauce.

1 SERVING: 174 cal., 14g fat (3g sat. fat), 51mg chol., 287mg sod., 2g carb. (1g sugars, 0 fiber), 8g pro.

FROM GRANDMA'S KITCHEN: To prevent your cutting board from slipping around on the counter when you're chopping or mincing ingredients, get a kitchen towel damp and put it under the cutting board.

CHICKEN SALAD IN BASKETS

When I first made these cute little cups, they were a big hit.
They make a yummy appetizer for an Easter gathering.
—*Gwendolyn Fae Trapp, Strongsville, OH*

PREP: 15 MIN. • BAKE: 15 MIN. + CHILLING • MAKES: 20 APPETIZERS

1 cup diced cooked chicken	**⅛** tsp. salt
3 bacon strips, cooked and crumbled	Dash pepper
⅓ cup chopped mushrooms	**20** slices bread
2 Tbsp. chopped pecans	**6** Tbsp. butter, melted
2 Tbsp. diced peeled apple	**2** Tbsp. minced fresh parsley
¼ cup mayonnaise	

1. In a small bowl, combine the first 5 ingredients. Combine mayonnaise, salt and pepper; add to chicken mixture and stir to coat. Cover and refrigerate until serving.

2. Preheat oven to 350°. Cut each slice of bread with a 3-in. round cookie cutter; brush both sides with butter. Press into ungreased mini muffin cups. Bake for 11-13 minutes or until golden brown and crisp.

3. Cool 3 minutes before removing from pans to wire racks to cool completely. Spoon 1 Tbsp. chicken salad into each bread basket. Cover and refrigerate up to 2 hours. Just before serving, sprinkle with parsley.

1 APPETIZER: 140 cal., 8g fat (3g sat. fat), 17mg chol., 223mg sod., 12g carb. (2g sugars, 1g fiber), 5g pro.

LEMONADE ICED TEA

I have always loved iced tea with lemon, and this delightful thirst quencher just takes it one step further.
Lemonade gives the drink a nice color too. I dress up each glass with a slice of lemon on the rim.
—*Gail Buss, New Bern, NC*

PREP: 15 MIN. + CHILLING • MAKES: 12 SERVINGS (3 QT.)

3 qt. water
9 tea bags
¾ to 1¼ cups sugar
1 can (12 oz.) frozen lemonade concentrate, thawed
Lemon slices, optional

In a Dutch oven, bring water to a boil. Remove from the heat; add tea bags. Cover and steep for 5 minutes. Discard tea bags. Stir in the sugar and lemonade concentrate. Cover and refrigerate until chilled. Serve over ice. If desired, garnish with lemon slices.

1 CUP: 100 cal., 0 fat (0 sat. fat), 0 chol., 1mg sod., 26g carb. (25g sugars, 0 fiber), 0 pro.

CHEESY CARAMELIZED
ONION SKILLET BREAD

CHEESY CARAMELIZED ONION SKILLET BREAD

This appetizer is perfect for a football game or informal party, but it came about because I have two sons who are always hungry. I needed time to get dinner on the table after coming home from work. They love the skillet bread for the flavor, and I love it because it keeps them in the kitchen to chat while I prepare the rest of dinner! If you'd like, you can use homemade biscuits instead of prepared.
—*Mary M. Leverette, Columbia, SC*

PREP: 45 MIN. • BAKE: 20 MIN. • MAKES: 8 SERVINGS

2 tsp. caraway seeds
1 Tbsp. olive oil
1 large onion, chopped
¼ tsp. salt
1 cup shredded sharp cheddar cheese
½ cup butter, melted
1 tube (16.3 oz.) large refrigerated buttermilk biscuits
1 Tbsp. minced fresh thyme, optional

1. Preheat oven to 350°. In a 10-in. cast-iron or other ovenproof skillet, toast caraway seeds until fragrant, about 1 minute. Remove and set aside.

2. In same skillet, heat oil over medium heat. Add onion; cook and stir until softened, 5-6 minutes. Reduce heat to medium-low; cook until deep golden brown, 30-40 minutes, stirring occasionally. Stir in salt; remove from the heat and cool slightly.

3. Sprinkle cheese over onions in skillet. Place melted butter and caraway seeds in a shallow bowl. Cut each biscuit into fourths. Dip biscuit pieces in butter mixture; place in a single layer over onion mixture in skillet.

4. Bake until puffed and golden brown, 20-25 minutes. Cool in skillet 5 minutes before inverting onto a serving plate. If desired, sprinkle with thyme. Serve warm.

1 SERVING: 352 cal., 25g fat (13g sat. fat), 45mg chol., 874mg sod., 27g carb. (4g sugars, 1g fiber), 7g pro.

ROASTED VEGETABLE DIP

While my children were always very good eaters, I came up with this recipe to get them to eat more veggies and like it. The dip doesn't last long in our house!
—*Sarah Vasques, Milford, NH*

PREP: 15 MIN. • BAKE: 25 MIN. + COOLING • MAKES: 20 SERVINGS

2 large sweet red peppers
1 large zucchini
1 medium onion
1 Tbsp. olive oil
½ tsp. salt
¼ tsp. pepper
1 pkg. (8 oz.) reduced-fat cream cheese
Assorted crackers or fresh vegetables

1. Preheat oven to 425°. Cut vegetables into 1-in. pieces. Place in a 15x10x1-in. baking pan coated with cooking spray; toss with oil, salt and pepper. Roast for 25-30 minutes or until tender, stirring occasionally. Cool completely.

2. Place the vegetables and cream cheese in a food processor; process until blended. Transfer to a bowl; refrigerate, covered, until serving. Serve with crackers or fresh vegetables.

2 TBSP. DIP: 44 cal., 3g fat (2g sat. fat), 8mg chol., 110mg sod., 3g carb. (2g sugars, 1g fiber), 2g pro.

MUSHROOM PASTRY PINWHEELS

Pinwheels make a pretty addition to any appetizer buffet, and when I serve them they disappear in a snap. These use purchased puff pastry, so they are very easy to make.
—*Mary Bettuchy, Saint Robert, MO*

PREP: 25 MIN. • BAKE: 20 MIN. • MAKES: 16 APPETIZERS

½ lb. fresh mushrooms, finely chopped
2 Tbsp. butter
1 shallot, finely chopped
2 garlic cloves, minced
1 tsp. dried thyme
½ cup dry red wine or beef broth
⅛ tsp. salt
⅛ tsp. pepper
1 sheet frozen puff pastry, thawed
4 oz. spreadable garlic and herb cream cheese

1. Preheat oven to 400°. In a large skillet, saute mushrooms in butter until tender. Add the shallot, garlic and thyme; saute 4-5 minutes longer.

2. Stir in the wine, salt and pepper; bring to a boil. Reduce heat; simmer, uncovered, for 8-10 minutes or until liquid is reduced by three-fourths. Remove from the heat; set aside.

3. On a lightly floured surface, unfold pastry. Roll into a 14x9-in. rectangle. Spread the cheese over pastry; top with mushroom mixture. Roll up jelly-roll style, starting from a short side; pinch seam to seal. Cut into ¾-in. pieces.

4. Place 2 in. apart on a parchment-lined baking sheet. Bake for 16-18 minutes or until golden brown. Serve warm.

1 APPETIZER: 119 cal., 8g fat (3g sat. fat), 13mg chol., 124mg sod., 10g carb. (1g sugars, 1g fiber), 2g pro.

HORSERADISH DEVILED EGGS

People say "Wow!" when they taste these flavorful tangy deviled eggs. The bold combination of ground mustard, dill and horseradish is so appealing. The plate is always emptied when I serve these eggs.
—*Ruth Roth, Linville, NC*

TAKES: 15 MIN. • MAKES: 1 DOZEN

6 hard-boiled large eggs
¼ cup mayonnaise
1 to 2 Tbsp. prepared horseradish
½ tsp. dill weed
¼ tsp. ground mustard
⅛ tsp. salt
Dash pepper
Dash paprika

Cut eggs in half lengthwise. Remove yolks; set whites aside. In a bowl, mash the yolks. Add mayonnaise, horseradish, dill, mustard, salt and pepper; mix well. Pipe or spoon into the egg whites. Sprinkle with paprika. Refrigerate until serving.

2 STUFFED EGG HALVES: 146 cal., 13g fat (3g sat. fat), 215mg chol., 169mg sod., 1g carb. (1g sugars, 0 fiber), 6g pro.

FROM GRANDMA'S KITCHEN: You can peel hard-boiled eggs using a spoon! To start, give the egg a good crack on a hard surface. Then carefully insert a spoon between the shell and the egg and rotate until the shell is completely separated. The shell should peel off easily, with minimal mess.

MUSHROOM
PASTRY
PINWHEELS

PEACHES & CREAM FIZZ

This recipe came about when I was a child living in peach country in eastern Washington. There were fresh peaches everywhere, so my mom and I came up with this beverage. We called it a fizz because there's a bit of bubbling from the ginger ale. By the way, there is no need to peel the peaches. Add more ginger ale to make it thinner, or more ice cream to make it thicker.
—*Teresa Jarnot, Monroe, WA*

TAKES: 10 MIN. • MAKES: 6 SERVINGS

3 medium peaches, pitted
⅓ cup ginger ale, chilled, plus additional for topping if desired

2 Tbsp. honey
1 qt. vanilla ice cream
Optional: Whipped cream and peach slices

Place peaches, ginger ale and honey in a blender; cover and process until smooth. Add the ice cream; cover and process until combined. Pour into serving glasses. If desired, top with whipped cream or additional ginger ale and garnish with peach slices. Serve immediately.

¾ CUP: 237 cal., 10g fat (6g sat. fat), 39mg chol., 72mg sod., 35g carb. (32g sugars, 2g fiber), 4g pro.

ORANGE-CINNAMON PECANS

With a burst of citrus and spice, these glazed pecan halves taste like Christmas in a bowl. Yuletide gatherings just aren't the same without this crunchy, munchy snack.
—*Cleo Gonske, Redding, CA*

PREP: 15 MIN. • BAKE: 30 MIN. + COOLING • MAKES: 3 CUPS

1 cup sugar
½ cup orange juice
2 tsp. ground cinnamon
¼ tsp. ground nutmeg
3 cups pecan halves
1 tsp. butter
1 tsp. vanilla extract

1. Preheat oven to 250°. Line a 15x10x1-in. baking pan with foil.

2. In a large heavy saucepan, combine sugar, orange juice, cinnamon and nutmeg. Bring to a boil, stirring occasionally. Cook over medium heat for 6-8 minutes or until a candy thermometer reads 236° (soft-ball stage), stirring occasionally.

3. Remove from heat; stir in pecans, butter and vanilla. Spread into prepared baking pan. Bake 30 minutes, stirring occasionally. Cool completely. Break apart; store in an airtight container up to 1 week.

⅓ CUP: 328 cal., 24g fat (2g sat. fat), 1mg chol., 4mg sod., 29g carb. (25g sugars, 3g fiber), 3g pro.

HAM CROQUETTES WITH MUSTARD SAUCE

PICTURED ON PAGE 38

Any leftover ham is set aside for these crispy croquettes. I shape them early in the day, then simply fry them at dinnertime. The mustard sauce is mild and pairs well with ham.
—*Kathy Vincek, Toms River, NJ*

PREP: 35 MIN. + CHILLING • COOK: 5 MIN./BATCH • MAKES: 1 DOZEN

2 cups finely chopped fully cooked ham
1 Tbsp. finely chopped onion
1 tsp. minced fresh parsley
¼ cup butter, cubed
¼ cup all-purpose flour
¼ tsp. salt
⅛ tsp. pepper
1 cup 2% milk
1 large egg
2 Tbsp. water
¾ cup dry bread crumbs
  Oil for deep-fat frying

SAUCE
1½ tsp. butter
1½ tsp. all-purpose flour
¼ tsp. salt
  Dash pepper
½ cup 2% milk
4½ tsp. yellow mustard

1. In a small bowl, combine the ham, onion and parsley; set aside.

2. In a small saucepan, melt butter. Stir in the flour, salt and pepper until smooth; gradually add milk. Bring to a boil; cook and stir for 1 minute or until thickened. Stir into ham mixture.

3. Spread into an 8-in. square baking dish; cover and refrigerate for at least 2 hours.

4. In a shallow bowl, combine egg and water. Place bread crumbs in a separate shallow bowl. Shape the ham mixture into 12 balls (mixture will be soft); roll each ball in egg mixture, then in bread crumbs. Cover and refrigerate 2 hours longer.

5. In an electric skillet or deep fryer, heat the oil to 375°. Fry croquettes, a few at a time, for 2-3 minutes or until golden brown, turning once. Drain on paper towels.

6. Meanwhile, for the sauce, in a small saucepan, melt butter. Stir in the flour, salt and pepper until smooth; gradually add milk. Bring to a boil; cook and stir 2 minutes or until thickened. Stir in mustard. Serve with croquettes.

1 CROQUETTE WITH 2 TSP. SAUCE: 188 cal., 14g fat (5g sat. fat), 44mg chol., 503mg sod., 8g carb. (2g sugars, 0 fiber), 7g pro.

PEANUT BUTTER
PUMPKIN BREAD,
PAGE 80

GRANDMA'S FAVORITE
BREADS, BISCUITS & MORE

From crusty loaves and buttery biscuits to tasty pastries and sugary scones, dozens of fresh-baked ways to fill your home with heavenly aromas await!

AIR-FRYER ONION CRESCENT ROLLS

French-fried onions aren't just for green bean casserole. Sprinkle them onto crescent roll dough before rolling up, and you'll end up with a crunchy treat inside flaky pastry.
—*Barbara Nowakowski, North Tonawanda, NY*

TAKES: 20 MIN. • MAKES: 8 SERVINGS

1 tube (8 oz.) refrigerated crescent rolls
1⅓ cups french-fried onions, divided
1 large egg
1 Tbsp. water

1. Do not preheat air fryer. Unroll crescent dough and separate into triangles. Sprinkle each with about 2 Tbsp. onions. Roll up each from the wide end. Curve ends down to form crescents.

2. In batches, place crescents in a single layer on greased tray in air-fryer basket. Beat egg and water; brush over the dough. Sprinkle with the remaining onions. Cook at 325° until golden brown, 7-8 minutes. Serve warm.

1 ROLL: 170 cal., 10g fat (4g sat. fat), 23mg chol., 301mg sod., 16g carb. (3g sugars, 0 fiber), 3g pro.

SOUR CREAM PEACH KUCHEN

For an old-fashioned sweet, there's nothing that beats my mom's peach kuchen. With a melt-in-your-mouth crust and a tasty filling, this treat is perfect after a big meal.
—*Cathy Eland, Hightstown, NJ*

PREP: 15 MIN. • BAKE: 45 MIN. • MAKES: 12 SERVINGS

3 cups all-purpose flour
1¼ cups sugar, divided
½ tsp. baking powder
¼ tsp. salt
1 cup cold butter, cubed
2 cans (29 oz. each) sliced peaches, drained or 13 small peaches, peeled and sliced
1 tsp. ground cinnamon

TOPPING
4 large egg yolks
2 cups sour cream
2 to 3 Tbsp. sugar
¼ tsp. ground cinnamon

1. In a large bowl, combine flour, ¼ cup sugar, baking powder and salt; cut in butter until mixture resembles coarse crumbs. Press onto bottom and 1 in. up sides of a greased 13x9-in. baking dish.

2. Arrange peaches over crust. Combine cinnamon and remaining sugar; sprinkle over peaches. Bake at 400° for 15 minutes.

3. Meanwhile, for topping, in a small bowl, combine egg yolks and sour cream. Spread evenly over peaches. Combine sugar and cinnamon; sprinkle over top.

4. Bake 30-35 minutes longer or until set. Serve warm or cold. Store leftovers in the refrigerator.

1 PIECE: 507 cal., 24g fat (15g sat. fat), 135mg chol., 197mg sod., 66g carb. (41g sugars, 2g fiber), 6g pro.

AIR-FRYER ONION
CRESCENT ROLLS

SLOW-COOKER MONKEY BREAD

I often take this monkey bread to church potlucks—
children and adults alike love it! The rum extract is optional.
—*Lisa Leaper, Worthington, OH*

PREP: 20 MIN. • **COOK:** 2½ HOURS +STANDING • **MAKES:** 10 SERVINGS

- 1 **cup sugar**
- ¾ **cup packed brown sugar**
- 2 **tsp. ground cinnamon**
- ½ **tsp. ground allspice**
- 4 **tubes (6 oz. each) refrigerated buttermilk biscuits, quartered**
- ¾ **cup butter, melted**
- ½ **cup apple juice**
- 1 **tsp. vanilla extract**
- 1 **tsp. rum extract**
  Toasted chopped pecans, optional

1. Line a 5-qt. slow cooker with a piece of aluminum foil, letting ends extend up the sides. Grease foil.

2. Combine the sugars, cinnamon and allspice in a large bowl; sprinkle 3 Tbsp. sugar mixture in bottom of prepared slow cooker. Add biscuit pieces to bowl; toss to coat. Transfer coated biscuits to slow cooker; sprinkle any remaining sugar mixture over biscuits.

3. Stir together butter, apple juice and extracts; pour over biscuits.

4. Cook, covered, on low 2½-3 hours. Remove lid and let stand for 10 minutes. Carefully invert onto serving platter. If desired, sprinkle with pecans.

8 BISCUIT PIECES: 473 cal., 22g fat (12g sat. fat), 37mg chol., 675mg sod., 68g carb. (41g sugars, 0 fiber), 4g pro.

HERB PARMESAN LOAF

Take your usual frozen bread dough to a whole new level
when you try this good-for-you recipe.
—*Shirley Sibit Rudder, Burkeville, TX*

PREP: 10 MIN. + RISING • **BAKE:** 20 MIN. • **MAKES:** 1 LOAF (12 PIECES)

- 1 **loaf (1 lb.) frozen whole wheat bread dough**
- ¼ **cup shredded Parmesan cheese**
- 1½ **tsp. dried parsley flakes**
- 1½ **tsp. dried minced garlic**
- ¼ **tsp. dill weed**
- ¼ **tsp. salt**
- 1 **Tbsp. butter, melted**

1. Place dough in a greased 8x4-in. loaf pan. Thaw according to package directions. In a small bowl, combine the cheese, parsley, garlic, dill and salt. Brush dough with butter; sprinkle with cheese mixture. Cover and let rise in a warm place until nearly doubled, about 2½ hours. Preheat oven to 350°.

2. Bake until golden brown, 20-25 minutes. Remove from pan to a wire rack to cool.

1 PIECE: 111 cal., 3g fat (1g sat. fat), 4mg chol., 250mg sod., 18g carb. (2g sugars, 2g fiber), 6g pro.

RHUBARB PINWHEELS

I love to make this colorful, tart-tasting dessert in the spring, just as Mother always did. As soon as the fresh rhubarb is long enough to pick, I make sure this special dish makes an appearance on our table.

—*Doris Natvig, Jesup, IA*

PREP: 25 MIN. • BAKE: 30 MIN. • MAKES: 12 SERVINGS

DOUGH
- 2 **cups all-purpose flour**
- 1 **Tbsp. sugar**
- 4 **tsp. baking powder**
- ½ **tsp. salt**
- ⅓ **cup shortening**
- 1 **large egg, room temperature, beaten**
- ½ **cup 2% milk**

FILLING
- 2 **Tbsp. butter, melted**
- 1 **cup sugar**
- 3 **to 4 cups diced fresh or frozen rhubarb**

SYRUP
- 1½ **cups water**
- 1 **cup sugar**
- **A few drops red food coloring, optional**
- **Whipped cream, optional**

1. In a large bowl, sift together dry ingredients. Cut in shortening until mixture resembles coarse crumbs. Combine egg and milk; add to crumb mixture, stirring just until moistened. Turn out onto a floured surface. Roll into a 12x10-in. rectangle. Brush dough with melted butter; sprinkle with the sugar and top with rhubarb. Carefully roll up dough, jelly-roll style, starting with the shorter side. Cut into 1-in. slices. Reshape the slices as needed to form round pinwheels.

2. Place in a 13x9-in. baking dish. For syrup, bring water and sugar to a boil in a saucepan. Cook and stir until the sugar has dissolved. Stir in food coloring if desired. Carefully pour hot syrup over pinwheels. Bake at 400° for 30 minutes or until golden brown. Serve warm, with cream if desired.

1 ROLL: 294 cal., 8g fat (3g sat. fat), 22mg chol., 286mg sod., 52g carb. (35g sugars, 1g fiber), 3g pro.

"I am so happy that I found this recipe. These taste great with ice cream, and I thought it was an excellent change for a dessert."
—SMURF007, TASTEOFHOME.COM

FRUITY PULL-APART BREAD

Who doesn't love to start the day with monkey bread? This skillet version is packed with bright berries and dolloped with irresistibly rich cream cheese. A sprinkle of fresh basil brings it all together.
—*Darla Andrews, Boerne, TX*

PREP: 15 MIN. • BAKE: 35 MIN. • MAKES: 8 SERVINGS

1 tube (16.3 oz.) large refrigerated flaky honey butter biscuits
½ cup packed dark brown sugar
½ cup sugar
⅓ cup butter, melted
1 cup fresh blueberries
1 cup chopped fresh strawberries
4 oz. cream cheese, softened
1 Tbsp. minced fresh basil

1. Preheat oven to 350°. Separate dough into 8 biscuits; cut biscuits into fourths.

2. In a shallow bowl, combine sugars. Dip biscuits in melted butter, then in sugar mixture. Place the biscuits in a greased 10¼-in. cast-iron skillet. Top with fresh berries; dollop with cream cheese. Bake until the biscuits are golden brown and cooked through, 35-40 minutes. Sprinkle with basil.

1 SERVING: 383 cal., 20g fat (9g sat. fat), 30mg chol., 641mg sod., 49g carb. (28g sugars, 2g fiber), 5g pro.

SESAME FRENCH BREAD

Homemade French bread isn't at all difficult to make, and it's perfect alongside Italian foods. If you're not serving a large group, freeze one loaf to enjoy later.
—*Peggy Van Arsdale, Trenton, NJ*

PREP: 25 MIN. + RISING • BAKE: 25 MIN. • MAKES: 2 LOAVES (16 PIECES EACH)

2 pkg. (¼ oz. each) active dry yeast
2½ cups water (110° to 115°)
2 Tbsp. sugar
2 Tbsp. canola oil
2 tsp. salt
6 to 6½ cups all-purpose flour
Cornmeal
1 large egg white
1 Tbsp. water
2 Tbsp. sesame seeds

1. In a large bowl, dissolve yeast in warm water. Add sugar, oil, salt and 4 cups of flour; beat until smooth. Add enough remaining flour to form a soft dough.

2. Turn onto a floured surface; knead until smooth and elastic, 6-8 minutes. Place in a greased bowl, turning once to grease top. Cover and let rise in a warm place until doubled, about 1 hour.

3. Punch dough down. Divide in half. Roll each half into a 15x10-in. rectangle. Roll up from a long side; seal well. Place with seam side down on greased baking sheet sprinkled with cornmeal. Cover and let rise until nearly doubled, about 30 minutes. Preheat oven to 400°

4. Beat the egg white and water; brush over loaves. Sprinkle with sesame seeds. With a sharp knife, make 4 shallow diagonal cuts across top. Bake until lightly browned, about 25 minutes. Remove from pan and cool on a wire rack.

1 PIECE: 99 cal., 1g fat (0 sat. fat), 0 chol., 150mg sod., 19g carb. (1g sugars, 1g fiber), 3g pro.

FRUITY
PULL-APART
BREAD

EASY CHEESY
BISCUITS

EASY CHEESY BISCUITS

I'm a big fan of homemade biscuits, but not the rolling and cutting that goes into making them. The drop-biscuit method solves everything!
—*Christy Addison, Clarksville, OH*

TAKES: 30 MIN. • MAKES: 1 DOZEN

3 cups all-purpose flour
3 tsp. baking powder
1 Tbsp. sugar
1 tsp. salt
¾ tsp. cream of tartar
½ cup cold butter
1 cup shredded sharp cheddar cheese
1 garlic clove, minced
¼ to ½ tsp. crushed red pepper flakes
1¼ cups 2% milk

1. Preheat oven to 450°. In a large bowl, whisk flour, baking powder, sugar, salt and cream of tartar. Cut in the butter until mixture resembles coarse crumbs. Stir in cheese, garlic and pepper flakes. Add milk; stir just until moistened.

2. Drop dough by heaping ¼ cupfuls 2 in. apart onto a greased baking sheet. Bake for 18-20 minutes or until golden brown. Serve warm.

1 BISCUIT: 237 cal., 12g fat (7g sat. fat), 32mg chol., 429mg sod., 26g carb. (2g sugars, 1g fiber), 7g pro.

VANILLA-GLAZED GINGER SCONES

Gingerbread is a flavor that works with all sorts of delicious holiday baked goods. To glaze these ginger scones, just dip a fork or spoon into the glaze mixture and then drizzle over the tops.
—*Colleen Delawder, Herndon, VA*

PREP: 25 MIN. • BAKE: 15 MIN. • MAKES: 12 SERVINGS

2 cups all-purpose flour
¼ cup packed light brown sugar
2½ tsp. baking powder
1½ tsp. ground cinnamon
1 tsp. ground ginger
¼ tsp. salt
6 Tbsp. cold butter
¾ cup heavy whipping cream
1 large egg, room temperature
¼ cup molasses
1 Tbsp. maple syrup

GLAZE
1 cup confectioners' sugar
¼ cup heavy whipping cream
1 tsp. vanilla extract
Dash salt
¼ cup finely chopped crystallized ginger

1. Preheat oven to 400°. In a large bowl, whisk first 6 ingredients. Cut in butter until mixture resembles coarse crumbs. In another bowl, whisk cream, egg, molasses and syrup until blended; stir into crumb mixture just until moistened.

2. Drop dough by ¼ cupfuls onto a parchment-lined baking sheet. Bake until golden brown, 12-15 minutes. In a small bowl, combine the confectioners' sugar, cream, vanilla and salt; stir until smooth. Drizzle over scones; sprinkle with ginger. Serve warm.

1 SCONE: 299 cal., 14g fat (8g sat. fat), 53mg chol., 226mg sod., 42g carb. (23g sugars, 1g fiber), 3g pro.

SOCCA

Socca is a traditional flatbread from Nice, France. It's common to see it cooked on grills as street food, served chopped in a paper cone and sprinkled with salt, pepper or other delicious toppings. Bonus: It's gluten free.
—Taste of Home *Test Kitchen*

PREP: 5 MIN. + STANDING • COOK: 5 MIN. • MAKES: 6 SERVINGS

1 cup chickpea flour
1 cup water
2 Tbsp. extra virgin olive oil, divided
¾ tsp. salt
Optional toppings: Za'atar seasoning, sea salt flakes, coarsely ground pepper and additional extra virgin olive oil

1. In a small bowl, whisk chickpea flour, water, 1 Tbsp. oil and salt until smooth. Let stand 30 minutes.

2. Meanwhile, preheat broiler. Place a 10-in. cast-iron skillet in oven until hot, about 5 minutes. Add remaining 1 Tbsp. oil to the pan; swirl to coat. Pour batter into the hot pan and tilt to coat evenly.

3. Broil 6 in. from heat until edge is crisp and browned and center just begins to brown, 5-7 minutes. Cut into wedges. If desired, top with optional ingredients.

1 WEDGE: 113 cal., 6g fat (1g sat. fat), 0 chol., 298mg sod., 12g carb. (2g sugars, 3g fiber), 4g pro. **DIABETIC EXCHANGES:** 1 fat, ½ starch.

CRAN-APPLE MUFFINS

I like to pile a fresh batch of these muffins on a plate when friends drop in for coffee. Even my grandkids enjoy the cranberry and apple flavor combination.
—*Millie Westland, Hayward, MN*

PREP: 20 MIN. • BAKE: 20 MIN. • MAKES: 1 DOZEN

½ cup whole-berry cranberry sauce
½ tsp. grated orange zest
1½ cups all-purpose flour
½ cup sugar
1 tsp. ground cinnamon
½ tsp. baking soda
¼ tsp. baking powder
¼ tsp. salt
1 large egg, room temperature
⅓ cup 2% milk
⅓ cup canola oil
1 cup shredded peeled tart apple
½ cup confectioners' sugar
1 Tbsp. orange juice

1. In a small bowl, combine cranberry sauce and orange zest; set aside.

2. In a large bowl, combine the flour, sugar, cinnamon, baking soda, baking powder and salt. Beat the egg, milk and oil; stir into dry ingredients just until moistened. Fold in apple.

3. Fill greased or paper-lined muffin cups half full. Make a well in the center of each muffin; fill with about 2 tsp. of reserved cranberry mixture.

4. Bake at 375° until a toothpick inserted in muffin comes out clean, 18-20 minutes. Cool for 5 minutes before removing from pan to a wire rack. Combine confectioners' sugar and orange juice; drizzle over warm muffins.

1 MUFFIN: 195 cal., 7g fat (1g sat. fat), 19mg chol., 122mg sod., 32g carb. (17g sugars, 1g fiber), 2g pro.

PACZKI

My mom used to make these when I was growing up.
She filled them with raspberry or apricot jam, but prune
filling is pretty traditional in Polish and Czech households.
—*Lisa Kaminski, Wauwatosa, WI*

PREP: 35 MIN. + RISING • COOK: 5 MIN./BATCH • MAKES: 2 DOZEN

1¼ cups sugar, divided
1 pkg. (¼ oz.) active
 dry yeast
1 tsp. salt
3¼ to 3¾ cups all-purpose
 flour
¾ cup 2% milk

¼ cup shortening
¼ cup water
1 large egg, room
 temperature
 Oil for deep-fat frying
1 cup seedless
 raspberry jam

1. In a large bowl, mix ¼ cup sugar, yeast, salt and 2 cups flour.
In a small saucepan, heat milk, shortening and water to 120°-
130°. Add to dry ingredients; beat on medium speed 2 minutes.
Add egg; beat on high 2 minutes. Stir in enough remaining flour
to form a soft dough (dough will be sticky).

2. Turn dough onto a floured surface; knead until smooth and
elastic, 6-8 minutes. Place in a greased bowl, turning once to
grease the top. Cover and let rise in a warm place until doubled,
about 1 hour.

3. Punch down dough. Turn onto a lightly floured surface; roll to
½-in. thickness. Cut with a floured 3-in. round cutter. Place 2 in.
apart on greased baking sheets. Cover and let rise in a warm
place until nearly doubled, about 1 hour.

4. In an electric skillet or deep fryer, heat the oil to 375°. Fry
doughnuts, a few at a time, until golden brown, 2-3 minutes
on each side. Drain on paper towels. Cool slightly; roll in the
remaining 1 cup sugar.

5. Cut a small hole in the tip of a pastry bag; insert a small pastry
tip. Fill bag with jam. With a small knife, pierce a hole into the side
of each doughnut; fill with jam.

1 DOUGHNUT: 183 cal., 6g fat (1g sat. fat), 8mg chol., 105mg sod.,
30g carb. (17g sugars, 1g fiber), 2g pro.

MAKEOVER
CHOCOLATE
ZUCCHINI BREAD

GRANDMA'S SECRET

There's no need to tightly pack the zucchini into the measuring cup. Loosely piling the shredded, peeled zucchini will get you the right amount of green goodness in your bread.

MAKEOVER CHOCOLATE ZUCCHINI BREAD

Enjoy all the sweet, satisfying flavors of everyone's
favorite sweet bread without all the guilt afterward!
—*Jennifer Sickels, Greenfield, IN*

PREP: 15 MIN. • BAKE: 40 MIN. + COOLING • MAKES: 2 LOAVES (12 PIECES EACH)

1¼ cups sugar
3 large eggs, room temperature
⅔ cup unsweetened applesauce
⅓ cup canola oil
3 tsp. vanilla extract
1½ cups all-purpose flour
1 cup cake flour
½ cup baking cocoa
1 tsp. salt
1 tsp. baking soda
1 tsp. ground cinnamon
¼ tsp. baking powder
2 cups shredded peeled zucchini

1. Preheat oven to 350°. In a large bowl, beat sugar, eggs, applesauce, oil and vanilla until well blended. Combine the flours, cocoa, salt, baking soda, cinnamon and baking powder; gradually beat into sugar mixture until blended. Stir in zucchini. Transfer to two 8x4-in. loaf pans coated with cooking spray.

2. Bake until a toothpick inserted in the center comes out clean, 40-45 minutes. Cool for 10 minutes before removing from pans to wire racks to cool completely.

1 PIECE: 137 cal., 4g fat (0 sat. fat), 26mg chol., 165mg sod., 23g carb. (12g sugars, 1g fiber), 3g pro.

ITALIAN GARLIC PARMESAN BREADSTICKS

I found this recipe in a farm newspaper many years ago. It is one of
my family's favorite appetizers, especially before Italian meals.
—*Loretta Fisher, Abbottstown, PA*

PREP: 25 MIN. + STANDING • BAKE: 20 MIN. • MAKES: 2½ DOZEN

3 tsp. active dry yeast
1½ cups warm water (110° to 115°)
4 Tbsp. canola oil, divided
1 Tbsp. sugar
¼ tsp. salt
4 cups all-purpose flour
½ cup butter, melted
3 Tbsp. grated Parmesan cheese
2 Tbsp. dried parsley flakes
1½ tsp. garlic powder

1. In a large bowl, dissolve the yeast in warm water. Add 1 Tbsp. oil, sugar, salt and 3 cups flour. Beat until smooth. Stir in enough remaining flour to form a soft dough (dough will be sticky). Cover and let rest for 10 minutes.

2. On a lightly floured surface, roll dough into a 15-in. square. Cut in half; cut each half widthwise into 1-in. strips.

3. In a shallow bowl, combine the butter, cheese, parsley, garlic powder and remaining oil. Dip each strip into the butter mixture, then twist 2 to 3 times.

4. Place 1 in. apart on greased baking sheets. Bake at 350° for 18-21 minutes or until golden brown. Serve warm.

1 SERVING: 109 cal., 5g fat (2g sat. fat), 8mg chol., 50mg sod., 13g carb. (1g sugars, 1g fiber), 2g pro.

CINNAMON-SUGAR SWEET POTATO PASTRIES

We always have leftover mashed sweet potatoes after our Thanksgiving Day meal. I take what's left to make an indulgent filling for empanadas. Convenient crescent roll dough makes this recipe easy as pie.
—*Sarah Vasques, Milford, NH*

PREP: 25 MIN. • BAKE: 10 MIN. • MAKES: 32 SERVINGS

½ cup mashed sweet potato
2 oz. cream cheese, softened
1 Tbsp. brown sugar
½ tsp. grated orange zest
2 tubes (8 oz. each) refrigerated crescent rolls
½ cup sugar
2 tsp. ground cinnamon
¼ cup butter, melted

1. Preheat oven to 375°. In a small bowl, combine sweet potato, cream cheese, brown sugar and orange zest. Unroll 1 tube of the crescent roll dough and separate into 4 rectangles; press perforations to seal. Cut each rectangle into 4 triangles. Repeat with remaining tube of dough. Place 1 tsp. potato filling in center of each triangle. Fold dough over filling and pinch seams to seal.

2. Place 2 in. apart on parchment-lined baking sheets. Bake 10-12 minutes or until golden brown. Cool slightly. In a small bowl, mix sugar and cinnamon. Brush pastries with butter; coat with cinnamon-sugar mixture.

1 PIECE: 88 cal., 5g fat (1g sat. fat), 6mg chol., 125mg sod., 11g carb. (5g sugars, 0 fiber), 1g pro.

OATMEAL DINNER ROLLS

These fluffy rolls go perfectly with any meal. They have a delicious homemade flavor that's irresistible. They're not hard to make, and they bake up nice and high.
—*Patricia Staudt, Marble Rock, IA*

PREP: 40 MIN. + RISING • BAKE: 20 MIN. • MAKES: 1½ DOZEN

2 cups water
1 cup quick-cooking oats
3 Tbsp. butter
1 pkg. (¼ oz.) active dry yeast
⅓ cup warm water (110° to 115°)
⅓ cup packed brown sugar
1 Tbsp. sugar
1½ tsp. salt
4¾ to 5¼ cups all-purpose flour

1. In a large saucepan, bring water to a boil; add oats and butter. Cook and stir for 1 minute. Remove from the heat; cool to lukewarm.

2. In a large bowl, dissolve yeast in warm water. Add the oat mixture, sugars, salt and 4 cups flour; beat until smooth. Add enough remaining flour to form a soft dough.

3. Turn onto a floured surface; knead until smooth and elastic, 6-8 minutes. Place in a greased bowl, turning once to grease top. Cover and let rise in a warm place until doubled, about 1 hour.

4. Punch the dough down; allow to rest for 10 minutes. Shape into 18 balls. Place in 2 greased 9-in. round baking pans. Cover and let rise until doubled, about 45 minutes.

5. Preheat oven to 350°; bake the rolls until golden brown, 20-25 minutes. Remove from pans to wire racks.

1 ROLL: 173 cal., 3g fat (1g sat. fat), 0 chol., 221mg sod., 33g carb. (5g sugars, 1g fiber), 4g pro.

CINNAMON-SUGAR
SWEET POTATO
PASTRIES

CINNAMON CRESCENT TWISTS

This is a true twist on an old favorite—refrigerated crescent rolls.
You'll love how tasty they are and how fast they come together.
—Ruth Vineyard, Plano, TX

TAKES: 20 MIN. • **MAKES:** 16 SERVINGS

1 pkg. (8 oz.) refrigerated
  crescent rolls
¼ cup packed brown sugar
2 Tbsp. butter, softened
1½ tsp. ground cinnamon

GLAZE
¼ cup confectioners' sugar
1 Tbsp. butter, melted
1½ tsp. hot water
⅛ tsp. almond extract

1. Separate crescent roll dough into 4 rectangles; press seams to seal. In a small bowl, combine the brown sugar, butter and cinnamon; spread over 2 rectangles. Top with the remaining 2 rectangles. Starting from a long side, cut each rectangle into 8 strips. Twist each strip several times; seal ends together.

2. Place on greased baking sheets. Bake at 375° until golden brown, 10-12 minutes. Immediately remove to wire racks. Combine glaze ingredients; brush over warm twists.

1 TWIST: 96 cal., 5g fat (2g sat. fat), 6mg chol., 128mg sod., 11g carb. (6g sugars, 0 fiber), 1g pro.

HERBED CHEESE STICKS

We love the breadsticks we get hot from the oven at our local pizza parlor.
Now I can serve that same wonderful goodness at home.
—Heather Bates, Athens, ME

TAKES: 30 MIN. • **MAKES:** 16 CHEESE STICKS

1 pkg. (6½ oz.) pizza
  crust mix
1½ tsp. garlic powder
1 Tbsp. olive oil
1 cup shredded part-skim
  mozzarella cheese
¼ cup shredded Parmesan
  cheese
1 tsp. Italian seasoning
  Pizza sauce

1. Preheat oven to 450°. Mix pizza dough according to package directions, adding garlic powder to dry mix. Cover; let rest for 5 minutes.

2. Knead dough 4-5 times or until easy to handle. On a greased baking sheet, press dough into an 8-in. square. Brush top with oil; sprinkle with cheeses and Italian seasoning.

3. Bake 6-8 minutes or until cheese is lightly browned. Cut square in half; cut each half crosswise into 8 strips. Serve with pizza sauce.

1 CHEESE STICK: 72 cal., 3g fat (1g sat. fat), 5mg chol., 117mg sod., 8g carb. (1g sugars, 0 fiber), 3g pro.

GRANDMA'S STOLLEN

When I was a child, my grandmother always prepared stollen at Christmas and Easter.
This recipe makes four loaves, which are great to share with family and friends.
—*Kathy Green, Layton, NJ*

PREP: 40 MIN. + STANDING • **BAKE:** 35 MIN. • **MAKES:** 4 LOAVES (12 PIECES EACH)

1½ **cups chopped almonds**
1½ **cups chopped candied citron**
1½ **cups red candied cherries**
¾ **cup chopped candied pineapple**
¾ **cup golden raisins**
¾ **cup brandy**
7 **to 8 cups all-purpose flour**
½ **cup sugar**
2 **pkg. (¼ oz. each) active dry yeast**
2 **tsp. salt**
1½ **cups 2% milk**
1½ **cups butter, cubed**
3 **large eggs, room temperature**
¼ **cup confectioners' sugar**

1. In a large bowl, combine the almonds, citron, cherries, pineapple and raisins. Stir in brandy. Cover and let stand for several hours or overnight, stirring occasionally.

2. In a large bowl, combine 4 cups flour, sugar, yeast and salt. In a small saucepan, heat milk and butter to 120°-130°. Add to dry ingredients; beat just until moistened. Add eggs; beat until smooth. Stir in enough remaining flour to form a soft dough.

3. Turn onto a floured surface; knead until smooth and elastic, 6-8 minutes. Place in a very large greased bowl, turning once to grease top. Cover and let rise in a warm place until doubled, about 1 hour.

4. Punch dough down; turn onto a floured surface. Knead fruit mixture into dough (knead in more flour if necessary). Divide into fourths. Roll each portion into a 10x8-in. oval. Fold a long side over to within 1 in. of opposite side; press edges lightly to seal. Place on greased baking sheets. Cover and let rise until doubled, about 30 minutes.

5. Bake at 350° for 35-40 minutes or until golden brown. Remove to wire racks to cool. Sprinkle with confectioners' sugar.

1 PIECE: 220 cal., 9g fat (4g sat. fat), 29mg chol., 173mg sod., 31g carb. (15g sugars, 1g fiber), 4g pro.

FROM GRANDMA'S KITCHEN: To chop almonds with ease, quickly pulse them in a food processor until they're the desired texture.

PEANUT BUTTER PUMPKIN BREAD

My husband brought this recipe home from the office more than 20 years ago.
Each fall, I bake several of these lovely loaves to share with family and friends.
Pumpkin and peanut butter are an unusual, delicious combination.
—*Anita Chicke, Frisco, TX*

> **PREP:** 10 MIN. • **BAKE:** 1 HOUR + COOLING • **MAKES:** 2 LOAVES (16 PIECES EACH)

3½ cups all-purpose flour
3 cups sugar
2 tsp. baking soda
1½ tsp. salt
1 tsp. ground cinnamon
1 tsp. ground nutmeg
1 can (15 oz.) pumpkin
4 large eggs, room temperature
1 cup canola oil
¾ cup water
⅔ cup peanut butter

1. In a large bowl, combine the flour, sugar, baking soda, salt, cinnamon and nutmeg. In another bowl, combine the pumpkin, eggs, oil, water and peanut butter. Stir into dry ingredients just until moistened.

2. Pour into 2 greased 9x5-in. loaf pans. Bake at 350° until a toothpick inserted in the center comes out clean, 60-70 minutes. Cool 10 minutes before removing from pans to wire racks.

NOTE: Six 5¾x3x2-in. loaf pans may be used; bake 40-45 minutes.

1 PIECE: 228 cal., 10g fat (2g sat. fat), 27mg chol., 223mg sod., 31g carb. (19g sugars, 1g fiber), 4g pro.

GRANDMA'S POPOVERS

Still warm from the oven, popovers are always a fun accompaniment to a homey meal. I was raised on these—my grandmother often made them for our Sunday dinners. The recipe could not be simpler.
—*Debbie Terenzini, Lusby, MD*

> **PREP:** 10 MIN. + STANDING • **BAKE:** 30 MIN. • **MAKES:** 6 POPOVERS

1 cup all-purpose flour
⅛ tsp. salt
3 large eggs
1 cup 2% milk

1. In a large bowl, combine flour and salt. Beat eggs and milk; whisk into dry ingredients just until combined. Cover and let stand at room temperature for 45 minutes. Grease cups of a popover pan well with butter or oil; fill cups of two-thirds full with batter.

2. Bake at 450° for 15 minutes. Reduce heat to 350° (do not open oven door). Bake 15 minutes longer or until deep golden brown (do not underbake).

3. Run a table knife or small metal spatula around edges of cups to loosen if necessary. Immediately remove the popovers from pan; prick with a small sharp knife to allow steam to escape. Serve immediately.

NOTE: You may use greased muffin tins instead of a popover pan. Fill every other cup two-thirds full with batter to avoid crowding the popovers; fill remaining cups with water. Bake at 450° for 15 minutes and 350°; for 10 minutes. Yield: 9 popovers.

1 POPOVER: 132 cal., 3g fat (1g sat. fat), 109mg chol., 105mg sod., 18g carb. (2g sugars, 1g fiber), 7g pro.

PEANUT BUTTER
PUMPKIN BREAD

GOOEY LEMON ROLLS

My mother made these hard-to-resist rolls when I was young.
I always warm up after having one, and so will your family.
—*Cora Patterson, Lewiston, ID*

PREP: 25 MIN. + RISING • BAKE: 20 MIN. • MAKES: 1 DOZEN

1 Tbsp. active dry yeast
½ cup warm water (110°
   to 115°)
½ cup warm 2% milk (110°
   to 115°)
¼ cup butter, melted
1 large egg, room
   temperature
½ cup sugar
1 tsp. salt
3 to 3½ cups all-purpose
   flour

FILLING
½ cup sugar
2 tsp. grated lemon zest
½ tsp. ground cinnamon
1 Tbsp. poppy seeds,
   optional
¼ cup butter, melted
1 cup slivered almonds,
   toasted

GLAZE
½ cup sugar
1 can (12 oz.) frozen
   lemonade concentrate,
   thawed
1 Tbsp. butter
2 tsp. grated lemon zest

1. In a small bowl, dissolve yeast in warm water. In a large bowl, combine milk, butter, egg, sugar, salt, yeast mixture and 2 cups flour; beat on medium speed until smooth. Stir in enough remaining flour to form a soft dough (dough will be sticky).

2. Turn dough onto a floured surface; knead until smooth and elastic, 6-8 minutes. Place in a greased bowl, turning once to grease the top. Cover and let rise in a warm place until doubled, about 1 hour.

3. For filling, in a small bowl, mix sugar, lemon zest, cinnamon and, if desired, poppy seeds. Punch down dough; roll into an 18x12-in. rectangle. Brush with melted butter to within ¼ in. of edges; sprinkle with sugar mixture and almonds. Roll up jelly-roll style, starting with a long side; pinch seam to seal. Cut into 12 slices.

4. Place in a greased 13x9-in. baking pan, cut side down. Cover with a kitchen towel; let rise in a warm place until almost doubled, about 45 minutes.

5. Preheat oven to 400°. Bake rolls for 15 minutes. Meanwhile, for glaze, in a small saucepan, combine sugar and lemonade concentrate. Cook and stir over medium-low heat until sugar is dissolved. Stir in butter and lemon zest; simmer, uncovered, until slightly thickened, 10-12 minutes. Remove rolls from oven; pour glaze over rolls. Bake until golden brown, 5-10 minutes longer. Cool in pan 5 minutes. Run a knife around sides of pan before inverting onto a serving plate. Serve warm.

1 ROLL: 430 cal., 15g fat (6g sat. fat), 39mg chol., 280mg sod., 71g carb. (42g sugars, 3g fiber), 7g pro.

BLUEBERRY CHEESE DANISH

A layer of fresh blueberries is the sweet surprise hidden inside this pretty,
delicious pastry. It's hard to not want to make it again and again!
—Taste of Home *Test Kitchen*

PREP: 20 MIN. + CHILLING • **BAKE:** 20 MIN. • **MAKES:** 10 SERVINGS

¾ cup 1% cottage cheese
⅓ cup sugar
⅓ cup 1% milk
¼ cup canola oil
1 tsp. vanilla extract
2 cups all-purpose flour
2 tsp. baking powder
½ tsp. salt

FILLING

4 oz. reduced-fat cream cheese
¼ cup sugar
1 large egg, separated
1 tsp. grated lemon zest
1 tsp. vanilla extract
1 cup fresh or frozen blueberries
1 Tbsp. water

GLAZE

½ cup confectioners' sugar
2 tsp. lemon juice

1. In a blender, cover and process cottage cheese until smooth. Add the sugar, milk, oil and vanilla; process until smooth. Combine the flour, baking powder and salt; add to cheese mixture. Process just until the dough forms a ball (dough will be sticky). Turn onto a floured surface; knead 4-5 times. Place in a large bowl; cover and refrigerate for 30 minutes.

2. In a large bowl, beat cream cheese and sugar until smooth. Beat in the egg yolk, lemon zest and vanilla. Turn dough onto a 17x13-in. piece of parchment. Roll into a 16x12-in. rectangle. Transfer with paper to a baking sheet.

3. Spread cream cheese mixture lengthwise in a 3½-in.-wide strip down center of dough; sprinkle with blueberries. On each long side, cut 1-in.-wide strips about 3¾ in. into center. Fold alternating strips at an angle across berries. Pinch ends to seal and tuck under. Beat egg white and water; brush over dough.

4. Bake at 400° for 20-22 minutes or until golden brown. Remove to a wire rack. Combine the glaze ingredients; drizzle over warm pastry. Refrigerate leftovers.

1 PIECE: 260 cal., 8g fat (1g sat. fat), 30mg chol., 339mg sod., 41g carb., 1g fiber), 7g pro.

CHICKEN CORN FRITTERS

I've always loved corn fritters, but they weren't satisfying as a main dish. I came up with this recipe and was thrilled when my husband and our three young boys gave it rave reviews. The chicken and zesty sauce make the fritters a wonderful brunch or lunch dish.

—*Marie Greene, Scottsbluff, NE*

PREP: 20 MIN. • **COOK:** 10 MIN./BATCH • **MAKES:** 1 DOZEN

1 can (15¼ oz.) whole kernel corn, drained
1 cup finely chopped cooked chicken
1 large egg, room temperature, lightly beaten
½ cup whole milk
2 Tbsp. butter, melted
½ tsp. salt
⅛ tsp. pepper
1¾ cups all-purpose flour
1 tsp. baking powder
Oil for deep-fat frying

GREEN CHILE SAUCE
⅓ cup butter, cubed
¼ cup all-purpose flour
¼ tsp. salt
⅛ tsp. pepper
⅛ tsp. garlic powder
⅛ tsp. ground cumin
1 can (4 oz.) chopped green chiles
1 cup whole milk
Shredded cheddar cheese, optional

1. Place corn in a large bowl; lightly crush with a potato masher. Stir in the chicken, egg, milk, butter, salt and pepper. Combine flour and baking powder; stir into the corn mixture just until combined.

2. In a deep-fat fryer or skillet, heat 2 in. of oil to 375°. Drop batter by ¼ cupfuls into oil. Fry for 3 minutes on each side or until golden brown. Drain on paper towels; keep warm.

3. In a large saucepan, melt butter over medium-low heat. Stir in flour and seasonings until smooth. Add chiles. Gradually stir in milk. Bring to a boil; cook and stir 2 minutes or until thickened. Serve with corn fritters; sprinkle with cheese if desired.

1 FRITTER: 254 cal., 15g fat (6g sat. fat), 48mg chol., 414mg sod., 21g carb. (4g sugars, 2g fiber), 8g pro.

"I have picky eaters at my house, and everyone loved this recipe. It worked out great!"
—RENEBRAN, TASTEOFHOME.COM

HOMEMADE BAGELS

Instead of going to a baker, head to the kitchen and surprise your family with homemade bagels. For variation and flavor, sprinkle the tops with cinnamon sugar instead of sesame and poppy seeds.
—*Rebecca Phillips, Burlington, CT*

PREP: 30 MIN. + RISING • BAKE: 20 MIN. • MAKES: 1 DOZEN

1 tsp. active dry yeast
1¼ cups warm 2% milk (110° to 115°)
½ cup butter, softened
2 Tbsp. sugar
1 tsp. salt
1 large egg yolk, room temperature
3¾ to 4¼ cups all-purpose flour
  Sesame or poppy seeds, optional

1. In a large bowl, dissolve yeast in warm milk. Add the butter, sugar, salt and egg yolk; mix well. Stir in enough flour to form a soft dough.

2. Turn onto a floured surface; knead until smooth and elastic, 6-8 minutes. Place in a greased bowl, turning once to grease top. Cover; let rise in a warm place until doubled, about 1 hour.

3. Punch dough down. Shape into 12 balls. Push thumb through centers to form a 1½-in. hole. Stretch and shape dough to form an even ring. Place on a floured surface. Cover and let rest for 10 minutes; flatten bagels slightly.

4. Fill a Dutch oven two-thirds full with water; bring to a boil. Drop bagels, 2 at a time, into boiling water. Cook for 45 seconds; turn and cook 45 seconds longer. Remove with a slotted spoon; drain well on paper towels.

5. Sprinkle with sesame or poppy seeds if desired. Place 2 in. apart on greased baking sheets. Bake at 400° 20-25 minutes or until golden brown. Remove from pans to wire racks to cool.

1 BAGEL: 237 cal., 9g fat (5g sat. fat), 38mg chol., 271mg sod., 33g carb. (3g sugars, 1g fiber), 5g pro.

FROM GRANDMA'S KITCHEN: The key to making fluffy bagels is to avoid overboiling. Doing so will cause them to sink and lose the air you incorporated during the rise. Cook for 45 seconds; turn and cook 45 seconds longer.

DOUBLE CHOCOLATE BANANA MUFFINS

Combining two favorite flavors like rich chocolate and soft banana makes these muffins doubly good.
—*Donna Brockett, Kingfisher, OK*

PREP: 15 MIN. • BAKE: 20 MIN. • MAKES: ABOUT 1 DOZEN

1½ cups all-purpose flour
1 cup sugar
¼ cup baking cocoa
1 tsp. baking soda
½ tsp. salt
¼ tsp. baking powder
1⅓ cups mashed ripe bananas (about 3 medium)
⅓ cup canola oil
1 large egg, room temperature
1 cup miniature semisweet chocolate chips

1. Preheat oven to 350°. Whisk together the first 6 ingredients. In a separate bowl, whisk bananas, oil and egg until blended. Add to flour mixture; stir just until moistened. Fold in chocolate chips.

2. Fill greased or paper-lined muffin cups three-fourths full. Bake until a toothpick inserted in the center comes out clean, 20-25 minutes. Cool 5 minutes before removing from pan to a wire rack. Serve warm.

1 MUFFIN: 278 cal., 11g fat (3g sat. fat), 16mg chol., 220mg sod., 45g carb. (28g sugars, 2g fiber), 3g pro.

OPTIONAL STREUSEL TOPPING: Combine ½ cup sugar, ⅓ cup all-purpose flour and ½ tsp. ground cinnamon; cut in ¼ cup cold butter until crumbly. Before baking, sprinkle over filled muffin cups; bake as directed.

AIR-FRYER HONEY-COCONUT STICKY BUNS

There's nothing better than a warm sticky bun on a chilly morning—or any morning for that matter. Hot out of the air fryer, dripping with buttery honey and lots of coconut, these are heavenly!
—*Diane Nemitz, Ludington, MI*

PREP: 20 MIN. + RISING • COOK: 20 MIN./BATCH • MAKES: 16 SERVINGS

1 loaf (1 lb.) frozen bread dough, thawed
4 oz. (½ cup) cream cheese, softened
½ cup sweetened shredded coconut
3 Tbsp. thawed orange juice concentrate
½ cup butter
½ cup honey
Optional: Toasted sweetened shredded coconut and grated orange zest

1. Grease two 8-in. round baking pans that fit in air fryer. Cut the thawed bread dough in half; roll each half into a 10x8-in. rectangle. Combine cream cheese, coconut and orange juice concentrate; spread mixture on dough. Roll up jelly-roll style, starting with long side. Cut each roll crosswise into 8 slices; place in prepared pans. Cover; let rise until almost doubled, about 1 hour.

2. Preheat air fryer to 325°. In a microwave, melt butter and honey. Spoon 1 Tbsp. butter-honey mixture over each bun. In batches, place pans in air fryer; cook until tops are golden brown, about 20 minutes. Immediately invert onto a serving plate. If desired, top with toasted coconut and orange zest.

NOTE: In our testing, we find cook times vary dramatically between brands of air fryers. As a result, we give wider than normal ranges on suggested cook times. Begin checking at the first time listed and adjust as needed.

1 BUN: 206 cal., 10g fat (6g sat. fat), 22mg chol., 235mg sod., 25g carb. (12g sugars, 1g fiber), 4g pro.

GRANDMA'S SECRET

If you want to ripen your bananas faster, try putting them in a folded paper bag. If you have any extra ripe fruit on hand, like an apple, throw that in there as well to speed up the process.

DOUBLE CHOCOLATE
BANANA MUFFINS

GRAHAM STREUSEL COFFEE CAKE

I use this sweet coffee cake recipe often. It's quick and easy to make.
—*Blanche Whytsell, Arnoldsburg, WV*

PREP: 20 MIN. • **BAKE:** 40 MIN. • **MAKES:** 16 SERVINGS

1½ cups graham cracker
crumbs
¾ cup packed brown sugar
¾ cup chopped pecans
1½ tsp. ground cinnamon

⅔ cup butter, melted
1 pkg. yellow cake mix
(regular size)
½ cup confectioners' sugar
1 Tbsp. 2% milk

1. In a small bowl, combine the cracker crumbs, brown sugar, pecans and cinnamon. Stir in butter; set aside. Prepare cake mix batter according to package directions.

2. Pour half the batter into a greased 13x9-in. baking pan. Sprinkle with half the graham cracker mixture. Carefully spoon remaining batter on top. Sprinkle with remaining graham cracker mixture.

3. Bake at 350° for 40-45 minutes or until a toothpick inserted in the center comes out clean. Cool on a wire rack. Combine confectioners' sugar and milk; drizzle over coffee cake.

1 PIECE: 329 cal., 15g fat (6g sat. fat), 21mg chol., 332mg sod., 46g carb. (30g sugars, 2g fiber), 3g pro.

SOUR CREAM BANANA BREAD

I just love this wonderful, moist banana bread! It's so easy to make, and no one can tell it's been lightened up.
—*Marge Schoessler, Warden, WA*

PREP: 15 MIN. • **BAKE:** 55 MIN. + COOLING • **MAKES:** 1 LOAF (18 PIECES)

1½ cups all-purpose flour
1 cup sugar
1 tsp. baking soda
½ tsp. salt
1 cup mashed ripe bananas
(about 3 medium)
½ cup egg substitute
½ cup canola oil
½ cup fat-free sour cream
1 tsp. vanilla extract

1. Coat a 9x5-in. loaf pan with cooking spray and dust with flour; set aside.

2. In a large bowl, combine the flour, sugar, baking soda and salt. Combine the bananas, egg substitute, oil, sour cream and vanilla; stir into the dry ingredients just until moistened.

3. Pour into prepared pan. Bake at 350° for 55-65 minutes or until a toothpick comes out clean. Cool for 10 minutes before removing from pan to a wire rack.

1 PIECE: 186 cal., 7g fat (1g sat. fat), 1mg chol., 332mg sod., 28g carb., 1g fiber), 3g pro. **DIABETIC EXCHANGES:** 1 starch, 1 fruit, 1 fat.

FLAKY DANISH KRINGLE

This traditional Scandinavian yeast bread has flaky layers of tender dough flavored with almond paste. The unique sugar cookie crumb coating adds the perfect amount of sweetness.

—*Lorna Jacobsen, Arrowwood, AB*

PREP: 30 MIN. + RISING • **BAKE:** 20 MIN. • **MAKES:** 20 SERVINGS

8 **Tbsp. butter, softened, divided**
1½ **to 2 cups all-purpose flour, divided**
1 **pkg. (¼ oz.) active dry yeast**
2 **Tbsp. warm water (110° to 115°)**
¼ **cup warm half-and-half cream (110° to 115°)**
2 **Tbsp. sugar**
¼ **tsp. salt**
1 **large egg, room temperature, beaten**
½ **cup almond paste**
1 **large egg white, beaten**
¼ **cup sugar cookie crumbs**
2 **Tbsp. sliced almonds**

1. In a small bowl, cream 6 Tbsp. butter and 2 Tbsp. flour. Spread into an 8x4-in. rectangle on a piece on waxed paper. Cover with waxed paper; refrigerate.

2. In a large bowl, dissolve yeast in warm water. Add the half-and-half, sugar, salt and egg; beat until smooth. Stir in enough remaining flour to form a soft dough.

3. Turn onto a floured surface; knead until smooth and elastic, 6-8 minutes. Do not let rise. Roll into an 8-in. square. Remove top sheet of waxed paper from butter mixture; invert onto the center of dough. Peel off waxed paper. Fold plain dough over butter layer. Fold widthwise into thirds. Roll out into a 12x6-in. rectangle. Fold into thirds. Repeat rolling and folding twice. Wrap in waxed paper; refrigerate for 30 minutes.

4. On a lightly floured surface, roll into a 24x5-in. rectangle. In a small bowl, beat almond paste and remaining butter; beat until smooth. Spread lengthwise down the center of dough. Fold the dough over filling to cover; pinch to seal. Place on a greased baking sheet. Shape into a pretzel. Flatten lightly with a rolling pin. Cover and let rise in a warm place until doubled, about 1 hour. Preheat oven to 350°.

5. Brush egg white over dough. Sprinkle with cookie crumbs and almonds. Bake for 20-25 minutes or until golden brown. Carefully remove from pan to a wire rack to cool.

1 PIECE: 121 cal., 7g fat (3g sat. fat), 24mg chol., 88mg sod., 12g carb. (3g sugars, 1g fiber), 2g pro.

FROM GRANDMA'S KITCHEN: You can also form this Danish kringle recipe into a rectangular or oval shape. Once the kringle is filled, gently stretch it out slightly longer—to at least 30 in.—on the baking sheet. Then, bring the ends of the kringle dough together and form to the shape you prefer. Proceed with letting the dough rise.

CREOLE CORNBREAD

Cornbread is a staple of Cajun and Creole cuisine. This version is an old favorite, and it really tastes wonderful. I found the recipe in the bottom of my recipe drawer.
—*Enid Hebert, Lafayette, LA*

PREP: 15 MIN. • **BAKE:** 45 MIN. • **MAKES:** 12 SERVINGS

2 cups cooked rice
1 cup yellow cornmeal
½ cup chopped onion
1 to 2 Tbsp. seeded chopped jalapeno pepper
1 tsp. salt
½ tsp. baking soda
2 large eggs, room temperature
1 cup 2% milk
¼ cup canola oil
1 can (16½ oz.) cream-style corn
3 cups shredded cheddar cheese
Additional cornmeal

1. In a large bowl, combine rice, cornmeal, onion, peppers, salt and baking soda.

2. In another bowl, beat eggs, milk and oil. Add corn; mix well. Stir into rice mixture until blended. Fold in cheese. Sprinkle a well-greased 10-in. ovenproof skillet with cornmeal. Pour the batter into skillet.

3. Bake at 350° for 45-50 minutes or until bread tests done. Cut into wedges and serve warm.

NOTE: Wear disposable gloves when cutting hot peppers; the oils can burn skin. Avoid touching your face.

1 PIECE: 272 cal., 14g fat (7g sat. fat), 68mg chol., 551mg sod., 26g carb. (3g sugars, 2g fiber), 10g pro.

SWEDISH DOUGHNUTS

One day, my father got a hankering for doughnuts and asked me to make him some. I ended up trying these. Dad—and everyone else—loved the results. They come out so golden and plump.
—*Lisa Bates, Dunham, QC*

PREP: 20 MIN. + CHILLING • **COOK:** 5 MIN./BATCH • **MAKES:** ABOUT 2½ DOZEN

2 large eggs, room temperature
1 cup sugar
2 cups cold mashed potatoes (mashed with milk and butter)
¾ cup buttermilk
2 Tbsp. butter, melted
1 tsp. vanilla or almond extract
4½ cups all-purpose flour
4 tsp. baking powder
1 tsp. baking soda
1 tsp. salt
2 tsp. ground nutmeg
⅛ tsp. ground ginger
Oil for deep-fat frying
Additional sugar, optional

1. In a large bowl, beat eggs and sugar. Add the potatoes, buttermilk, butter and vanilla. Combine flour, baking powder, baking soda, salt, nutmeg and ginger; gradually add to egg mixture and mix well. Cover and refrigerate for 1-2 hours.

2. Turn onto a lightly floured surface; roll to ½-in. thickness. Cut with a floured 2½-in. doughnut cutter. In an electric skillet or deep-fat fryer, heat oil to 375°.

3. Fry doughnuts, a few at a time, until golden brown on both sides, about 2 minutes. Drain on paper towels. Roll warm doughnuts in sugar if desired.

1 DOUGHNUT: 170 cal., 7g fat (1g sat. fat), 16mg chol., 252mg sod., 24g carb. (7g sugars, 1g fiber), 3g pro.

CREOLE
CORNBREAD

PEANUT BUTTER & COOKIE KNOTS

These braided pastries are filled with chunks of cookies and peanut butter. They are perfect for dessert or with your morning coffee. You could use any type of chocolate cookie or chocolate candy that would pair well with peanut butter. You can even substitute hazelnut spread for the peanut butter.

—*Daniel Carberg, Roxbury, NH*

PREP: 1 HOUR + RISING • BAKE: 20 MIN. + COOLING • MAKES: 16 SERVINGS

2 pkg. (¼ oz. each) active dry yeast
1 cup warm buttermilk (110°-115°)
2 large eggs, room temperature
½ cup unsalted butter, softened
½ cup sugar
1 tsp. salt
4 to 4½ cups all-purpose flour

FILLING
2 cups creamy peanut butter or Nutella
24 Oreo cookies, crushed (about 2⅔ cups)

TOPPING
1 large egg, beaten
1 cup confectioners' sugar
1 to 2 Tbsp. 2% milk
Coarse sea salt

1. In a small bowl, dissolve yeast in warm buttermilk. In a large bowl, combine the eggs, butter, sugar, salt, yeast mixture and 2 cups flour; beat on medium speed until smooth. Stir in enough remaining flour to form a soft dough (dough will be sticky).

2. Turn dough onto a floured surface; knead until smooth and elastic, 6-8 minutes. Place in a greased bowl, turning once to grease the top. Cover and let rise in a warm place until doubled, about 1¼ hours.

3. Punch down the dough. Turn onto a lightly floured surface; divide into 16 portions. Roll each into 12x4-in. rectangle. Spread 1 rectangle with ¼ cup peanut butter to within ½ in. of the edges; sprinkle with ⅓ cup crushed Oreos. Top with another rectangle of dough. Pinch around edges to seal.

4. Using a sharp knife, cut rectangle lengthwise in half; carefully turn each half cut side up. Loosely twist strips around each other, keeping cut surfaces facing up. Shape into a ring, pinching ends together to seal. Place on parchment-lined baking sheets. Repeat with remaining dough, peanut butter and crushed Oreos. Cover with kitchen towels; let rise in a warm place until almost doubled, about 30 minutes.

5. Preheat oven to 350°. Brush rolls with beaten egg. Bake until golden brown, 20-25 minutes. Cool on pans on wire racks for 30 minutes.

6. Combine confectioners' sugar and milk; drizzle over cooled rolls. Sprinkle the knots with sea salt and, if desired, additional crushed Oreos.

½ ROLL: 510 cal., 27g fat (8g sat. fat), 45mg chol., 397mg sod., 58g carb. (25g sugars, 3g fiber), 13g pro.

FROM GRANDMA'S KITCHEN: You can make your own homemade peanut butter for this recipe by combining 4 cups unsalted dry roasted peanuts and 1 tsp. salt in a food processor and blending to your desired consistency. Add 2 Tbsp. honey and blend to taste.

POT ROAST WITH
GRAVY, PAGE 123

GRANDMA'S FAVORITE
MAIN COURSES

It's never been easier to have a satisfying supper on the table thanks to these bubbling bakes, cozy casseroles, simmering skillets and so much more!

AU GRATIN HAM POTPIE

We first had Aunt Dolly's potpie at a family get-together. We loved it and were so happy she shared the recipe. Now we make it almost every time we bake a ham.
—Mary Zinsmeister, Slinger, WI

PREP: 15 MIN. • BAKE: 40 MIN. • MAKES: 6 SERVINGS

1 pkg. (4.9 oz.) au gratin potatoes
1½ cups boiling water
2 cups frozen peas and carrots
1½ cups cubed fully cooked ham
1 can (10¾ oz.) condensed cream of chicken soup, undiluted
1 can (4 oz.) mushroom stems and pieces, drained
½ cup 2% milk
½ cup sour cream
1 jar (2 oz.) diced pimientos, drained
1 sheet refrigerated pie crust

1. Preheat oven to 400°. In a large bowl, combine the potatoes, contents of sauce mix and water. Stir in peas and carrots, ham, soup, mushrooms, milk, sour cream and pimientos. Transfer to an ungreased 2-qt. round baking dish.

2. Unroll crust; roll out to fit top of dish. Place over potato mixture; flute edge and cut slits in crust. Bake for 40-45 minutes or until golden brown. Let stand for 5 minutes before serving.

1 PIECE: 434 cal., 20g fat (9g sat. fat), 45mg chol., 1548mg sod., 47g carb. (7g sugars, 3g fiber), 14g pro.

FROM GRANDMA'S KITCHEN: If you don't like peas and carrots, feel free to swap in your favorite veggie mix. You can also use any kind of cream soup; for instance, cream of mushroom soup is a natural go-to instead of cream of chicken.

VEGETARIAN FARRO SKILLET

Farro is a type of wheat that was popular in ancient Rome. A good source of fiber, it includes more protein than most grains, making it a smart choice for meatless meals.
—Taste of Home *Test Kitchen*

PREP: 20 MIN. • COOK: 25 MIN. • MAKES: 4 SERVINGS

1 Tbsp. canola oil
1 medium onion, chopped
1 medium sweet red pepper, chopped
3 garlic cloves, minced
1 can (14½ oz.) vegetable broth
1 can (14½ oz.) diced tomatoes
1 can (15 oz.) garbanzo beans or chickpeas, rinsed and drained
1 small zucchini, halved and cut into ½-in. slices
1 cup farro, rinsed
1 cup frozen corn
¾ tsp. ground cumin
¼ tsp. salt
¼ tsp. pepper
Chopped fresh cilantro

Heat oil in a large skillet over medium-high heat. Add onion and pepper; cook and stir until tender, 2-3 minutes. Add garlic; cook 1 minute longer. Stir in broth, tomatoes, beans, zucchini, farro, corn, cumin, salt and pepper. Bring to a boil. Reduce heat; cover and simmer until farro is tender, 25-30 minutes. Sprinkle with cilantro.

1½ CUPS: 416 cal., 8g fat (0 sat. fat), 0 chol., 757mg sod., 73g carb. (10g sugars, 15g fiber), 14g pro.

FROM GRANDMA'S KITCHEN: Serve this dish over a swirl of Greek (or vegan) yogurt for creaminess.

SWEET BARBECUED PORK CHOPS

I often prepare a double batch of these tangy chops, then freeze half to keep on hand for fast family dinners. They are so easy and taste so fresh, no one ever guesses my quick entree was frozen!
—Susan Holderman, Fostoria, OH

TAKES: 25 MIN. • MAKES: 8 SERVINGS

2 Tbsp. canola oil
8 boneless pork loin chops (¾ in. thick and 8 oz. each)
½ cup packed brown sugar
½ cup chopped sweet onion
½ cup each ketchup, barbecue sauce, French salad dressing and honey

1. In a large skillet, heat oil over medium heat. In batches, brown pork chops 2-3 minutes on each side. Return all to pan.

2. In a small bowl, mix remaining ingredients; pour over chops. Bring to a boil. Reduce heat; simmer, covered, 4-5 minutes or until a thermometer inserted in pork reads 145°. Let stand for 5 minutes before serving.

FREEZE OPTION: Place pork chops in freezer containers; top with sauce. Cool and freeze. To use, partially thaw in the refrigerator overnight. Heat through in a covered saucepan, gently stirring sauce; add water if necessary.

1 PORK CHOP: 282 cal., 12g fat (3g sat. fat), 14mg chol., 533mg sod., 41g carb. (37g sugars, 1g fiber), 6g pro.

ENCHILADAS VERDES

These enchiladas are easy to make ahead and refrigerate until you're ready to bake. After quickly cooking the tortillas in hot oil, I layer them between paper napkins to soak up excess oil.
—*Joan Hallford, North Richland Hills, TX*

PREP: 45 MIN. • BAKE: 25 MIN. • MAKES: 6 SERVINGS

- 1 **lb. lean ground beef (90% lean)**
- 1 **large onion, chopped**
- ¼ **tsp. salt**
- 1 **small garlic clove, minced**
- 2 **cups shredded cheddar cheese**
- 1 **can (10¾ oz.) condensed cream of chicken soup, undiluted**
- 1 **pkg. (8 oz.) Velveeta, cubed**
- ¾ **cup evaporated milk**
- 1 **can (4 oz.) chopped green chiles, drained**
- 1 **jar (2 oz.) diced pimientos, drained**
- 12 **corn tortillas (6 in.)**
- ¼ **cup canola oil**
  Minced fresh cilantro, optional

1. In a large skillet, cook the beef, onion and salt over medium heat until meat is no longer pink. Add garlic; cook for 1 minute longer. Drain. Stir in cheddar cheese; set aside.

2. Meanwhile, in a large saucepan, cook and stir the soup, Velveeta and milk over medium heat until cheese is melted. Stir in chiles and pimientos.

3. In a large skillet, fry tortillas, 1 at a time, in oil 5 seconds on each side or until golden brown. Drain on paper towels.

4. Place a scant ¼ cup of reserved meat mixture down the center of each tortilla. Roll up and place seam side down in greased 13x9-in. baking dish. Pour cheese sauce over top.

5. Cover and bake at 350° for 25-30 minutes or until heated through. If desired, sprinkle with cilantro before serving.

2 ENCHILADAS: 676 cal., 41g fat (19g sat. fat), 121mg chol., 1406mg sod., 40g carb. (8g sugars, 4g fiber), 36g pro.

FROM GRANDMA'S KITCHEN: You can use flour tortillas instead of the traditional corn tortillas. Also, feel free to skip the step of browning the tortillas, but do let them warm up so they're pliable and less likely to tear or break.

GRANDMA'S SECRET
Do you have puff pastry left over after assembling this dish? If you're feeling creative, save the scraps—they can be used to cut out decorative and seasonal shapes.

BEEF WELLINGTON WITH MADEIRA SAUCE

This very impressive-looking yet easy-to-make dish can be
made ahead. Just finish when your guests arrive.
—*Janaan Cunningham, Greendale, WI*

PREP: 45 MIN. + CHILLING • BAKE: 40 MIN. + STANDING • MAKES: 16 SERVINGS

1 **beef tenderloin roast (4 to 5 lbs.)**

MADEIRA SAUCE
2 **cans (10½ oz. each) condensed beef consomme, undiluted**
2 **Tbsp. tomato paste**
½ **tsp. beef bouillon granules**
2 **Tbsp. butter, softened**
2 **Tbsp. all-purpose flour**
½ **cup Madeira wine**

FILLING
2 **cups chopped fresh mushrooms**
4 **shallots, chopped**
¼ **lb. sliced deli ham, chopped**
¼ **cup minced fresh parsley**
1 **pkg. (17.3 oz.) frozen puff pastry sheets, thawed**
2 **Tbsp. 2% milk**
1 **large egg, lightly beaten, optional**

1. Preheat oven to 475°. Place the tenderloin in a greased 15x10x1-in. baking pan; fold ends under tenderloin. Bake, uncovered, for 20-25 minutes or until browned. Cover and refrigerate for at least 2 hours or until chilled.

2. For sauce, in a large saucepan, combine the consomme, tomato paste and bouillon granules. Bring to a boil. Reduce the heat; simmer, uncovered, for 20 minutes or until reduced to 2 cups.

3. Combine the butter and flour until smooth. Stir into sauce 1 tsp. at a time. Bring to a boil; cook and stir for 2 minutes or until thickened. Remove from the heat; stir in wine.

4. For the filling, in a large skillet, combine the mushrooms, shallots, ham and 2 Tbsp. Madeira sauce. Cook over low heat for 10 minutes, stirring occasionally. Stir in the parsley; cook 10 minutes longer or until the liquid has evaporated, stirring occasionally. Set aside.

5. Preheat oven to 425°. On a lightly floured surface, unfold both puff pastry sheets; moisten short side of 1 sheet with water. Slightly overlap the edge of the remaining sheet over the moistened edge; press edges together. Transfer to an ungreased baking sheet.

6. Spread half of the filling down the center of pastry. Place the tenderloin on the filling. Spread the remaining filling over the top of meat. Bring edges of pastry over the filling and pinch together. Roll to place seam side down. Brush pastry edges with milk; fold edges under meat. If desired, lightly score the puff pastry with a sharp knife to form a diamond pattern and brush with beaten egg.

7. Bake, uncovered, until deep golden brown, about 40 minutes, covering lightly with foil if needed to prevent overbrowning (meat will be medium-rare). Transfer to a serving platter. Let stand for 15 minutes before slicing. Rewarm Madeira sauce if necessary. Serve with tenderloin.

1 PIECE: 363 cal., 17g fat (5g sat. fat), 56mg chol., 453mg sod., 21g carb. (2g sugars, 3g fiber), 30g pro.

MY MOM'S BEST MEAT LOAF

The Rice Krispies used in this recipe are my mom's secret ingredient. While they may seem odd or out of place, they help hold the meat loaf together. And once they are cooked, no one realizes they're even there.
—*Kelly Simmons, Hopkinsville, KY*

PREP: 10 MIN. • BAKE: 1 HOUR + STANDING • MAKES: 8 SERVINGS

½ cup chili sauce
¼ cup ketchup
2 cups Rice Krispies
1 medium onion, finely chopped
1 small green or sweet red pepper, finely chopped
¾ cup shredded part-skim mozzarella cheese
1 large egg, lightly beaten
½ tsp. salt
¼ tsp. pepper
2 lbs. ground beef

1. Preheat oven to 350°. In a small bowl, mix chili sauce and ketchup. In a large bowl, combine Rice Krispies, onion, green pepper, cheese, egg, salt and pepper; stir in half of the chili sauce mixture. Add beef; mix lightly but thoroughly.

2. Transfer beef mixture to an ungreased 9x5-in. loaf pan. Make a shallow indentation down center of loaf. Spread remaining chili sauce mixture over loaf, being sure to fill indentation.

3. Bake 60-70 minutes or until a thermometer reads 160°; use a turkey baster to remove drippings every 20 minutes. Let stand for 10 minutes before slicing.

1 PIECE: 303 cal., 16g fat (6g sat. fat), 100mg chol., 654mg sod., 15g carb. (7g sugars, 0 fiber), 24g pro.

SLOW-COOKER BARBECUE PULLED PORK SANDWICHES

Foolproof and wonderfully delicious describes my barbecue pork recipe. Just four ingredients and a slow cooker make a fabulous dish with little effort from you.
—*Sarah Johnson, Chicago, IL*

PREP: 15 MIN. • COOK: 7 HOURS • MAKES: 6 SERVINGS

1 lemon-garlic pork loin filet (about 1⅓ lbs.)
1 can (12 oz.) Dr Pepper
1 bottle (18 oz.) barbecue sauce
6 hamburger buns, split

1. Place pork in a 3-qt. slow cooker. Pour Dr Pepper over top. Cover and cook on low 7-9 hours or until meat is tender.

2. Remove meat; cool slightly. Discard cooking juices. Shred meat with 2 forks and return to slow cooker. Stir in the barbecue sauce; heat through. Serve on buns.

FREEZE OPTION: Place individual portions of cooled meat mixture and juice in freezer containers. To use, partially thaw in refrigerator overnight. Microwave, covered, on high in a microwave-safe dish until heated through, stirring occasionally; add broth or water if necessary.

1 SANDWICH: 348 cal., 8g fat (2g sat. fat), 45mg chol., 1695mg sod., 43g carb. (22g sugars, 2g fiber), 25g pro.

SAUSAGE, PEAR & SWEET POTATO SHEET-PAN DINNER

This healthy, foolproof weeknight dinner is naturally gluten free, uses one pan and is on your table in no time! The recipe is also easily adaptable to whatever seasonal fruits or veggies are lying around.

—*Melissa Erdelac, Valparaiso, IN*

PREP: 15 MIN. • **BAKE:** 45 MIN. • **MAKES:** 5 SERVINGS

2 **large sweet potatoes, peeled and cut into ½-in. cubes**
1 **large sweet onion, cut into wedges**
2 **Tbsp. olive oil**
1 **Tbsp. brown sugar**
½ **tsp. salt**
½ **tsp. ground allspice**
¼ **tsp. ground cinnamon**
⅛ **tsp. pepper**
3 **small pears, quartered**
1 **pkg. (19 oz.) Italian sausage links**

1. Preheat oven to 425°. Place sweet potatoes and onion in a 15x10x1-in. baking pan; drizzle with oil. Sprinkle with brown sugar and seasonings; toss to coat. Bake 15 minutes. Gently stir in pears; top with sausages.

2. Bake for 20 minutes longer, stirring once. Increase oven temperature to 450°. Bake until sausages are golden brown and a thermometer inserted in sausage reads at least 160°, 8-10 minutes longer, turning once.

1 SERVING: 533 cal., 29g fat (8g sat. fat), 58mg chol., 912mg sod., 56g carb. (28g sugars, 8g fiber), 15g pro.

FROM GRANDMA'S KITCHEN: It's best to leave the sausages whole while cooking. Cut sausages cook much faster than whole links, so they'd be fully cooked long before the veggies are done.

COWBOY SPAGHETTI

Cowboy spaghetti starts on the stovetop and finishes in the oven, giving you plenty of hands-off time to prepare a salad or dessert for after dinner. If you don't have a cast-iron skillet, transfer the spaghetti to a 13x9-in. baking dish before putting it in the oven.

—*Kerry Whitaker, Carthage, TX*

PREP: 20 MIN. **BAKE:** 20 MIN. • **MAKES:** 16 SERVINGS

- 1 **pkg. (12 oz.) spaghetti**
- 8 **bacon strips, chopped**
- 1½ **lbs. lean ground beef (90% lean)**
- 1 **large onion, chopped**
- 1 **can (15 oz.) kidney beans, rinsed and drained**
- 1 **can (15 oz.) tomato sauce**
- 1 **can (10 oz.) chili-seasoned diced tomatoes and green chiles, undrained**
- 2 **Tbsp. chili powder**
- 2 **Tbsp. Worcestershire sauce**
- 1 **tsp. ground cumin**
- 1 **tsp. dried oregano**
- ½ **tsp. garlic powder**
- 3 **cups shredded pepper jack cheese, divided Chopped green onions, optional**

1. Preheat oven to 350°. Cook the spaghetti according to the package directions.

2. In a 12-in. cast iron skillet, cook the bacon over medium heat until crisp, stirring occasionally. Remove with a slotted spoon; drain on paper towels. Add the beef and onion to the drippings. Cook and stir for 5-7 minutes or until beef is no longer pink, breaking meat into crumbles. Stir in the tomato sauce, beans, diced tomatoes, chili powder, Worcestershire sauce, cumin, oregano and garlic powder.

3. Drain spaghetti; stir into skillet. Stir in 1½ cups cheese and half the bacon. Top with remaining 1½ cups cheese. Bake until heated through, 20-25 minutes. Sprinkle with the green onions and remaining bacon.

1 CUP: 303 cal., 17g fat (8g sat. fat), 59mg chol., 469mg sod., 20g carb. (2g sugars, 2g fiber), 19g pro.

FROM GRANDMA'S KITCHEN: Try swapping in a different protein like ground turkey or ground pork for the ground beef.

MEAT-AND-POTATO CASSEROLE

For variety, you can use another kind of cream soup (cream of mushroom, for example). But try it this way first!
—*Marna Heitz, Farley, IA*

PREP: 10 MIN. • BAKE: 50 MIN. • MAKES: 6 SERVINGS

4 **cups thinly sliced peeled potatoes**
2 **Tbsp. butter, melted**
½ **tsp. salt**
1 **lb. ground beef**
1 **pkg. (10 oz.) frozen corn**
1 **can (10¾ oz.) condensed cream of celery soup, undiluted**
⅓ **cup 2% milk**
¼ **tsp. garlic powder**
⅛ **tsp. pepper**
1 **Tbsp. chopped onion**
1 **cup shredded cheddar cheese, divided**
  Minced fresh parsley, optional

1. Toss potatoes with butter and salt; arrange on the bottom and up the sides of a greased 13x9-in. baking dish. Bake, uncovered, at 400° for 25-30 minutes or until potatoes are almost tender.

2. Meanwhile, in a large skillet, cook the beef over medium heat until no longer pink; drain. Sprinkle beef and corn over potatoes. Combine the soup, milk, garlic powder, pepper, onion and ½ cup cheese; pour over beef mixture.

3. Bake, uncovered, at 400° for 20 minutes or until vegetables are tender. Sprinkle with remaining cheese. Bake 2-3 minutes longer or until cheese is melted. Sprinkle with parsley if desired.

1 CUP: 374 cal., 19g fat (11g sat. fat), 71mg chol., 778mg sod., 31g carb. (3g sugars, 3g fiber), 22g pro.

MOM'S BEEF LASAGNA

One of my mom's special recipes, this Italian classic is requested time and again. The made-from-scratch sauce gives each cheesy slice home-style flavor and a softer texture than many other versions of lasagna.
—*Kim Orr, West Grove, PA*

PREP: 40 MIN. • **BAKE:** 45 MIN. + STANDING • **MAKES:** 12 SERVINGS

1 **lb. ground beef**
2 **garlic cloves, minced**
1½ **cups water**
1 **can (15 oz.) tomato sauce**
1 **can (6 oz.) tomato paste**
½ **to 1 envelope onion soup mix**
1 **tsp. dried oregano**
½ **tsp. sugar**
¼ **tsp. pepper**
9 **lasagna noodles, cooked and drained**
2 **cups 4% cottage cheese**
4 **cups shredded part-skim mozzarella cheese**
2 **cups grated Parmesan cheese**

1. In a large saucepan, cook beef over medium heat until meat is no longer pink. Add garlic; cook 1 minute longer. Drain. Stir in water, tomato sauce and paste, soup mix, oregano, sugar and pepper. Bring to a boil. Reduce heat; cover and simmer for 30 minutes.

2. Spoon ½ cup meat sauce into a greased 13x9-in. baking dish. Layer with 3 noodles and a third of the cottage cheese, mozzarella, meat sauce and Parmesan cheese. Repeat the layers twice.

3. Cover and bake at 350° for 40 minutes or until bubbly and heated through. Uncover; bake 5-10 minutes longer. Let stand for 10 minutes before cutting.

1 PIECE: 367 cal., 18g fat (9g sat. fat), 62mg chol., 901mg sod., 25g carb. (5g sugars, 2g fiber), 27g pro.

TUNA CRESCENT RING

Here's my on-the-fly recipe for those days when I haven't shopped and have to invent something. It's so good, and I always keep the ingredients on hand.

—Julia Bivens, Martinsburg, WV

TAKES: 30 MIN. • MAKES: 4 SERVINGS

1 tube (8 oz.) refrigerated crescent rolls
1 can (12 oz.) albacore white tuna in water
1 cup frozen peas and carrots (about 5 oz.)
½ cup shredded cheddar cheese
¼ cup mayonnaise
1 Tbsp. Dijon mustard
1½ tsp. dried minced onion
1 tsp. Italian seasoning

1. Preheat oven to 375°. Unroll crescent dough and separate into triangles. On an ungreased 12-in. pizza pan, arrange triangles in a ring with points toward the outside and wide ends overlapping. Press overlapping dough to seal.

2. In a small bowl, combine the remaining ingredients. Spoon across wide end of triangles. Fold pointed end of triangles over filling, tucking points under to form a ring (filling will be visible).

3. Bake 15-20 minutes or until golden brown and heated through.

1 PIECE: 506 cal., 30g fat (8g sat. fat), 56mg chol., 1044mg sod., 28g carb. (6g sugars, 1g fiber), 28g pro.

LAZY MAN'S RIBS

I'll have to admit these ribs are finger-lickin' good and fall-off-the-bone tender! I've made them for a lot of my buddies—including my preacher—and some have even suggested that I try bottling my sauce and selling it to the public!

—Allan Stackhouse Jr., Jennings, LA

PREP: 20 MIN. • COOK: 5 HOURS • MAKES: 4 SERVINGS

2½ lbs. pork baby back ribs, cut into 8 pieces
2 tsp. Cajun seasoning
1 medium onion, sliced
1 cup ketchup
½ cup packed brown sugar
⅓ cup orange juice
⅓ cup cider vinegar
¼ cup molasses
2 Tbsp. Worcestershire sauce
1 Tbsp. barbecue sauce
1 tsp. stone-ground mustard
1 tsp. paprika
½ tsp. garlic powder
½ tsp. liquid smoke, optional
  Dash salt
5 tsp. cornstarch
1 Tbsp. cold water

1. Rub ribs with Cajun seasoning. Layer ribs and onion in a 5-qt. slow cooker. In a small bowl, combine the ketchup, brown sugar, orange juice, vinegar, molasses, Worcestershire sauce, barbecue sauce, mustard, paprika, garlic powder, liquid smoke if desired, and salt. Pour over ribs. Cover and cook on low until the meat is tender, 5-6 hours.

2. Remove ribs and keep warm. Strain cooking juices and skim fat; transfer to a small saucepan. Combine cornstarch and water until smooth; stir into juices. Bring to a boil; cook and stir until thickened, about 2 minutes. Serve with ribs.

1 SERVING: 753 cal., 39g fat (14g sat. fat), 153mg chol., 1335mg sod., 70g carb. (52g sugars, 2g fiber), 33g pro.

TUNA
CRESCENT
RING

CHIPPED BEEF ON TOAST

This fast-to-fix dish makes a hearty breakfast or light lunch. A creamy sauce prepared in the microwave coats convenient packaged dried beef and is served over toast.

—*Jane Fry, Lancaster, PA*

TAKES: 10 MIN. • MAKES: 4 SERVINGS

¼ cup butter, cubed	2 pkg. (2½ oz. each) thinly sliced dried beef
¼ cup all-purpose flour	
2 cups 2% milk	4 slices bread, toasted

1. In a microwave-safe bowl, microwave the butter on high for 35 seconds or until melted. Stir in flour until smooth. Gradually stir in milk.

2. Microwave, uncovered, on high for 2-3 minutes or until thickened, stirring every minute. Stir in beef; cook on high for 1 minute or until heated through. Serve on toast.

¾ CUP BEEF MIXTURE WITH 2 PIECES TOAST: 400 cal., 17g fat (10g sat. fat), 68mg chol., 1422mg sod., 41g carb. (10g sugars, 2g fiber), 21g pro.

CREAMY CELERY BEEF STROGANOFF

Cream of celery soup adds richness to a recipe that has become a family favorite. Besides the delicious flavor of the dish, I love the ease of preparing it.

—*Kimberly Wallace, Dennison, OH*

PREP: 20 MIN. • COOK: 8 HOURS • MAKES: 6 SERVINGS

2 lbs. beef stew meat, cut into 1-in. cubes
1 can (10¾ oz.) condensed cream of celery soup, undiluted
1 can (10¾ oz.) condensed cream of mushroom soup, undiluted
1 medium onion, chopped
1 jar (6 oz.) sliced mushrooms, drained
1 envelope onion soup mix
½ tsp. pepper
1 cup sour cream
Hot cooked noodles

In a 3-qt. slow cooker, combine the first 7 ingredients. Cover and cook on low for 8 hours or until beef is tender. Stir in sour cream. Serve with noodles.

1 CUP: 405 cal., 22g fat (10g sat. fat), 125mg chol., 1340mg sod., 16g carb. (4g sugars, 2g fiber), 33g pro.

SUMMER BOUNTY RATATOUILLE

Make use of your garden's surplus with this comforting dish from the Provence region of France. It's a vegetable dish traditionally made with eggplant, tomatoes, onions, zucchini, garlic, bell peppers and various herbs. I highly recommend accompanying it with some freshly baked bread.

—*Phyllis Jacques, Venice, FL*

PREP: 20 MIN. + STANDING • **COOK:** 1 HOUR • **MAKES:** 12 SERVINGS

1 large eggplant, peeled and cut into 1-in. cubes
1½ tsp. kosher salt, divided
3 Tbsp. olive oil
2 medium sweet red peppers, cut into ½-in. strips
2 medium onions, peeled and chopped
4 garlic cloves, minced
¼ cup tomato paste
1 Tbsp. herbes de Provence
½ tsp. pepper
3 cans (14½ oz. each) diced tomatoes, undrained
1½ cups water
4 medium zucchini, quartered lengthwise and sliced ½-in. thick
¼ cup chopped fresh basil
2 Tbsp. minced fresh rosemary
2 Tbsp. minced fresh parsley
2 French bread baguettes (10½ oz. each), cubed and toasted

1. Place eggplant in a colander over a plate; toss with 1 tsp. kosher salt. Let stand 30 minutes. Rinse and drain well.

2. In a Dutch oven, heat oil over medium-high heat; saute peppers and onions until tender, 8-10 minutes. Add the garlic; cook and stir for 1 minute. Stir in the tomato paste, herbs de Provence, pepper, remaining salt, tomatoes and water. Add zucchini and eggplant; bring to a boil. Reduce heat; simmer, uncovered, until flavors are blended, 40-45 minutes, stirring occasionally.

3. Stir in fresh herbs. Serve over baguette cubes.

1 CUP RATATOUILLE WITH 1 CUP BREAD CUBES: 205 cal., 4g fat (1g sat. fat), 0 chol., 542mg sod., 38g carb. (8g sugars, 6g fiber), 7g pro.

GRANDMA'S SECRET

If you want to chop an onion without having to experience that unpleasant eye-burning sensation, try putting your onion in the freezer 15-20 minutes before you chop it.

GARLIC BEEF ENCHILADAS

Enchiladas are typically prepared with corn tortillas, but we prefer
flour tortillas in this saucy casserole with a subtle kick.

—Jennifer Standridge, Dallas, GA

PREP: 30 MIN. • **BAKE:** 40 MIN. • **MAKES:** 5 SERVINGS

1 lb. ground beef
1 medium onion, chopped
2 Tbsp. all-purpose flour
1 Tbsp. chili powder
1 tsp. salt
1 tsp. garlic powder
½ tsp. ground cumin
¼ tsp. rubbed sage
1 can (14½ oz.) stewed
tomatoes, cut up

SAUCE
⅓ cup butter
4 to 6 garlic cloves, minced
½ cup all-purpose flour
1 can (14½ oz.) beef broth
1 can (15 oz.) tomato sauce
1 to 2 Tbsp. chili powder
1 to 2 tsp. ground cumin
1 to 2 tsp. rubbed sage
½ tsp. salt
10 flour tortillas (6 in.),
warmed
2 cups shredded Colby-
Monterey Jack cheese,
divided
Optional toppings: Halved
grape tomatoes, minced
fresh cilantro, sliced
jalapeno peppers,
chopped or sliced red
onion and cubed avocado

1. Preheat oven to 350°. In a large skillet, cook beef and onion over medium heat until the beef is no longer pink, 6-8 minutes, breaking meat into crumbles; drain. Stir in flour and seasonings. Add tomatoes; bring to a boil. Reduce heat; simmer, covered, 15 minutes.

2. In a saucepan, heat butter over medium-high heat. Add garlic; cook and stir 1 minute or until tender. Stir in flour until blended; gradually whisk in the broth. Bring to a boil; cook and stir until thickened, about 2 minutes. Stir in tomato sauce and seasonings; heat through.

3. Pour 1½ cups sauce into an ungreased 13x9-in. baking dish. Place about ¼ cup beef mixture off-center on each tortilla; top with 1-2 Tbsp. cheese. Roll up and place over sauce, seam side down. Top with remaining sauce.

4. Bake, covered, until heated through, 30-35 minutes. Sprinkle with remaining cheese. Bake, uncovered, until cheese is melted, 10-15 minutes longer. Serve with toppings as desired.

2 ENCHILADAS: 751 cal., 43g fat (21g sat. fat), 128mg chol., 2536mg sod., 56g carb. (8g sugars, 4g fiber), 38g pro.

"I'm not the best cook, but this was easy, fun and delicious. I could have drunk the sauce with a straw! I took it to work and let people sample it. I ended up giving the recipe out multiple times."
—NANCY709, TASTEOFHOME.COM

MOM'S ROAST CHICKEN

This is the best way to cook a whole chicken that roasts up super juicy with crisp, golden skin. It's simply seasoned, but packs in so much flavor.
—*James Schend, Pleasant Prairie, WI*

PREP: 15 MIN. + CHILLING • **BAKE:** 35 MIN. + STANDING • **MAKES:** 6 SERVINGS

1 broiler/fryer chicken
  (4 to 5 lbs.)
2 tsp. kosher salt
1 tsp. coarsely
  ground pepper
2 tsp. olive oil
  Optional: Minced fresh
  thyme or rosemary

1. Rub outside of chicken with salt and pepper. Transfer chicken to a rack on a rimmed baking sheet. Refrigerate, uncovered, overnight.

2. Preheat oven to 450°. Remove chicken from refrigerator while oven heats. Heat a 12-in. cast-iron or ovenproof skillet in the oven for 15 minutes.

3. Place chicken on a work surface, neck side down. Cut through skin where legs connect to body. Press thighs down so joints pop and legs lie flat.

4. Carefully place chicken, breast side up, into hot skillet; press legs down so they lie flat on bottom of pan. Brush with oil. Roast until a thermometer inserted in thickest part of the thigh reads 170°-175°, 35-40 minutes. Remove the chicken from oven; let stand for 10 minutes before carving. If desired, top with herbs before serving.

5 OZ. COOKED CHICKEN: 405 cal., 24g fat (6g sat. fat), 139mg chol., 760mg sod., 0 carb. (0 sugars, 0 fiber), 44g pro.

ITALIAN BEEF HOAGIES

You'll need just a few ingredients to feed a crowd these tender tangy sandwiches. On weekends, I start the roast the night before, so I can shred it in the morning.
—*Lori Piatt, Danville, IL*

PREP: 25 MIN. • **COOK:** 8 HOURS • **MAKES:** 18 SERVINGS

1 beef sirloin tip roast
  (4 lbs.), halved
2 envelopes Italian salad
  dressing mix
2 cups water
1 jar (16 oz.) mild pickled
  pepper rings, undrained
18 hoagie buns, split

1. Place roast in a 5-qt. slow cooker. Combine the salad dressing mix and water; pour over roast. Cover and cook on low 8-10 hours or until meat is tender.

2. Remove meat; shred with 2 forks and return to the slow cooker. Add pepper rings; heat through. Spoon ½ cup meat mixture onto each bun.

1 SANDWICH: 346 cal., 9g fat (4g sat. fat), 53mg chol., 674mg sod., 39g carb. (8g sugars, 2g fiber), 26g pro.

GRANDMA'S POTPIE

My husband and father-in-law are both picky eaters, but they enjoy this savory
meat pie with a flaky golden crust. The recipe is from my husband's grandmother.
—*Annette Wheatley, Syracuse, NY*

PREP: 30 MIN. • BAKE: 45 MIN. • MAKES: 6 SERVINGS

1½ **lbs. ground beef**
1 **tsp. onion powder**
  Salt to taste
1 **cup diced peeled**
  potatoes
1 **cup frozen mixed**
  vegetables, thawed
¼ **cup butter, cubed**
¼ **cup all-purpose flour**
1 **can (14½ oz.) beef broth**

CRUST
2 **cups all-purpose flour**
1 **Tbsp. baking powder**
1 **tsp. salt**
¼ **cup shortening**
¾ **cup 2% milk**
1 **Tbsp. butter, melted**

1. In a large skillet, cook beef over medium heat until no longer
pink; drain. Stir in onion powder and salt. Transfer to a greased
9-in. square baking dish. Top with potatoes and vegetables.

2. Meanwhile, in a small saucepan, melt the butter. Stir in flour
until smooth; gradually add broth. Bring to a boil. Cook and stir
for 2 minutes or until thickened. Pour over vegetables.

3. For crust, in a small bowl, combine the flour, baking powder
and salt in a bowl. Cut in shortening until mixture resembles
coarse crumbs. Stir in milk until a soft dough forms.

4. On a floured surface, roll dough into a 9-in. square. Place over
filling; flute edges and cut slits in top. Brush with melted butter.
Bake at 350° for 45 minutes or until golden brown.

1 PIECE: 572 cal., 29g fat (13g sat. fat), 84mg chol., 1051mg sod., 47g
carb. (3g sugars, 3g fiber), 28g pro.

*"This is a great recipe—easy and so delicious. My 3-year-
old eats every bite. It's so, so good for the winter blues!"*
—WISCONSINMAMA, TASTEOFHOME.COM

HOMEMADE FISH STICKS

I am a nutritionist and needed a healthy fish fix. With a moist inside and crunchy outside, these are amazing with oven fries or roasted veggies and low-fat homemade tartar sauce.
—*Jennifer Rowland, Elizabethtown, KY*

TAKES: 25 MIN. • MAKES: 2 SERVINGS

½ cup dry bread crumbs
½ tsp. salt
½ tsp. paprika
½ tsp. lemon-pepper seasoning
½ cup all-purpose flour
1 large egg, beaten
¾ lb. cod fillets, cut into 1-in. strips
Butter-flavored cooking spray

1. Preheat oven to 400°. In a shallow bowl, mix bread crumbs and seasonings. Place flour and egg in separate shallow bowls. Dip fish in flour to coat both sides; shake off excess. Dip in egg, then in crumb mixture, patting to help coating adhere.

2. Place on a baking sheet coated with cooking spray; spritz fish with butter-flavored cooking spray. Bake 10-12 minutes or until fish just begins to flake easily with a fork, turning once.

1 SERVING: 278 cal., 4g fat (1g sat. fat), 129mg chol., 718mg sod., 25g carb. (2g sugars, 1g fiber), 33g pro. **DIABETIC EXCHANGES:** 4 lean meat, 1½ starch.

MOM'S SLOPPY TACOS

No matter how hectic the weeknight, there's always time to serve your family a healthy meal with recipes this easy and delicious!
—*Kami Jones, Avondale, AZ*

TAKES: 30 MIN. • MAKES: 6 SERVINGS

1½ lbs. extra-lean ground beef (95% lean)
1 can (15 oz.) tomato sauce
¾ tsp. garlic powder
½ tsp. salt
¼ tsp. pepper
¼ tsp. cayenne pepper
12 taco shells, warmed
Optional: Shredded lettuce, shredded cheese, chopped tomatoes, avocado and olives

1. In a large skillet, cook beef over medium heat until no longer pink, crumbling beef. Stir in the tomato sauce, garlic powder, salt, pepper and cayenne. Bring to a boil. Reduce the heat; simmer, uncovered, for 10 minutes.

2. Fill each taco shell with ¼ cup beef mixture and toppings of your choice.

2 TACOS: 264 cal., 10g fat (4g sat. fat), 65mg chol., 669mg sod., 17g carb. (1g sugars, 1g fiber), 25g pro. **DIABETIC EXCHANGES:** 3 lean meat, 1 starch, 1 fat.

CHICKEN
TOSTADA
CUPS

CHICKEN TOSTADA CUPS

Years ago, I tried a version of these cups at a restaurant in Santa Fe, and I wanted to make my own spin. They're perfect party fare; it's easy to let everyone add their own favorite toppings.
—*Marla Clark, Moriarty., NM*

PREP: 25 MIN. • BAKE: 15 MIN. • MAKES: 6 SERVINGS

12 corn tortillas (6 in.),
  warmed
  Cooking spray
2 cups shredded
  rotisserie chicken
1 cup salsa
1 can (16 oz.) refried beans
1 cup shredded reduced-
  fat Mexican cheese blend
  Optional toppings:
  Shredded lettuce,
  reduced-fat sour cream,
  chopped cilantro, diced
  avocado, sliced jalapeno,
  lime wedges, sliced ripe
  olives, sliced green
  onions, sliced radishes,
  and pico de gallo or
  additional salsa

1. Preheat oven to 425°. Press warm tortillas into 12 muffin cups coated with cooking spray, pleating the sides as needed. Spritz tortillas with additional cooking spray.

2. Bake until lightly browned, 5-7 minutes. Toss chicken with salsa. Layer each cup with beans, chicken mixture and cheese.

3. Bake until heated through, 9-11 minutes. Serve with toppings as desired.

2 TOSTADA CUPS: 338 cal., 11g fat (4g sat. fat), 52mg chol., 629mg sod., 35g carb. (2g sugars, 6g fiber), 25g pro. DIABETIC EXCHANGES: 3 lean meat, 2 starch, 1 fat.

CHEESY STUFFED PEPPERS

This is my favorite summertime dinner because I can use peppers and tomatoes fresh from my garden.
—*Betty DeRaad, Sioux Falls, SD*

PREP: 20 MIN. • BAKE: 20 MIN. • MAKES: 6 SERVINGS

6 medium green peppers
1½ lbs. ground beef
1 medium onion, chopped
½ tsp. salt
2 cups shredded cheddar
  cheese
2½ cups chopped tomatoes
  (3 medium)
1½ cups cooked rice

1. Cut tops off peppers and remove seeds. In a Dutch oven, cook peppers in boiling water 6-8 minutes or until crisp-tender.

2. Meanwhile, brown beef, onion and salt in a skillet; drain. Cool slightly. Stir in the cheese, tomatoes and rice.

3. Drain peppers and stuff with meat mixture. Place in a baking dish. Bake, uncovered, at 350° 20 minutes or until heated through.

1 STUFFED PEPPER: 419 cal., 21g fat (13g sat. fat), 96mg chol., 509mg sod., 26g carb. (7g sugars, 4g fiber), 31g pro.

VEGETABLE PAD THAI

Classic flavors of Thailand abound in this fragrant and flavorful dish featuring peanuts, tofu and noodles. Tofu gives the entree its satisfying protein.

—*Sara Landry, Brookline, MA*

PREP: 25 MIN. • **COOK:** 15 MIN. • **MAKES:** 6 SERVINGS

12 oz. uncooked thick rice noodles
¼ cup rice vinegar
3 Tbsp. reduced-sodium soy sauce
2 Tbsp. brown sugar
2 Tbsp. fish sauce or additional reduced-sodium soy sauce
1 Tbsp. lime juice
Dash Louisiana-style hot sauce
3 tsp. canola oil, divided
1 pkg. (12 oz.) extra-firm tofu, drained and cut into ½-in. cubes
2 medium carrots, grated
2 cups fresh snow peas
3 garlic cloves, minced
2 large eggs, lightly beaten
2 cups bean sprouts
3 green onions, chopped
½ cup minced fresh cilantro
¼ cup unsalted peanuts, chopped

1. Cook noodles according to package directions. Meanwhile, in a small bowl, combine vinegar, soy sauce, brown sugar, fish sauce, lime juice and hot sauce until smooth; set aside.

2. In a large skillet or wok, heat 2 tsp. oil over medium-high heat. Add tofu; cook and stir until golden brown, 4-6 minutes. Remove and keep warm. Cook and stir carrots and snow peas in remaining 1 tsp. oil until crisp-tender, 3-5 minutes. Add the garlic; cook 1 minute longer. Add eggs; cook and stir until set.

3. Drain pasta; add to vegetable mixture. Stir vinegar mixture and add to the skillet. Bring to a boil. Add the tofu, bean sprouts and onions; heat through. Sprinkle with cilantro and peanuts.

1⅓ CUPS: 402 cal., 10g fat (2g sat. fat), 62mg chol., 1054mg sod., 63g carb. (12g sugars, 4g fiber), 15g pro.

GERMAN-STYLE SHORT RIBS

Our whole family is excited when I plug in the slow cooker to make these amazing ribs. We like them served over rice or egg noodles.
—*Bregitte Rugman, Shanty Bay, ON*

PREP: 15 MIN. • **COOK:** 8 HOURS • **MAKES:** 8 SERVINGS

- ¾ **cup dry red wine or beef broth**
- ½ **cup mango chutney**
- 3 **Tbsp. quick-cooking tapioca**
- ¼ **cup water**
- 3 **Tbsp. brown sugar**
- 3 **Tbsp. cider vinegar**
- 1 **Tbsp. Worcestershire sauce**
- ½ **tsp. salt**
- ½ **tsp. ground mustard**
- ½ **tsp. chili powder**
- ½ **tsp. pepper**
- 4 **lbs. bone-in beef short ribs**
- 2 **medium onions, sliced**
  Optional: Egg noodles or spaetzle and minced fresh parsley

1. In a 5-qt. slow cooker, combine the first 11 ingredients. Add ribs and turn to coat. Top with onions.

2. Cover and cook on low for 8-10 hours or until meat is tender. Remove ribs from slow cooker. Skim fat from cooking juices; serve with ribs. If desired, serve ribs with noodles or spaetzle and parsley.

3 OZ. COOKED BEEF: 302 cal., 11g fat (5g sat. fat), 55mg chol., 378mg sod., 28g carb. (17g sugars, 1g fiber), 19g pro.

CAJUN MACARONI

When I prepare my favorite meat loaf, I usually end up with an extra half-pound of ground beef. I created this Cajun-flavored dish as a way to use it up.
—*June Ellis, Erie, IL*

PREP: 15 MIN. • **COOK:** 20 MIN, • **MAKES:** 4 SERVINGS

- ½ **lb. ground beef**
- ⅓ **cup chopped onion**
- ⅓ **cup chopped green pepper**
- ⅓ **cup chopped celery**
- 1 **can (14½ oz.) diced tomatoes, undrained**
- 1½ **tsp. Cajun seasoning**
- 1 **pkg. (7¼ oz.) macaroni and cheese dinner mix**
- 2 **Tbsp. 2% milk**
- 1 **Tbsp. butter**

1. In a large saucepan or skillet, cook beef, onion, green pepper and celery over medium heat until meat is no longer pink; drain. Add the tomatoes and Cajun seasoning. Cook, uncovered, for 15-20 minutes, stirring occasionally.

2. Meanwhile, prepare the macaroni and cheese according to package directions, using 2 Tbsp. milk and 1 Tbsp. butter. Stir into beef mixture; cook for 2-3 minutes or until heated through.

1 CUP: 353 cal., 12g fat (6g sat. fat), 46mg chol., 797mg sod., 19g carb. (10g sugars, 3g fiber), 18g pro.

SPINACH SALMON BUNDLES

Rich salmon encased in a flaky golden brown pastry will delight
family and guests—and no one has to know how easy it is.
—*Larissa Gedney, Myrtle Beach, SC*

TAKES: 30 MIN. • MAKES: 4 SERVINGS

2 tubes (8 oz. each) refrigerated crescent rolls
4 salmon fillets (6 oz. each)
¼ tsp. salt
¼ tsp. pepper
⅓ cup garlic-herb spreadable cheese
1 pkg. (10 oz.) frozen chopped spinach, thawed and squeezed dry

1. Unroll crescent dough and separate into 4 rectangles; seal perforations. Place a salmon fillet in the center of each rectangle; sprinkle with salt and pepper. Spoon spreadable cheese over each; top with spinach. Fold dough over filling and pinch edges to seal.

2. Place on an ungreased baking sheet. Bake at 400° until golden brown, 20-25 minutes.

1 BUNDLE: 854 cal., 52g fat (16g sat. fat), 124mg chol., 1311mg sod., 48g carb. (8g sugars, 2g fiber), 45g pro.

MOM'S SCALLOPED POTATOES & HAM

Mom's friend gave her this recipe years ago, and she shared it with me.
When we have leftover ham to use up, it's the most-requested recipe at my house.
—*Kelly Graham, St. Thomas, ON*

PREP: 20 MIN. • COOK: 8 HOURS • MAKES: 9 SERVINGS

10 medium potatoes (about 3 lbs.), peeled and thinly sliced
3 cups cubed fully cooked ham
2 large onions, thinly sliced
2 cups shredded cheddar cheese
1 can (10¾ oz.) condensed cream of mushroom soup, undiluted
½ tsp. paprika
¼ tsp. pepper

1. In a greased 6-qt. slow cooker, layer half of the potatoes, ham, onions and cheese. Repeat layers. Pour soup over top. Sprinkle with paprika and pepper.

2. Cover and cook on low 8-10 hours or until potatoes are tender.

1½ CUPS: 344 cal., 13g fat (7g sat. fat), 53mg chol., 995mg sod., 40g carb. (4g sugars, 3g fiber), 17g pro.

FROM GRANDMA'S KITCHEN: Make this dish even creamier by adding a tablespoon or two of milk into your slow cooker.

POT ROAST WITH GRAVY
PICTURED ON PAGE 96

My family loves this tangy slow-cooked roast with its rich onion and mushroom gravy. We even look forward to the leftovers.
—*Deborah Dailey, Vancouver, WA*

PREP: 30 MIN. • COOK: 6½ HOURS • MAKES: 10 SERVINGS

1   **beef rump roast or bottom round roast (5 lbs.)**
6   **Tbsp. balsamic vinegar, divided**
1   **tsp. salt**
½   **tsp. garlic powder**
¼   **tsp. pepper**
2   **Tbsp. canola oil**
3   **garlic cloves, minced**
4   **bay leaves**
1   **large onion, thinly sliced**
3   **tsp. beef bouillon granules**
½   **cup boiling water**
1   **can (10¾ oz.) condensed cream of mushroom soup, undiluted**
4   **to 5 Tbsp. cornstarch**
¼   **cup cold water**

1. Cut roast in half; rub with 2 Tbsp. vinegar. Combine salt, garlic powder and pepper; rub over meat. In a large skillet, brown roast in oil on all sides. Transfer to a 5-qt. slow cooker.

2. Place garlic, bay leaves and onion on roast. In a small bowl, dissolve bouillon in boiling water; stir in soup and remaining vinegar. Slowly pour over roast. Cover and cook on low until meat is tender, 6-8 hours.

3. Remove the roast; keep warm. Discard bay leaves. Whisk cornstarch and cold water until smooth; stir into cooking juices. Cover and cook on high until gravy is thickened, about 30 minutes. Slice roast; return to slow cooker and heat through.

2 PIECES: 365 cal., 15g fat (4g sat. fat), 137mg chol., 769mg sod., 9g carb. (2g sugars, 1g fiber), 45g pro.

EASY TAMALE PIE WITH PEPPERS

My family loves anything with southwestern flavor, so this recipe is a big hit. It's super quick and easy to prepare, and cleanup afterward is fast because everything cooks in one dish.
—*Joan Hallford, North Richland Hills, TX*

PREP: 20 MIN. + STANDING • BAKE: 30 MIN. • MAKES: 6 SERVINGS

2   **poblano peppers**
6   **chicken or beef tamales**
1   **can (15 oz.) chili with beans**
2   **cups shredded sharp cheddar cheese**
1   **small onion, chopped**
    Chopped fresh cilantro and thinly sliced green onions

1. Cut peppers lengthwise in half; remove stems and seeds. Place peppers on a foil-lined baking sheet, skin side up. Broil 4 in. from heat until skins blister, about 5 minutes. Immediately place the peppers in a large bowl; let stand, covered, 20 minutes. Reduce oven setting to 350°.

2. Peel off and discard charred skin. Place peppers in a greased 11x7-in. baking dish. Remove husks from tamales. Cut tamales into quarters; place over peppers. Top with the chili, cheese and chopped onion. Bake until hot and bubbly, 30-35 minutes. Serve with cilantro and green onions.

1 SERVING: 439 cal., 25g fat (9g sat. fat), 59mg chol., 1152mg sod., 34g carb. (3g sugars, 5g fiber), 23g pro.

HAMBURGER STIR-FRY

Here's a quick, easy teriyaki stir-fry that uses hamburger instead of the traditional beef strips. It has a nice sauce and is different enough to be a treat for the taste buds.

—Kathie and John Horst, Westfield, NY

TAKES: 25 MIN. • MAKES: 4 SERVINGS

1 Tbsp. sugar
1 Tbsp. cornstarch
1 Tbsp. ground mustard
⅓ cup cold water
⅓ cup reduced-sodium teriyaki sauce
1 lb. lean ground beef (90% lean)
1 pkg. (16 oz.) frozen asparagus stir-fry vegetable blend
1 medium onion, halved and thinly sliced
2 tsp. canola oil
2 cups hot cooked rice
2 tsp. sesame seeds
Julienned green onions, optional

1. In a small bowl, combine sugar, cornstarch and mustard. Stir in water and teriyaki sauce until smooth.

2. In a large nonstick skillet or wok over medium heat, cook beef until no longer pink, 5-7 minutes, breaking into crumbles; drain and set aside. In the same pan, heat oil over medium heat; add the vegetable blend and onion. Cook and stir until crisp-tender, 6-8 minutes.

3. Stir cornstarch mixture and add to pan. Bring to a boil; cook and stir until thickened, 1-2 minutes. Add beef; heat through. Serve with rice. Sprinkle with sesame seeds and, if desired, top with green onions.

1 SERVING: 399 cal., 12g fat (4g sat. fat), 56mg chol., 516mg sod., 42g carb. (9g sugars, 3g fiber), 28g pro. DIABETIC EXCHANGES: 3 lean meat, 2 starch, 2 vegetable, ½ fat.

GRANDMA'S KITCHEN: Udon noodles, ramen, chow mein, spaghetti or rice noodles are also great sides for this stir-fry. You can make it even healthier by using a whole-grain option or zucchini noodles as your base.

CHEESY CHICKEN & RICE

When autumn winds start to blow here in the Northeast, I keep this recipe close at hand. There are never any leftovers when I serve this to my family—much to their disappointment!

—Rebekah Thurlow, New Wilmington, PA

PREP: 15 MIN. • **BAKE:** 45 MIN. • **MAKES:** 6 SERVINGS

3 cups cooked long grain rice

3 cups frozen chopped broccoli, thawed and drained

½ lb. sliced fresh mushrooms

2 Tbsp. butter

2 cups diced cooked chicken

½ cup chopped green onions

4 large eggs

1 cup whole milk

½ tsp. salt

½ tsp. pepper

2 cups shredded cheddar cheese, divided

1 can (10¾ oz.) condensed cream of chicken soup, undiluted

1. Combine rice and broccoli; spoon into a greased 13x9-in. baking dish.

2. In a large skillet, saute mushrooms in butter until tender. Remove from the heat. Add chicken and green onions; spoon over rice mixture. Beat eggs, milk, salt and pepper; pour over all. Sprinkle with 1 cup cheese. Spread soup over top.

3. Bake, uncovered, at 350° for 30 minutes. Sprinkle with remaining cheese and bake 15 minutes longer.

1½ CUPS: 532 cal., 28g fat (13g sat. fat), 221mg chol., 969mg sod., 36g carb. (5g sugars, 4g fiber), 34g pro.

CREAMY CHICKEN & MUSHROOM RICE CASSEROLE

Gravy, chicken soup and sour cream make this rich and hearty dish one you'll want to curl up with. Be prepared to make it often, as it fills 'em up fast and tastes fantastic!

—Nancy Foust, Stoneboro, PA

PREP: 20 MIN. • BAKE: 50 MIN. • MAKES: 9 SERVINGS

3 cups shredded cooked chicken

2⅔ cups chicken gravy

2 cups uncooked instant rice

1 can (10¾ oz.) condensed cream of chicken soup, undiluted

1 cup sour cream

1 can (8 oz.) mushroom stems and pieces, drained

1 medium onion, chopped

⅔ cup chopped celery

⅔ cup water

¼ cup chopped pitted green olives

¼ cup chopped ripe olives

2 tsp. dried parsley flakes

⅛ tsp. pepper

Chopped green onions, optional

1. Preheat oven to 375°. In a large bowl, combine the first 13 ingredients. Transfer to a greased 13x9-in. baking dish.

2. Cover and bake 30 minutes. Uncover and stir; bake until bubbly and rice and vegetables are tender, 20-25 minutes. If desired, top with chopped green onions.

FREEZE OPTION: Freeze the cooled casserole mixture in freezer containers. To use, partially thaw in refrigerator overnight. Heat in a saucepan, stirring occasionally; add a little water if necessary.

1⅓ CUPS: 305 cal., 12g fat (5g sat. fat), 68mg chol., 790mg sod., 28g carb. (3g sugars, 2g fiber), 19g pro. **DIABETIC EXCHANGES:** 2 starch, 2 lean meat, 1 fat.

FROM GRANDMA'S KITCHEN: If you have a few minutes before heading out the door in the morning, mix up the ingredients, put the mixture in the greased 13x9-in. dish and store it in the fridge, covered. Unbaked, it will last up to 2 days; after baking you can keep it for about 4 days (if it's not eaten before then).

BISCUIT NUGGET
CHICKEN BAKE

BISCUIT NUGGET CHICKEN BAKE

Topped with seasoned biscuits, this yummy casserole is a fun, easy way to please everyone in the family. It's one of my favorite recipes for a quick dinner.
—Kayla Dempsey, O'Fallon, IL

TAKES: 30 MIN. • MAKES: 6 SERVINGS

- 3 cups cubed cooked chicken
- 1 can (10¾ oz.) condensed cream of chicken soup, undiluted
- 1 cup 2% milk
- 1 jar (4½ oz.) sliced mushrooms, drained
- ½ tsp. dill weed
- ½ tsp. paprika

TOPPING
- ¼ cup grated Parmesan cheese
- 1 Tbsp. dried minced onion
- 1 tsp. dried parsley flakes
- ½ tsp. paprika
- 2 tubes (6 oz. each) refrigerated buttermilk biscuits

1. In a large saucepan, combine the first 6 ingredients. Cook and stir over medium heat 5-7 minutes or until heated through; keep warm.

2. In a bowl, combine the cheese, onion, parsley and paprika. Separate biscuits and cut into quarters; add to bowl and toss to coat. Place on an ungreased baking sheet. Bake at 400° for 5 minutes.

3. Transfer chicken mixture to a greased 8-in. square baking dish; top with biscuits. Bake, uncovered, for 10-13 minutes or until bubbly and biscuits are golden brown.

1 CUP: 570 cal., 25g fat (12g sat. fat), 75mg chol., 3144mg sod., 57g carb. (6g sugars, 2g fiber), 30g pro.

CHUCK ROAST DINNER

A tasty tomato sauce nicely coats this comforting combination of beef, potatoes and carrots. My father gave me the recipe. It was one of our favorites when we used to hike all day—it takes only minutes to throw together!
—Cindy Miller, Estes Park, CO

PREP: 10 MIN. • COOK: 6 HOURS • MAKES: 10 SERVINGS

- 1 boneless beef chuck roast (3 lbs.), cut into serving-size pieces
- 3 medium potatoes, peeled and cut into chunks
- 4 medium carrots, cut into chunks
- 2 cans (11½ oz. each) tomato juice
- ¼ cup Worcestershire sauce
- 3 Tbsp. quick-cooking tapioca
  Chopped fresh parsley, optional

In a 5-qt. slow cooker, combine first 6 ingredients. Cover and cook on high until meat is tender, 6-8 hours. If desired, top with chopped parsley.

1 CUP: 300 cal., 13g fat (5g sat. fat), 88mg chol., 250mg sod., 17g carb. (3g sugars, 1g fiber), 28g pro.

DEEP-DISH PIZZA

My family devours this crusty pan pizza with easy-to-swap toppings.
Use a combination of green, red and yellow peppers for extra color.
—*Patricia Howson, Carstairs, AB*

PREP: 15 MIN. + STANDING • **BAKE:** 20 MIN. • **MAKES:** 8 SERVINGS

1 pkg. (¼ oz.) active
dry yeast
1 cup warm water
(110° to 115°)
1 tsp. sugar
1 tsp. salt
2 Tbsp. canola oil
2½ cups all-purpose flour
1 lb. ground beef, cooked
and drained
1 can (10¾ oz.) condensed
tomato soup, undiluted
1 tsp. each dried basil,
oregano and thyme
1 tsp. dried rosemary,
crushed
¼ tsp. garlic powder
1 small green pepper,
julienned
1 can (8 oz.) mushroom
stems and pieces,
drained
1 cup shredded part-skim
mozzarella cheese

1. In a large bowl, dissolve yeast in warm water. Add sugar, salt, oil and 2 cups flour. Beat until smooth. Stir in enough remaining flour to form a soft dough. Cover and let rest for 20 minutes.

2. On a floured surface, roll into a 13x9-in. rectangle. Transfer to a greased 13x9-in. baking pan. Sprinkle with beef.

3. In a small bowl, combine soup and seasonings; spoon over beef. Top with the green pepper, mushrooms and cheese.

4. Bake at 425° for 20-25 minutes or until crust and cheese are lightly browned.

FREEZE OPTION: Cover and the freeze unbaked pizza. To use, partially thaw in the refrigerator overnight. Remove from the refrigerator 30 minutes before baking. Preheat oven to 425°. Bake pizza as directed, increasing time as necessary.

1 PIECE: 364 cal., 14g fat (5g sat. fat), 49mg chol., 704mg sod., 39g carb. (5g sugars, 3g fiber), 20g pro.

"I have to admit, I was a little afraid that my kids wouldn't like it, but they really did. They ate every bite!"
—EFWYNNE, TASTEOFHOME.COM

CHICKEN PARMESAN BURGERS

A restaurant-quality burger that's topped with
marinara and loaded with cheese—what's not to love?
Fresh basil adds even more flavor if you'd like.

—Brooke Petras, Alpine, CA

TAKES: 30 MIN. • **MAKES:** 4 SERVINGS

3 **Tbsp. olive oil, divided**
1 **small onion, finely chopped**
2 **garlic cloves, minced**
¾ **cup marinara sauce, divided**
½ **cup finely chopped or shredded part-skim mozzarella cheese**
½ **cup dry bread crumbs**
1 **tsp. Italian seasoning**
1 **tsp. dried oregano**
½ **tsp. salt**
½ **tsp. pepper**
1 **lb. ground chicken**
4 **slices part-skim mozzarella cheese**
4 **hamburger buns, split and toasted**
¼ **cup shredded Parmesan cheese**
Fresh basil leaves, optional

1. In a large skillet, heat 1 Tbsp. oil over medium-high heat. Add onion; cook and stir until tender, about 3 minutes. Add garlic; cook 1 minute longer. Remove from heat; cool slightly.

2. In a large bowl, combine ¼ cup marinara sauce with chopped mozzarella cheese, bread crumbs, seasonings and onion mixture. Add chicken; mix lightly but thoroughly. With wet hands, shape into four ½-in.-thick patties.

3. In the same skillet, heat remaining 2 Tbsp. oil over medium heat. Cook burgers until a thermometer reads 165°, 4-5 minutes on each side. Top with sliced mozzarella cheese; cook, covered, until cheese is melted, 1-2 minutes.

4. Serve on buns; top with remaining ½ cup marinara sauce, Parmesan cheese and, if desired, basil leaves.

1 BURGER: 603 cal., 33g fat (10g sat. fat), 108mg chol., 1275mg sod., 41g carb. (8g sugars, 3g fiber), 38g pro.

SAUSAGE-STUFFED SHELLS

I wanted to make manicotti one day but was out of the noodles. So I came up with this recipe, using jumbo shells instead. They were much easier to work with.
—*Lori Daniels, Beverly, WV*

PREP: 25 MIN. • BAKE: 20 MIN. • MAKES: 2 SERVINGS

⅓ lb. bulk Italian sausage
1 can (8 oz.) tomato sauce
¼ cup tomato paste
2 Tbsp. water
1 tsp. brown sugar
½ tsp. Italian seasoning
⅓ cup 4% cottage cheese
¾ cup shredded part-skim mozzarella cheese, divided
2 Tbsp. beaten egg
½ tsp. minced fresh parsley
6 jumbo pasta shells, cooked and drained
Grated Parmesan cheese, optional

1. Preheat oven to 350°. In a small saucepan, cook sausage over medium heat until no longer pink; drain. Set half of the sausage aside for filling. Add tomato sauce, tomato paste, water, brown sugar and Italian seasoning to sausage in pan. Bring to a boil. Reduce the heat; simmer, uncovered, for 15 minutes, stirring mixture occasionally.

2. In a small bowl, combine the cottage cheese, ½ cup mozzarella cheese, egg, parsley and reserved sausage. Stuff into the shells. Spread ¼ cup meat sauce in an ungreased 1-qt. shallow baking dish. Place the stuffed shells in dish; drizzle with the remaining meat sauce.

3. Sprinkle with remaining mozzarella cheese and, if desired, Parmesan cheese. Bake, uncovered, until filling reaches 160°, 20-25 minutes. If desired, garnish with additional parsley.

3 STUFFED SHELLS: 437 cal., 14g fat (7g sat. fat), 67mg chol., 1371mg sod., 40g carb. (13g sugars, 4g fiber), 36g pro.

FROM GRANDMA'S KITCHEN: You can use a spoon to scoop the mixture into each pasta shell, but you'll probably have to get another utensil dirty to get the mixture off of the spoon. Instead, use a piping bag with no tip or a large plain tip for squeezing the mixture into each shell. (Make sure the hole is big enough that Italian sausage crumbles don't get stuck!)

TURKEY TENDERLOIN SUPREME

We're a busy hockey and figure skating family, so we're always on the go. Served over rice, this fast skillet supper makes a good home-cooked meal when there's little time.
—Nancy Levin, Chesterfield, MO

TAKES: 25 MIN. • MAKES: 4 SERVINGS

4 turkey breast tenderloin slices (¾ in. thick and 4 oz. each)
½ cup all-purpose flour
1 Tbsp. butter
3 green onions, thinly sliced
1 can (10¾ oz.) condensed cream of chicken soup, undiluted
½ cup water

Lightly dredge turkey with flour, shaking off excess. In a large skillet, heat butter over medium heat. Add turkey; cook until browned. Add onions; cook and stir 1-2 minutes. Combine the soup and water; pour over turkey. Bring to a boil. Reduce heat; cover and simmer until a thermometer reads 165°, 8-10 minutes.

1 SERVING: 174 cal., 3g fat (1g sat. fat), 59mg chol., 323mg sod., 8g carb. (5g sugars, 1g fiber), 28g pro. DIABETIC EXCHANGES: 3 lean meat, 1 fruit, 1 vegetable.

SUPER SHORT RIBS

This came from an old oven recipe my mom had for short ribs.
I added a few ingredients to the original to suit my taste.
—Coleen Carter, Malone, NY

PREP: 20 MIN. • COOK: 8 HOURS • MAKES: 6 SERVINGS

3 medium onions, cut into wedges
3 to 3½ lbs. bone-in beef short ribs
1 bay leaf
1 bottle (12 oz.) beer or nonalcoholic beer
2 Tbsp. brown sugar
2 Tbsp. Dijon mustard
2 Tbsp. tomato paste
2 tsp. dried thyme
2 tsp. beef bouillon granules
1 tsp. salt
¼ tsp. pepper
3 Tbsp. all-purpose flour
½ cup cold water
Hot cooked noodles

1. Place onions in a 5-qt. slow cooker; add the ribs and bay leaf. Combine the beer, brown sugar, mustard, tomato paste, thyme, bouillon, salt and pepper. Pour over meat.

2. Cover and cook on low for 8-10 hours or until meat is tender.

3. Remove meat and vegetables to a serving platter; keep warm. Discard bay leaf. Skim fat from cooking juices; transfer juices to a small saucepan. Bring liquid to a boil.

4. Combine flour and water until smooth. Gradually stir into the pan. Bring to a boil; cook and stir for 2 minutes or until thickened. Serve with meat and noodles.

1 SERVING: 257 cal., 11g fat (5g sat. fat), 55mg chol., 818mg sod., 16g carb. (7g sugars, 1g fiber), 20g pro.

GRANDMA'S SECRET

Make an alternative to cream of chicken soup by combining ½ cup chicken broth and ½ cup whole milk. Whisk together and bring to a low boil, whisking occasionally until slightly thickened.

TURKEY
TENDERLOIN
SUPREME

BUFFALO SHRIMP WITH SWEET POTATO GRITS

This dish is the perfect combination of spicy, cheesy, and creamy with just a touch of sweetness. The creamy, ultra fluffy sweet potato grits make a perfect pairing for the slightly spicy Buffalo-flavored shrimp!
—*Julie Peterson, Crofton, MD*

TAKES: 30 MIN. • MAKES: 6 SERVINGS

1 cup quick-cooking grits
1 can (16 oz.) cut sweet potatoes in syrup, drained and mashed
3 Tbsp. butter
½ tsp. salt
½ tsp. pepper
½ cup reduced-fat Monterey Jack cheese

1 lb. uncooked shrimp (26-30 per lb.), peeled and deveined
1 tsp. paprika
¼ tsp. cayenne pepper
3 Tbsp. olive oil
⅓ cup Buffalo wing sauce Sliced green onions, optional

1. In a large saucepan, cook grits according to package directions. Stir in the mashed sweet potatoes, butter, salt and pepper until heated through; stir in cheese until melted.

2. Toss the shrimp with paprika and cayenne pepper. In a large skillet, heat the oil over medium heat. Add the shrimp; cook until shrimp turn pink and become opaque, about 2-3 minutes, stirring occasionally. Stir in Buffalo sauce and heat through. Serve shrimp over grits. If desired, top with sliced green onions.

1 SERVING: 361 cal., 16g fat (6g sat. fat), 114mg chol., 837mg sod., 38g carb. (12g sugars, 3g fiber), 18g pro.

SLOW-COOKER BEEF TOSTADAS

I dedicate these slow-simmered tostadas to my husband, the only Italian man
I know who can't get enough of Mexican flavors. Pile on your best toppings.

—*Teresa DeVono, Red Lion, PA*

PREP: 20 MIN. • COOK: 6 HOURS • MAKES: 6 SERVINGS

1 **large onion, chopped**
¼ **cup lime juice**
1 **jalapeno pepper, seeded**
   and minced
1 **serrano pepper, seeded**
   and minced
1 **Tbsp. chili powder**
3 **garlic cloves, minced**
½ **tsp. ground cumin**
1 **beef top round steak**
   (about 1½ lbs.)
1 **tsp. salt**
½ **tsp. pepper**
¼ **cup chopped fresh**
   cilantro
12 **corn tortillas (6 in.)**
   Cooking spray

TOPPINGS
1½ **cups shredded lettuce**
1 **medium tomato, finely**
   chopped
¾ **cup shredded sharp**
   cheddar cheese
¾ **cup reduced-fat sour**
   cream, optional

1. Place the first 7 ingredients in a 3- or 4-qt. slow cooker. Cut steak in half and sprinkle with salt and pepper; add to slow cooker. Cook, covered, on low until meat is tender, 6-8 hours.

2. Remove meat; cool slightly. Shred meat with 2 forks. Return beef to slow cooker and stir in cilantro; heat through. Spritz both sides of the tortillas with cooking spray. Place in a single layer on baking sheets; broil 1-2 minutes on each side or until crisp. Spoon beef mixture over tortillas; top with lettuce, tomato, cheese and, if desired, sour cream.

NOTE: Wear disposable gloves when cutting hot peppers; the oils can burn skin. Avoid touching your face.

2 TOSTADAS: 372 cal., 13g fat (6g sat. fat), 88mg chol., 602mg sod., 30g carb. (5g sugars, 5g fiber), 35g pro. DIABETIC EXCHANGES: 4 lean meat, 2 starch, ½ fat.

"I made this, and it was so good and easy! The meat would also be tasty wrapped in a flour tortilla and eaten like a burrito. The options are endless with this."
—BILLIEPOCK, TASTEOFHOME.COM

BAKED LEMON CHICKEN

I found this recipe many years ago when my children were toddlers. I've changed it a little over the years to make it my own. Everyone in my family just loves it!
—*Aida Babbel, Bowen Island, BC*

PREP: 25 MIN. • BAKE: 25 MIN. • MAKES: 4 SERVINGS

3 Tbsp. all-purpose flour
¼ tsp. pepper
4 boneless skinless chicken breast halves (1½ lbs.)
2 Tbsp. canola oil
1 medium onion, chopped
1 Tbsp. butter
1 cup chicken broth
3 Tbsp. lemon juice
2 tsp. dried basil
½ tsp. dried thyme
4 lemon slices
2 Tbsp. minced fresh parsley
   Hot cooked rice, optional

1. In a shallow bowl, combine flour and pepper; dredge chicken. Set remaining flour mixture aside. In a skillet, brown chicken in oil; transfer to an ungreased 9-in. square baking dish.

2. In a saucepan, saute onion in butter. Add the reserved flour mixture; stir to form a thick paste. Gradually add broth, lemon juice, basil and thyme; mix well. Bring to boil; cook and stir for 2 minutes or until thickened and bubbly. Pour over the chicken. Top each half with a lemon slice. Sprinkle with parsley. Cover and bake at 350° for 25-30 minutes or until the juices run clear. Serve over rice if desired.

1 CHICKEN BREAST HALF: 312 cal., 14g fat (4g sat. fat), 103mg chol., 353mg sod., 9g carb. (2g sugars, 1g fiber), 36g pro. DIABETIC EXCHANGES: 5 lean meat, ½ starch.

HERBY CHICKEN WITH APRICOTS & FETA

Mix up your weeknight menu with an herby braised chicken dish with Middle Eastern flair. I love to serve it with couscous.
—*Sally Sibthorpe, Shelby Township, MI*

PREP: 20 MIN. • COOK: 25 MIN. • MAKES: 8 SERVINGS

1½ tsp. salt
1 tsp. dill weed
½ tsp. dried oregano
½ tsp. dried thyme
½ tsp. pepper
8 boneless skinless chicken thighs (about 2 lbs.)
3 Tbsp. canola oil
1 small onion, chopped
8 dried apricots
8 pitted dates
½ cup chicken stock
¼ cup lemon juice
1 cup crumbled feta cheese
2 green onions, thinly sliced
   Hot cooked couscous, optional

1. Combine the first 5 ingredients; sprinkle over chicken. In a large skillet, heat oil over medium heat. Brown chicken in batches; return all to skillet. Add onion, apricot and dates; cook 5 minutes longer.

2. Stir in stock and lemon juice; bring to a boil. Reduce heat; simmer, covered, until a thermometer reads 170°, 5-7 minutes. Uncover and top with feta and green onions. If desired, serve with couscous.

1 CHICKEN THIGH WITH ¼ CUP APRICOT MIXTURE: 282 cal., 16g fat (4g sat. fat), 83mg chol., 674mg sod., 10g carb. (7g sugars, 2g fiber), 24g pro. DIABETIC EXCHANGES: 3 lean meat, 2 fat, ½ starch.

BAKED LEMON
CHICKEN

PRETZEL-TOPPED
SWEET POTATOES,
PAGE 170

GRANDMA'S FAVORITE

SIDE
DISHES

No entree is complete without the perfect
accompaniment, so why not steal the suppertime
spotlight with a tasty array of sweet and savory sides!

SIDE DISHES

SPECIAL RADICCHIO-SPINACH SALAD

When you hear of mint, chipotle pepper and honey blended together, you may wonder
how it will taste. Well, prepare to be amazed—my spicy-sweet salad is simply delicious.
—*Roxanne Chan, Albany, CA*

TAKES: 20 MIN. • **MAKES:** 12 SERVINGS

6 cups fresh baby spinach
1 head radicchio, torn
2 cups fresh raspberries
½ cup raisins
¼ cup pine nuts, toasted
¼ cup thinly sliced
    red onion
¼ cup minced fresh mint
3 Tbsp. lime juice
2 Tbsp. olive oil
2 tsp. honey
1½ to 3 tsp. chopped chipotle
    pepper in adobo sauce
¼ tsp. salt
½ cup crumbled feta cheese

In a large salad bowl, combine the first 7 ingredients. In a small
saucepan over medium heat, combine the lime juice, oil, honey,
chipotle pepper and salt. Cook and stir until blended and heated
through. Immediately pour over salad; toss to coat. Sprinkle with
feta cheese.

¾ **CUP:** 92 cal., 5g fat (1g sat. fat), 3mg chol., 117mg sod., 11g carb.
(6g sugars, 3g fiber), 3g pro. **DIABETIC EXCHANGES:** 1 vegetable,
1 fat, ½ starch.

SAVORY ZUCCHINI BREAD PUDDING

I've been serving this dish for years and always receive compliments on it. If you don't have day-old
bread in your pantry, simply slice fresh bread and bake it at 300° for 10 minutes before cubing it.
—*Mary Ann Dell, Phoenixville, PA*

PREP: 25 MIN. • **BAKE:** 40 MIN. • **MAKES:** 12 SERVINGS

1 small onion, chopped
1 celery rib, chopped
3 Tbsp. butter
1 cup all-purpose flour
2 Tbsp. sugar
1 tsp. baking powder
1 tsp. salt
1 tsp. ground cinnamon
1 tsp. poultry seasoning
½ cup canned pumpkin
2 large eggs
⅓ cup 2% milk
¼ cup butter, melted
4 cups cubed day-old bread
3 medium zucchini,
    chopped
½ cup shredded
    cheddar cheese

1. In a small skillet, saute onion and celery in butter until tender;
set aside.

2. In a large bowl, combine the flour, sugar, baking powder,
salt, cinnamon and poultry seasoning. In a small bowl, whisk
pumpkin, eggs, milk and butter; stir into dry ingredients just
until moistened. Fold in the bread cubes, zucchini, cheese and
onion mixture.

3. Transfer to a greased 13x9-in. baking dish. Cover and bake at
325° for 30 minutes. Uncover; bake 10-15 minutes longer or until
lightly browned.

¾ **CUP:** 182 cal., 10g fat (6g sat. fat), 58mg chol., 408mg sod., 20g
carb. (5g sugars, 2g fiber), 5g pro.

SPECIAL
RADICCHIO-SPINACH
SALAD

ROYAL BROCCOLI
SOUFFLE

ROYAL BROCCOLI SOUFFLE

Talk about impressive! This side dish never fails to impress even the toughest of critics.
—*Linda Evancoe-Coble, Leola, PA*

PREP: 30 MIN. • BAKE: 30 MIN. • MAKES: 6 SERVINGS

4 **large egg whites**
2 **cups chopped fresh broccoli florets**
¼ **cup water**
2 **Tbsp. butter**
3 **Tbsp. all-purpose flour**
¼ **tsp. cayenne pepper**
¾ **cup fat-free milk**
2 **Tbsp. grated Parmesan cheese**
1 **tsp. ground mustard**
½ **tsp. salt**
¼ **tsp. pepper**
1 **large egg yolk, beaten**
¼ **tsp. cream of tartar**

1. Let egg whites stand at room temperature 30 minutes. Grease a 1½-qt. souffle dish; dust lightly with flour.

2. Preheat oven to 350°. Microwave broccoli and water, covered, on high until broccoli is tender, 2-3 minutes. Let stand 5 minutes; drain. Pulse broccoli in a food processor until blended.

3. In a small saucepan, melt butter over medium heat. Stir in flour and cayenne pepper until smooth. Gradually whisk in milk. Bring to a boil, stirring constantly; cook and stir for 1-2 minutes or until thickened. Transfer to a large bowl; stir in cheese, mustard, salt, pepper and broccoli. Whisk a small amount of hot mixture into egg yolk; return all to bowl, whisking constantly. Cool slightly.

4. In another bowl, beat egg whites with cream of tartar until stiff but not dry. With a rubber spatula, gently stir a fourth of egg whites into broccoli mixture until no white streaks remain. Fold in remaining egg whites. Transfer to prepared dish. Bake until the top is puffed and center appears set, 30-35 minutes. Serve immediately.

⅔ CUP: 100 cal., 5g fat (3g sat. fat), 43mg chol., 318mg sod., 7g carb. (2g sugars, 1g fiber), 6g pro. **DIABETIC EXCHANGES:** 1 fat, ½ starch.

SPECIAL CREAMED CORN

This corn has earned a permanent place on our special-occasion menus. While my whole family loves it, my son would be especially disappointed if I forgot to include our corn dish.
—*Deb Hauptmann, Mohnton, PA*

TAKES: 20 MIN. • MAKES: 8 SERVINGS

⅓ **cup butter**
⅓ **cup all-purpose flour**
1 **cup heavy whipping cream**
1 **cup whole milk**
¼ **cup sugar**
1 **tsp. salt**
  Dash white pepper
5 **cups frozen corn, thawed**
¼ **cup grated Parmesan cheese**

1. In a saucepan, melt butter over medium heat. Stir in flour until smooth. Gradually add cream, milk, sugar, salt and pepper. Bring to a boil; boil and stir for 2 minutes. Add corn; heat through.

2. Transfer to an ungreased 1½-qt. broiler-proof dish. Sprinkle with Parmesan cheese. Broil 5 in. from the heat for 3-5 minutes or until lightly browned and bubbly.

⅔ CUP: 317 cal., 21g fat (13g sat. fat), 59mg chol., 425mg sod., 31g carb. (11g sugars, 2g fiber), 6g pro.

GREEN BEAN MUSHROOM PIE

Fresh green bean flavor stands out in this pretty lattice-topped pie. A flaky golden crust holds the savory bean, mushroom and cream cheese filling. It tastes wonderfully different every time I make it, depending on the variety of mushrooms I use.
—*Tara Walworth, Maple Park, IL*

PREP: 45 MIN. • **BAKE:** 25 MIN. • **MAKES:** 10 SERVINGS

- 3 cups sliced fresh mushrooms
- 4 Tbsp. butter, divided
- 2½ cups chopped onions
- 6 cups cut fresh green beans (1-in. pieces)
- 2 tsp. minced fresh thyme or ¾ tsp. dried thyme
- ½ tsp. salt
- ¼ tsp. pepper
- 1 pkg. (8 oz.) cream cheese, cubed
- ½ cup 2% milk

CRUST
- 2½ cups all-purpose flour
- 2 tsp. baking powder
- 1 tsp. dill weed
- ¼ tsp. salt
- 1 cup cold butter, cubed
- 1 cup sour cream
- 1 large egg
- 1 Tbsp. heavy whipping cream

1. In a large skillet, saute mushrooms in 1 Tbsp. butter until tender; drain and set aside. In the same skillet, saute onions and beans in remaining butter until beans are crisp-tender, 18-20 minutes. Add the thyme, salt, pepper, cream cheese, milk and mushrooms. Cook and stir until the cheese is melted. Remove from the heat; set aside.

2. In a large bowl, combine the flour, baking powder, dill and salt. Cut in butter until mixture resembles coarse crumbs. Stir in sour cream to form a soft dough.

3. Divide dough in half. On a well-floured surface, roll out 1 portion to fit a deep-dish 9-in. pie plate; trim crust even with edge.

4. Pour green bean mixture into crust. Roll out remaining dough; make a lattice crust. Trim, seal and flute edge.

5. In a small bowl, beat the egg and cream; brush over lattice top. Bake at 400° until golden brown, 25-35 minutes.

1 PIECE: 503 cal., 37g fat (23g sat. fat), 127mg chol., 587mg sod., 35g carb. (7g sugars, 4g fiber), 9g pro.

FRIED CABBAGE

When I was young, my family grew our own cabbage. It was fun to put the cabbage to use in the kitchen, just like I did with this comforting side. It's so good with potatoes, deviled eggs and cornbread.
—*Bernice Morris, Marshfield, MO*

TAKES: 20 MIN. • **MAKES:** 6 SERVINGS

- 2 Tbsp. butter
- 1 tsp. sugar
- ½ tsp. salt
- ¼ tsp. crushed red pepper flakes
- ⅛ tsp. pepper
- 6 cups coarsely chopped cabbage
- 1 Tbsp. water

In a large skillet, melt butter over medium heat. Stir in the sugar, salt, pepper flakes and pepper. Add the cabbage and water. Cook 5-6 minutes or until tender, stirring occasionally.

1 CUP: 59 cal., 4g fat (2g sat. fat), 10mg chol., 251mg sod., 6g carb. (3g sugars, 2g fiber), 1g pro. **DIABETIC EXCHANGES:** 1 vegetable, 1 fat.

CREAMY POLENTA WITH BALSAMIC GLAZE

This delicious, easy side dish goes incredibly well with braised meat. It makes any meal feel a little more elevated.
—*Sarah Vasques, Milford, NH*

PREP: 15 MIN. • **COOK:** 2 HOURS • **MAKES:** 4 SERVINGS

4 Tbsp. butter, divided
1½ cups half-and-half cream, divided
1 cup 2% milk
¼ tsp. salt
⅓ cup cornmeal
1 cup balsamic vinegar
1 Tbsp. sugar
½ cup grated Parmesan cheese

1. In a medium saucepan, melt 2 Tbsp. butter over medium heat. Add 1 cup cream, milk and salt. Bring to a low simmer. Gradually whisk in cornmeal. Cook and stir for 3 minutes.

2. Pour the polenta into a 3-qt. slow cooker coated with cooking spray. Cook, covered, on low 2 hours, stirring every 30 minutes. Meanwhile, in a small saucepan, bring vinegar and sugar to a boil. Reduce heat; simmer, uncovered, until reduced to ⅓ cup. Just before serving, stir cheese and the remaining cream and butter into polenta. To serve, drizzle with balsamic glaze.

½ CUP POLENTA WITH 1 TBSP. GLAZE: 415 cal., 25g fat (16g sat. fat), 89mg chol., 494mg sod., 37g carb. (25g sugars, 1g fiber), 9g pro.

GRANDMA'S SECRET

Don't try to speed this polenta recipe along by cooking it on high heat. Doing so will likely cause the outer edge to get browned.

MAPLE-GLAZED
ACORN SQUASH

MAPLE-GLAZED ACORN SQUASH

With a maple syrup and brown sugar glaze, this squash becomes pleasantly sweet.
This is comfort food—easy to prepare and a tasty pairing with a pork entree.
—*Nancy Mueller, Menomonee Falls, WI*

PREP: 10 MIN. • **BAKE:** 55 MIN. • **MAKES:** 2 SERVINGS

1 medium acorn squash, halved
¾ cup water
¼ cup maple syrup
2 Tbsp. brown sugar
½ tsp. ground cinnamon
¼ tsp. ground ginger
¼ tsp. salt

1. Preheat oven to 350°. Scoop out and discard seeds from squash. Place cut side down in a 13x9-in. baking dish; add water. Bake, uncovered, for 45 minutes.

2. If necessary, drain water from pan; turn squash cut side up. Combine syrup, brown sugar, cinnamon, ginger and salt; pour into squash halves. Bake, uncovered, 10 minutes or until glaze is heated through.

½ SQUASH: 251 cal., 0 fat (0 sat. fat), 0 chol., 311mg sod., 65g carb. (43g sugars, 4g fiber), 2g pro.

OLD-FASHIONED MACARONI & CHEESE

Bring back the taste of days gone by with this ooey-gooey mac-and-cheese classic.
A little ground mustard and hot pepper sauce give it just the right spice.
—*James Backman, Centralia, WA*

PREP: 15 MIN. • **BAKE:** 45 MIN. • **MAKES:** 16 SERVINGS

3½ cups uncooked elbow macaroni
¼ cup butter, cubed
¼ cup all-purpose flour
1 tsp. salt
¾ tsp. ground mustard
½ tsp. pepper
  Few dashes hot pepper sauce
3½ cups whole milk
5 cups shredded cheddar cheese, divided
  Optional: Crumbled cooked bacon and coarsely ground pepper

1. Preheat oven to 350°. Cook macaroni in boiling water until almost tender; drain. Meanwhile, in a Dutch oven, melt butter over medium heat. Stir in the flour, salt, mustard, pepper and pepper sauce until smooth. Cook and stir until bubbly, about 1 minute. Stir in cooked macaroni, milk and 4 cups cheese.

2. Transfer to an ungreased 13x9-in. baking dish. Cover and bake until bubbly, 45-50 minutes. Uncover; sprinkle with the remaining 1 cup cheese. Let stand for 5 minutes before serving. If desired, top with bacon and pepper.

1 CUP: 267 cal., 17g fat (10g sat. fat), 48mg chol., 425mg sod., 17g carb. (3g sugars, 1g fiber), 12g pro.

FROM GRANDMA'S KITCHEN: One of the best options for topping this old-fashioned baked macaroni and cheese is a buttered bread crumb topping—combine 1 Tbsp. of melted butter per 2 Tbsp. dry bread crumbs and sprinkle over the mac and cheese before baking.

POLISH PIEROGI

I'm from a small town in New Jersey where a number of Polish immigrants settled, including my parents. My mother was a great cook who taught me lots of Polish recipes like this one, which I have adapted to use in my catering business. Also called Polish lasagna, it's a real crowd-pleaser!

—*Adeline Piscitelli, Sayreville, NJ*

PREP: 1 HOUR • COOK: 15 MIN./ BATCH • MAKES: 4½ DOZEN

DOUGH
- **4 cups all-purpose flour**
- **2 large eggs**
- **½ cup sour cream**
- **1 tsp. salt**
- **⅔ cup warm water**

POTATO FILLING
- **½ lb. potatoes, peeled, cooked, drained and mashed, about 2 medium**
- **¼ medium onion, chopped**
- **2 Tbsp. butter, softened**
- **¼ tsp. salt**
- **¼ tsp. pepper**

CHEESE FILLING
- **1 cup 4% cottage cheese, drained and patted dry**
- **1 large egg yolk, beaten**
- **¼ tsp. salt**
- **2 Tbsp. butter, melted**

COOKING LIQUID
- **3 chicken bouillon cubes**
- **8 cups water**
- **1 tsp. canola oil**

TOPPING
- **½ cup butter**
- **1 large onion, chopped**
- **2 cups sliced mushrooms**

1. To make dough, mix flour, eggs, sour cream, salt and water (a little at a time). Knead the dough until firm and elastic; cover and let rest 10 minutes.

2. For potato filling, combine ingredients; set aside. For cheese filling, combine ingredients; set aside.

3. Divide dough into 3 parts. On floured surface, roll the dough to ⅛-in. thickness; cut into 3-in. rounds with cutter, rerolling dough as needed. Place 1 tsp. potato or cheese filling in center of each round; fold and press edges together firmly to seal.

4. Dissolve bouillon cubes in water in large saucepan; add oil. Heat to a simmer over medium heat. Working in batches, drop pierogi into simmering water. Do not crowd. Simmer until tender, about 15 minutes, stirring gently with wooden spoon to prevent sticking. Remove with slotted spoon; drain well.

5. Melt butter in a large skillet over medium heat; add the onion. Cook until lightly browned, 2-3 minutes. Add mushrooms; cook until tender, stirring occasionally, about 5 minutes. Place drained pierogi on serving platter. Top evenly with mushroom mixture.

3 PIECES: 223 cal., 11g fat (6g sat. fat), 54mg chol., 366mg sod., 26g carb. (2g sugars, 1g fiber), 6g pro.

FRIED ONIONS & APPLES

Since a lot of delicious onions are grown in our state, they are always part of my menu. This tangy side dish is good with pork and beef. The inspiration for this unusual combination was a prolific apple tree!
—*Janice Mitchell, Aurora, CO*

TAKES: 30 MIN. • MAKES: 12 SERVINGS

3 large yellow onions, sliced
3 Tbsp. butter
6 large tart red apples, sliced

½ cup packed brown sugar
1 tsp. salt
½ tsp. paprika
⅛ tsp. ground nutmeg

1. In a large cast-iron or other heavy skillet, saute onions in butter until tender. Place apples on top of onions. Combine remaining ingredients; sprinkle over apples.

2. Cover and simmer for 10 minutes. Uncover and simmer for 5 minutes or until apples are tender. Serve with a slotted spoon.

1 CUP: 137 cal., 3g fat (2g sat. fat), 8mg chol., 230mg sod., 28g carb. (24g sugars, 4g fiber), 1g pro.

CARROT RAISIN COUSCOUS

Golden raisins add a slightly sweet flavor to this unique side dish featuring couscous and carrots. The recipe will brighten any holiday table.
—*Jordan Sucher, Brooklyn, NY*

PREP: 15 MIN. • COOK: 20 MIN. • MAKES: 10 SERVINGS

⅓ cup port wine or chicken broth
⅓ cup golden raisins
1 medium onion, chopped
3 Tbsp. olive oil, divided
1 pkg. (10 oz.) couscous
2 cups chicken broth
¼ tsp. salt, divided
¼ tsp. pepper, divided
4 medium carrots, julienned
1 Tbsp. sugar
1 tsp. molasses

1. In a small saucepan, heat wine until hot. In a small bowl, soak raisins in wine 5 minutes. Drain raisins, reserving wine.

2. In a large saucepan, saute onion in 1 Tbsp. oil until tender. Stir in couscous. Cook and stir until lightly browned. Stir in the broth, raisins and half each of the salt and pepper. Bring to a boil. Cover and remove from heat. Let stand for 5 minutes; fluff with a fork.

3. In a small skillet, saute carrots in remaining oil until crisp-tender. Combine sugar, molasses, reserved wine and the remaining salt and pepper. Stir into carrots; heat through.

4. In a large bowl, combine couscous mixture and carrots; toss to combine.

¾ CUP: 188 cal., 5g fat (1g sat. fat), 1mg chol., 277mg sod., 32g carb. (8g sugars, 2g fiber), 5g pro. **DIABETIC EXCHANGES:** 1½ starch, 1 vegetable, 1 fat.

HERBED PECAN STUFFING

I updated a basic stuffing recipe by using wholesome multigrain bread in place of customary white bread. It adds a hearty, crunchy taste.
—*Edie DeSpain, Logan, UT*

PREP: 35 MIN. • BAKE: 45 MIN. • MAKES: 12 SERVINGS

8   cups cubed day-old multigrain bread
¾   cup golden raisins
½   cup apple juice
¼   cup olive oil
4   celery ribs, diced
1   large onion, chopped
3   garlic cloves, minced
1   cup minced fresh parsley
1½ tsp. salt
1½ tsp. rubbed sage
¾   tsp. dried thyme
½   tsp. fennel seeds, crushed
¼   tsp. pepper
1   large egg
1½ to 2 cups chicken broth
1½ cups coarsely chopped pecans, toasted

1. Preheat oven to 225°. Place bread cubes in a single layer on an ungreased baking sheet. Bake until partially dried, tossing occasionally, 30-40 minutes. Set aside. Increase the oven temperature to 325°.

2. Meanwhile, combine raisins and apple juice in a saucepan; bring to a boil. Remove from the heat; let stand for 15 minutes. In a large skillet or Dutch oven, heat the oil over medium-high heat. Add celery, onion and garlic; cook and stir until tender, 5-7 minutes. Stir in the parsley, salt, sage, thyme, fennel seeds and pepper; remove from heat. Beat the egg and broth; add to vegetable mixture with bread cubes and raisin mixture. Toss well. Stir in pecans. Transfer to a greased 13x9-in. baking dish.

3. Cover and bake for 30 minutes. Uncover; bake until lightly browned, 15-20 minutes longer.

1 CUP: 255 cal., 17g fat (2g sat. fat), 18mg chol., 564mg sod., 24g carb. (10g sugars, 4g fiber), 5g pro.

BUTTERY ALMOND GREEN BEANS

Toasted almonds add crunch to this timeless treatment for fresh beans. They get extra flavor from onion soup mix and Parmesan cheese.
—*Edna Hoffman, Hebron, IN*

TAKES: 30 MIN. • MAKES: 8 SERVINGS

2   lbs. fresh green beans, trimmed
2   cups water
1   envelope onion soup mix
⅔   cup slivered almonds, toasted
2   Tbsp. grated Parmesan cheese
1   tsp. paprika
6   Tbsp. butter, melted

1. In a large saucepan, combine beans, water and soup mix. Bring to a boil. Reduce heat; cover and simmer until beans are crisp-tender, 15-20 minutes.

2. In a small bowl, combine the almonds, cheese and paprika. Drain beans; drizzle with the butter and sprinkle with almond mixture. Toss to coat.

¾ CUP: 179 cal., 14g fat (6g sat. fat), 24mg chol., 407mg sod., 13g carb. (4g sugars, 5g fiber), 5g pro.

GRANDMA'S CORNBREAD DRESSING

Growing up, we didn't have turkey. We had chicken, chopped and baked in my grandmother's dressing. Now we leave out the chicken and keep the cornbread dressing.
—*Suzanne Mohme, Bastrop, TX*

PREP: 40 MIN. + COOLING • **BAKE:** 45 MIN. • **MAKES:** 12 SERVINGS

1 cup all-purpose flour
1 cup cornmeal
2 tsp. baking powder
1 tsp. salt
2 large eggs
1 cup buttermilk
¼ cup canola oil

DRESSING
1 Tbsp. canola oil
1 medium onion, chopped
2 celery ribs, chopped
3 large eggs
2 cans (10¾ oz. each) condensed cream of chicken soup, undiluted
3 tsp. poultry seasoning
1 tsp. pepper
½ tsp. salt
2 cups chicken broth

1. Preheat oven to 400°. In a large bowl, whisk flour, cornmeal, baking powder and salt. In another bowl, whisk the eggs and buttermilk. Pour oil into an 8-in. ovenproof skillet; place skillet in oven 4 minutes.

2. Meanwhile, add buttermilk mixture to flour mixture; stir just until moistened.

3. Carefully tilt and rotate skillet to coat bottom with oil; add batter. Bake for 20-25 minutes or until a toothpick inserted in center comes out clean. Cool completely in pan on a wire rack.

4. Reduce oven setting to 350°. For dressing, in a large skillet, heat oil over medium-high heat. Add onion and celery; cook and stir 4-6 minutes or until tender. Remove from the heat. Coarsely crumble cornbread into skillet; toss to combine. In a small bowl, whisk eggs, condensed soup and seasonings; stir into the bread mixture. Stir in broth.

5. Transfer to a greased 13x9-in. baking dish. Bake 45-55 minutes or until lightly browned.

⅔ CUP: 236 cal., 12g fat (2g sat. fat), 83mg chol., 969mg sod., 25g carb. (2g sugars, 2g fiber), 7g pro.

GRANDMA'S SECRET

When washing celery, make sure to always separate the stalks before washing (don't wash the whole bunch together) to make sure you get into all the nooks and crannies.

GARLIC-ROASTED
BRUSSELS SPROUTS
WITH MUSTARD SAUCE

GARLIC-ROASTED BRUSSELS SPROUTS WITH MUSTARD SAUCE

Don't be afraid to bring out the Brussels sprouts. Mellowed by roasting and tossed with mustard sauce, they may just delight even the most skeptical folks.
—*Becky Walch, Orland, CA*

TAKES: 20 MIN. • MAKES: 6 SERVINGS

1½ lbs. fresh Brussels
    sprouts, halved
2 Tbsp. olive oil
3 garlic cloves, minced
½ cup heavy whipping
    cream
3 Tbsp. Dijon mustard
⅛ tsp. white pepper
    Dash salt

1. Place Brussels sprouts in an ungreased 15x10x1-in. baking pan. Combine oil and garlic; drizzle over sprouts and toss to coat.

2. Bake, uncovered, at 450° for 10-15 minutes or until tender, stirring occasionally.

3. Meanwhile, in a small saucepan, combine the cream, mustard, pepper and salt. Bring to a gentle boil; cook until slightly thickened, 1-2 minutes. Spoon over Brussels sprouts.

¾ CUP: 167 cal., 12g fat (5g sat. fat), 27mg chol., 241mg sod., 13g carb. (3g sugars, 4g fiber), 4g pro.

EGGPLANT PARMESAN

We really like eggplant and would rather have it baked than fried. This can be served as a side dish or main dish.
—*Donna Wardlow-Keating, Omaha, NE*

PREP: 10 MIN. • BAKE: 50 MIN. + COOLING • MAKES: 2 SERVINGS

2 Tbsp. olive oil
1 garlic clove, minced
1 small eggplant, peeled
    and cut into ¼-in. slices
1 Tbsp. minced fresh basil
    or 1 tsp. dried basil
1 Tbsp. grated Parmesan
    cheese
1 medium tomato, thinly
    sliced
½ cup shredded mozzarella
    cheese
    Additional basil, optional

1. Combine oil and garlic; brush over both sides of eggplant slices. Place on a greased baking sheet. Bake at 425° for 15 minutes; turn. Bake until golden brown, about 5 minutes longer. Cool on a wire rack.

2. Place half the eggplant in a greased 1-qt. baking dish. Sprinkle with half the basil and Parmesan cheese. Arrange tomato slices over top; sprinkle with remaining basil and Parmesan. Layer with half the mozzarella cheese and the remaining eggplant; top with remaining mozzarella. Cover and bake at 350° for 20 minutes. Uncover; bake until cheese is melted, 5-7 minutes longer. Garnish with additional basil if desired.

1 SERVING: 275 cal., 21g fat (6g sat. fat), 24mg chol., 164mg sod., 16g carb. (9g sugars, 5g fiber), 9g pro.

LEMON RISOTTO WITH PEAS

Lemon adds a refreshing taste to this lovely risotto dish that's perfect
for spring. This easy side is festively sprinkled with baby peas.
—*Sue Dannahower, Fort Pierce, FL*

PREP: 10 MIN. • COOK: 30 MIN. • MAKES: 8 SERVINGS

4 to 4½ cups reduced-sodium chicken broth
2 shallots, finely chopped
1 Tbsp. butter
1½ cups uncooked arborio rice
½ tsp. dried thyme
¼ tsp. pepper
⅓ cup white wine or additional reduced-sodium chicken broth
3 Tbsp. lemon juice
1 cup frozen peas, thawed
½ cup grated Parmesan cheese
1½ tsp. grated lemon zest

1. In a small saucepan, heat broth and keep warm. In a large nonstick skillet, saute shallots in butter until tender, 2-3 minutes. Add the rice, thyme and pepper; cook and stir 2-3 minutes. Stir in the wine and lemon juice; cook and stir until all the liquid is absorbed.

2. Stir in heated broth, ½ cup at a time, stirring constantly. Allow the liquid to absorb between additions. Cook just until risotto is creamy and rice is almost tender, about 20 minutes. Add peas, cheese and lemon zest; cook until heated through. Serve immediately.

½ CUP: 206 cal., 3g fat (2g sat. fat), 8mg chol., 407mg sod., 36g carb. (2g sugars, 1g fiber), 7g pro. **DIABETIC EXCHANGES:** 2 starch, ½ fat.

HONEY-GLAZED CARROTS

My mother used sugar in this recipe, but a local man who keeps bees
on our farm shares honey with us, so I use that instead.
—*Judie Anglen, Riverton, WY*

TAKES: 10 MIN. • MAKES: 4 SERVINGS

1 pkg. (16 oz.) baby carrots
1 Tbsp. water
2 Tbsp. butter
2 Tbsp. honey
1 Tbsp. lemon juice

1. Place carrots and water in a 1½-qt. microwave-safe dish. Cover and microwave until crisp-tender, 3-5 minutes.

2. Meanwhile, melt butter in a skillet over low heat; stir in honey and lemon juice. Cook, stirring constantly, 3-4 minutes. Add the carrots; cook and stir until glazed, about 1 minute.

½ CUP: 124 cal., 6g fat (4g sat. fat), 15mg chol., 126mg sod., 20g carb. (14g sugars, 3g fiber), 1g pro.

FROM GRANDMA'S KITCHEN: You can use other kinds of carrots to make this honey-glazed recipe! However, make sure you cut up whatever carrot you use into equally sized slices to guarantee even cooking.

LENTIL WHITE BEAN PILAF

Vegetarians will be happy to see this hearty meatless grain pilaf on the holiday buffet table. I like to make this when I have extra cooked lentils, barley, quinoa and rice on hand.
—*Juli Meyers, Hinesville, GA*

PREP: 35 MIN. • COOK: 15 MIN. • MAKES: 10 SERVINGS

1 cup dried lentils, rinsed
½ cup quick-cooking barley
½ cup quinoa, rinsed
⅓ cup uncooked long grain rice
½ lb. sliced baby portobello mushrooms
3 medium carrots, finely chopped
3 celery ribs, finely chopped
1 large onion, finely chopped

¼ cup butter, cubed
3 garlic cloves, minced
2 tsp. minced fresh rosemary or ½ tsp. dried rosemary, crushed
½ cup vegetable broth
½ tsp. salt
½ tsp. pepper
2 cups canned cannellini beans, rinsed and drained

1. Cook the lentils, barley, quinoa and rice according to the package directions.

2. In a Dutch oven, saute the mushrooms, carrots, celery and onion in butter until tender. Add the garlic and rosemary; cook 1 minute longer. Add broth, salt and pepper, stirring to loosen browned bits from pan. Stir in beans and the cooked lentils, barley, quinoa and rice; heat through.

¾ CUP: 259 cal., 6g fat (3g sat. fat), 12mg chol., 290mg sod., 41g carb. (3g sugars, 11g fiber), 11g pro.

HERBED LENTIL WHITE BEAN PILAF: Omit rosemary. With the broth, add ¾ tsp. dried basil, ½ tsp. dried oregano, ½ tsp. dried thyme and ¼ tsp. garlic powder.

CRANBERRY RICOTTA GNOCCHI
WITH BROWN BUTTER SAUCE

CRANBERRY RICOTTA GNOCCHI WITH BROWN BUTTER SAUCE

To make light and airy gnocchi, work quickly and handle the dough as little as possible. You'll be pleased with the resulting pillowy dumplings.
—*Sally Sibthorpe, Shelby Township, MI*

PREP: 30 MIN. + STANDING • COOK: 15 MIN. • MAKES: 8 SERVINGS

¾ cup dried cranberries, divided
2 cups ricotta cheese
1 cup all-purpose flour
½ cup grated Parmesan cheese
1 large egg, lightly beaten
¾ tsp. salt, divided
¾ cup butter, cubed
2 Tbsp. minced fresh sage
½ cup chopped walnuts, toasted
⅛ tsp. white pepper

1. Finely chop ¼ cup cranberries. In a large bowl, combine ricotta cheese, flour, Parmesan cheese, egg, ½ tsp. salt and chopped cranberries; mix until blended. On a lightly floured surface, knead 10-12 times, forming a soft dough. Cover and let rest for 10 minutes.

2. Divide dough into 4 portions. On a floured surface, roll each portion into a ¾-in.-thick rope; cut into ¾-in. pieces. Press and roll each piece with a lightly floured fork.

3. In a Dutch oven, bring 4 qt. water to a boil. Cook the gnocchi in batches 30-60 seconds or until they float. Remove with a slotted spoon; keep warm.

4. In a large heavy saucepan, cook butter over medium heat 5 minutes. Add sage; cook 3-5 minutes longer or until butter is golden brown, stirring occasionally. Stir in walnuts, white pepper, and the remaining cranberries and salt. Add gnocchi; stir gently to coat.

¾ CUP: 411 cal., 30g fat (16g sat. fat), 101mg chol., 503mg sod., 26g carb. (11g sugars, 1g fiber), 13g pro.

CREAMY SKILLET NOODLES WITH PEAS

I've made this creamy noodle side for years. Since kids and adults go for it, I keep the ingredients on hand at all times.
—*Anita Groff, Perkiomenville, PA*

TAKES: 25 MIN. • MAKES: 6 SERVINGS

¼ cup butter, cubed
2 Tbsp. canola oil
5 cups uncooked fine egg noodles
2½ cups frozen peas (about 10 oz.)
2½ cups chicken broth
1 cup half-and-half cream
½ tsp. salt
¼ tsp. pepper

In a large skillet, heat butter and oil over medium heat. Add noodles; cook and stir 2-3 minutes or until lightly browned. Stir in peas, broth, cream, salt and pepper. Bring to a boil. Reduce heat; simmer, covered, for 10-12 minutes or until noodles are tender, stirring occasionally.

¾ CUP: 329 cal., 31g fat (8g sat. fat), 76mg chol., 757mg sod., 31g carb. (6g sugars, 4g fiber), 9g pro.

STUFFED BAKED TOMATOES

I make this side dish often—my family really likes it. Besides being flavorful, the tomatoes make a colorful, zesty addition to any dinner.
—*Edna Jackson, Kokomo, IN*

PREP: 15 MIN. • BAKE: 30 MIN. • MAKES: 6 SERVINGS

6 **medium tomatoes**

STUFFING
1 **cup garlic/cheese croutons, crushed**
2 **Tbsp. grated Parmesan cheese**
2 **Tbsp. grated American or cheddar cheese**
4 **Tbsp. melted butter**
½ **tsp. salt**
¼ **tsp. freshly ground pepper**
   Chopped fresh parsley for garnish

1. Preheat oven to 350°. Cut a thin slice off the top of each tomato. Scoop out pulp, leaving a ½-in. shell. Invert the shells onto paper towels to drain. Mix stuffing ingredients except parsley; spoon stuffing into tomatoes. Sprinkle with parsley.

2. Place tomatoes in a baking dish; cover with foil to prevent overbrowning of stuffing. Bake until tomatoes are tender and stuffing is hot, about 30 minutes.

1 STUFFED TOMATO: 146 cal., 11g fat (6g sat. fat), 24mg chol., 434mg sod., 11g carb. (4g sugars, 2g fiber), 3g pro.

ROASTED PEPPERS & CAULIFLOWER

Caramelization really enhances the flavors in this easy side dish. The roasted peppers and cauliflower are seasoned just right to go with nearly any main course.
—*Cheryl Wilt, Eglon, WV*

PREP: 10 MIN. • BAKE: 30 MIN. • MAKES: 6 SERVINGS

1 **medium head cauliflower, broken into florets**
2 **medium sweet red peppers, cut into strips**
2 **small onions, cut into wedges**
2 **Tbsp. olive oil**
½ **tsp. salt**
½ **tsp. pepper**
1 **Tbsp. grated Parmesan cheese**
1 **Tbsp. minced fresh parsley**

1. Place the cauliflower, red peppers and onions in a shallow roasting pan. Add the oil, salt and pepper; toss to coat. Roast, uncovered, at 425° for 20 minutes.

2. Stir; roast 10 minutes longer or until vegetables are tender and lightly browned. Transfer to a serving bowl; sprinkle with Parmesan cheese and parsley.

⅔ **CUP:** 88 cal., 5g fat (1g sat. fat), 1mg chol., 243mg sod., 10g carb. (5g sugars, 4g fiber), 3g pro. **DIABETIC EXCHANGES:** 2 vegetable, 1 fat.

"I made this today for our Sunday lunch, and it was wonderful. The vegetables were al dente, which is how I like them!"
—DENNYMENTESSI, TASTEOFHOME.COM

ASPARAGUS & GREEN BEANS WITH TARRAGON LEMON DIP

Tarragon balances the tangy flavor from lemon in the creamy sauce covering colorful asparagus and green beans. I serve this as a side dish as well as an appetizer.
—*Bonnie Hawkins, Elkhorn, WI*

TAKES: 20 MIN. • MAKES: 10 SERVINGS

- 1 lb. fresh asparagus, trimmed
- 1 lb. fresh green beans, trimmed
- 1 cup mayonnaise
- ¼ cup lemon juice
- 1 shallot, finely chopped
- 2 Tbsp. minced fresh tarragon or 2 tsp. dried tarragon
- 2 Tbsp. minced fresh parsley or 2 tsp. dried parsley flakes
- 2 tsp. grated lemon zest
  Dash pepper

1. Place 1 in. of water in a Dutch oven; add asparagus and beans. Bring to a boil. Reduce heat; cover and simmer for 3-5 minutes or until crisp-tender.

2. Meanwhile, in a small bowl, combine the remaining ingredients. Drain vegetables; transfer to a serving platter. Drizzle with dip.

1 SERVING: 183 cal., 18g fat (2g sat. fat), 8mg chol., 126mg sod., 5g carb. (2g sugars, 2g fiber), 1g pro.

SOUR CREAM NOODLES

This fast and flavorful dish is requested often at my house, where it will be a mainstay for years to come. I think noodles and sour cream make the perfect pair.
—*Judy Robertson, Russell Springs, KY*

PREP: 20 MIN. • BAKE: 35 MIN. • MAKES: 8 SERVINGS

- 1 pkg. (10 oz.) fine egg noodles
- 1¼ cups 4% cottage cheese
- 1¼ cups sour cream
- 1 medium onion, finely chopped
- 1 Tbsp. Worcestershire sauce
- ⅛ tsp. garlic salt
- 2 Tbsp. grated Parmesan cheese
  Paprika, optional

1. Preheat oven to 350°. Cook the noodles according to package directions; drain. Transfer to a large bowl. Add cottage cheese, sour cream, onion, Worcestershire sauce and garlic salt. Spoon into a greased 2-qt. baking dish. Sprinkle with Parmesan cheese.

2. Bake, uncovered, until top is lightly browned, 35-40 minutes. If desired, sprinkle with paprika.

¾ CUP: 258 cal., 11g fat (6g sat. fat), 42mg chol., 201mg sod., 30g carb. (4g sugars, 1g fiber), 10g pro.

LATTICE CORN PIE

This unique side dish is full of diced potatoes and a fresh, sweet corn flavor. Once you've tasted this delicious pie, you'll never want to serve corn any other way!
—*Kathy Spang, Manheim, PA*

PREP: 25 MIN. • BAKE: 35 MIN. • MAKES: 8 SERVINGS

1 cup diced peeled potatoes
⅓ cup 2% milk
2 large eggs, room temperature
2 cups fresh or frozen corn, thawed
1 tsp. sugar
½ tsp. salt
2 sheets refrigerated pie crust

1. Preheat oven to 375°. Place potatoes in a small saucepan and cover with water. Bring to a boil. Reduce heat; cover and cook until tender, 6-8 minutes. Drain and set aside.

2. In a blender, combine the milk, eggs, corn, sugar and salt; cover and process until blended.

3. Unroll 1 sheet crust into a 9-in. pie plate. Trim crust to ½ in. beyond rim of plate; flute edge. Spoon potatoes into crust; top with corn mixture (crust will be full). Roll out remaining crust; make a lattice top with crust. Seal and flute edge.

4. Bake until the crust is golden brown and filling is bubbly, 35-40 minutes.

1 PIECE: 308 cal., 16g fat (7g sat. fat), 57mg chol., 373mg sod., 37g carb. (5g sugars, 1g fiber), 5g pro.

FROM GRANDMA'S KITCHEN: You can also add hard-boiled eggs to this pie for more texture. For a pie that's more meal-like, add cubed cooked chicken.

SUMMERTIME PASTA SALAD

Nothing says summer quite like a cool pasta salad with loads of vegetables! Best of all, this recipe calls for frozen vegetables, so it's perfect when you don't have time to slice and dice fresh produce.
—Taste of Home *Test Kitchen*

TAKES: 20 MIN. • MAKES: 6 SERVINGS

2½ cups uncooked spiral pasta
1 pkg. (10 oz.) frozen mixed vegetables
⅔ cup ranch salad dressing
⅓ cup Italian salad dressing
½ tsp. dill weed
½ tsp. garlic salt
2 small tomatoes, diced

In a large kettle, cook pasta according to package directions. Place frozen vegetables in strainer. Pour the cooked pasta and water over vegetables to thaw; rinse and drain well. In a small bowl or jar with tight-fitting lid, combine salad dressings, dill and garlic salt until smooth. Place pasta mixture in a large bowl. Add tomatoes and dressing; stir gently to coat.

1 CUP: 291 cal., 12g fat (2g sat. fat), 9mg chol., 575mg sod., 37g carb. (6g sugars, 4g fiber), 6g pro.

CLASSIC CREAMED SPINACH

Using fresh spinach instead of frozen really enhances the flavor of this classic recipe. The hint of nutmeg makes this side dish even more appealing.
—*Ann Van Dyk, Wrightstown, WI*

TAKES: 25 MIN. • MAKES: 4 SERVINGS

¾ **lb. fresh spinach, torn**
2 **Tbsp. olive oil**
6 **Tbsp. butter, cubed**
¼ **cup chopped onion**
¼ **cup all-purpose flour**
½ **tsp. salt**
⅛ **tsp. ground nutmeg**
1½ **cups whole milk**

1. In a Dutch oven, cook spinach in oil 3 minutes or until wilted. Remove from pan; set aside. Melt butter in the Dutch oven; add onion and saute until crisp-tender, about 2 minutes.

2. Stir in flour, salt and nutmeg until combined. Gradually whisk in milk until blended. Bring to a boil; cook and stir until thickened, about 2 minutes. Add the chopped spinach. Reduce heat to low; cook, uncovered, until heated through, about 5 minutes.

½ CUP: 318 cal., 27g fat (14g sat. fat), 58mg chol., 581mg sod., 14g carb. (5g sugars, 3g fiber), 7g pro.

DIRTY RICE

This is an old Louisiana recipe that I've had longer than I can remember. It's a very popular southern dish. To turn this into a main meal, simply add more sausage and chicken livers.
—*Lum Day, Bastrop, LA*

TAKES: 30 MIN. • MAKES: 12 SERVINGS

½ **lb. bulk pork sausage**
½ **lb. chicken livers, chopped**
3 **Tbsp. butter**
1 **large onion, chopped**
1 **celery rib, chopped**
3 **green onions, chopped**
2 **Tbsp. minced fresh parsley**
1 **garlic clove, minced**
1 **can (10½ oz.) condensed chicken broth, undiluted**
½ **tsp. dried basil**
½ **tsp. dried thyme**
½ **tsp. salt**
¼ **tsp. pepper**
¼ **tsp. hot pepper sauce**
3 **cups cooked rice**

1. In a large cast-iron or other heavy skillet, cook the sausage for 2-3 minutes; stir in chicken livers. Cook until sausage and chicken livers are no longer pink, 5-7 minutes; drain and set aside.

2. In the same skillet, melt butter over medium heat. Add onion, celery and green onions. Cook and stir until vegetables are tender, 3-5 minutes. Add parsley and garlic; cook for 1 minute longer. Add broth, basil, thyme, salt, pepper and hot pepper sauce. Stir in rice, sausage and chicken livers. Heat through, stirring constantly.

1 CUP: 148 cal., 7g fat (3g sat. fat), 97mg chol., 325mg sod., 14g carb. (1g sugars, 1g fiber), 6g pro.

FROM GRANDMA'S KITCHEN: The general rice-to-water ratio is as easy to remember as 1, 2, 3: 1 cup rice + 2 cups water = 3 cups cooked rice. However, the actual ratio varies depending on the cooking method and the type of rice that you're using. The ratio is generally 1:1 if you're using a rice cooker, but be sure to follow the manufacturer's instructions.

CLASSIC
CREAMED
SPINACH

FAVORITE
MEDITERRANEAN
SALAD

FAVORITE MEDITERRANEAN SALAD

Do you have a crowd coming over for a potluck? This big crisp
salad can accompany any main dish you have planned.
—*Pat Stevens, Granbury, TX*

TAKES: 20 MIN. • MAKES: 28 SERVINGS

18 cups torn romaine (about
   2 large bunches)
1 medium cucumber, sliced
1 cup crumbled feta cheese
1 cup cherry tomatoes,
   quartered
1 small red onion, thinly
   sliced
½ cup julienned roasted
   sweet red peppers
½ cup pitted Greek olives,
   halved

DRESSING
⅔ cup olive oil
¼ cup red wine vinegar
1 garlic clove, minced
1 tsp. Italian seasoning
¼ tsp. salt
¼ tsp. pepper

In a very large salad bowl, combine first 7 ingredients. In
a small bowl, whisk the dressing ingredients. Drizzle over
salad and toss to coat.

¾ CUP: 69 cal., 6g fat (1g sat. fat), 2mg chol., 117mg sod., 2g carb.
(1g sugars, 1g fiber), 1g pro. DIABETIC EXCHANGES: 1 vegetable,
1 fat.

FROM GRANDMA'S KITCHEN: If you want to add more protein to this
salad, toss in lean grilled chicken or cooked fresh calamari.

MAPLE HORSERADISH BEETS

Even folks who say they don't like beets will think this simple treatment is
a winner. An easy glaze gives them a rich flavor with a little zip.
—*Leslie Palmer, Swampscott, MA*

PREP: 50 MIN. • COOK: 10 MIN. • MAKES: 6 SERVINGS

1¾ lbs. fresh beets
1 Tbsp. canola oil
2 Tbsp. butter
¼ cup maple syrup
3 Tbsp. prepared
   horseradish
2 Tbsp. cider vinegar
¼ tsp. salt
¼ tsp. pepper

1. Preheat oven to 400°. Peel beets and cut into wedges. Place in
a 15x10x1-in. baking pan; drizzle with oil and toss to coat. Bake
until beets are tender, 40-50 minutes.

2. In a small saucepan, melt butter. Stir in syrup, horseradish,
vinegar, salt and pepper. Bring to a boil. Carefully stir in beets;
cook until the liquid is slightly thickened, 5-6 minutes, gently
stirring occasionally.

¾ CUP: 152 cal., 6g fat (3g sat. fat), 10mg chol., 252mg sod.,
23g carb. (19g sugars, 3g fiber), 2g pro. DIABETIC EXCHANGES:
2 vegetable, 1 fat, ½ starch.

PRETZEL-TOPPED SWEET POTATOES

PICTURED ON PAGE 140

Everyone with whom I've shared this recipe says it's the tastiest way to serve sweet potatoes. I like to make it for special dinners, and even for brunch as a colorful go-with dish. The mingled sweet, tart and salty flavors are an unusual treat.

—*Sue Mallory, Lancaster, PA*

PREP: 20 MIN. • BAKE: 25 MIN. • MAKES: 12 SERVINGS

2 cups chopped pretzel rods (about 13)
1 cup chopped pecans
1 cup fresh or frozen cranberries
1 cup packed brown sugar
1 cup butter, melted, divided
1 can (2½ lbs.) sweet potatoes, drained
1 can (5 oz.) evaporated milk
½ cup sugar
1 tsp. vanilla extract

1. In a large bowl, combine the pretzels, pecans, cranberries, brown sugar and ½ cup butter; set aside.

2. In a large bowl, beat the sweet potatoes until smooth. Add the milk, sugar, vanilla and remaining butter; beat until well blended.

3. Spoon into a greased shallow 2-qt. baking dish; sprinkle with pretzel mixture. Bake, uncovered, at 350° for 25-30 minutes or until the edges are bubbly.

¾ CUP: 484 cal., 24g fat (11g sat. fat), 44mg chol., 606mg sod., 66g carb. (43g sugars, 4g fiber), 5g pro.

BACON COLLARD GREENS

Collard greens are a staple vegetable of southern cuisine. This side dish is often made with smoked or salt-cured meats, such as ham hocks, pork or fatback.

—*Marsha Ankeney, Niceville, FL*

PREP: 25 MIN. • COOK: 55 MIN. • MAKES: 9 SERVINGS

2 lbs. collard greens
4 thick-sliced bacon strips, chopped
1 cup chopped sweet onion
5 cups reduced-sodium chicken broth
1 cup sun-dried tomatoes (not packed in oil), chopped
½ tsp. garlic powder
¼ tsp. salt
¼ tsp. crushed red pepper flakes

1. Trim thick stems from collard greens; coarsely chop leaves. In a Dutch oven, saute bacon for 3 minutes. Add onion; cook until onion is tender and bacon is crisp, 8-9 minutes longer. Add greens; cook just until wilted.

2. Stir in remaining ingredients. Bring to a boil. Reduce heat; cover and simmer until greens are tender, 45-50 minutes.

¾ CUP: 157 cal., 10g fat (4g sat. fat), 12mg chol., 651mg sod., 11g carb. (4g sugars, 5g fiber), 7g pro.

CREAMY TWICE-BAKED POTATOES

With a yummy cream cheese filling, these rich, delicious potatoes
are sure winners. They look fancy but are not tricky to make.
—*Linda Wheeler, Harrisburg, PA*

PREP: 1¼ HOURS • BAKE: 20 MIN. • MAKES: 2 SERVINGS

2 **medium baking potatoes**	2 **Tbsp. sour cream**
2 **Tbsp. butter, softened**	**Paprika**
1 **Tbsp. 2% milk**	**Optional: Minced fresh**
¼ **tsp. salt**	**parsley and green onions**
3 **oz. cream cheese, cubed**	

1. Preheat oven to 350°. Pierce potatoes and bake on a baking sheet until tender, about 1 hour. When cool enough to handle, cut a thin slice off the top of each potato and discard. Scoop out pulp, leaving a thin shell.

2. In a small bowl, mash the pulp with butter, milk and salt. Stir in cream cheese and sour cream. Spoon into potato shells. Sprinkle with paprika.

3. Place on a baking sheet. Bake, uncovered, until heated through and tops are golden brown, 20-25 minutes. If desired, sprinkle with parsley and green onions.

1 POTATO: 448 cal., 30g fat (18g sat. fat), 78mg chol., 541mg sod., 40g carb. (4g sugars, 4g fiber), 8g pro.

SAUTEED GARLIC MUSHROOMS

These tasty mushrooms are so delicious served with steak, chicken
or pork. You just can't beat mushrooms, garlic and butter together!
—*Joan Schroeder, Mesquite, NV*

TAKES: 15 MIN. • MAKES: 6 SERVINGS

¾ **lb. sliced fresh
  mushrooms**
2 **to 3 tsp. minced garlic**
1 **Tbsp. seasoned
  bread crumbs**
⅓ **cup butter, cubed**

In a large cast-iron or other heavy skillet, saute the mushrooms, garlic and bread crumbs in butter until mushrooms are tender, 3-5 minutes.

½ CUP: 109 cal., 10g fat (6g sat. fat), 27mg chol., 123mg sod., 3g carb. (1g sugars, 1g fiber), 2g pro.

TOMATO PIE

Make sure your tomatoes are firm and not too ripe. Ripe tomatoes will add too much moisture to the pie.
—*Lois Morgan, Edisto Beach, SC*

PREP: 50 MIN. + CHILLING • BAKE: 30 MIN. + STANDING • MAKES: 8 SERVINGS

1 cup plus 2 Tbsp.
  all-purpose flour
¼ tsp. salt
½ cup cold butter, cubed
2 to 3 Tbsp. ice water

FILLING
¾ cup mayonnaise
½ cup shredded
  cheddar cheese
⅓ cup thinly sliced
  green onions
1 Tbsp. minced
  fresh oregano
½ tsp. ground coriander
¼ tsp. salt
¼ tsp. pepper
6 medium tomatoes
  (1¾ lbs.), cut into
  ¼-in. slices
4 bacon strips, cooked
  and crumbled

1. In a large bowl, mix flour and salt; cut in butter until crumbly. Gradually add ice water, tossing with a fork until dough holds together when pressed. Shape into a disk; cover and refrigerate 30 minutes or overnight.

2. Preheat oven to 350°. On a lightly floured surface, roll dough to a ⅛-in.-thick circle; transfer to a 9-in. pie plate. Trim crust to ½ in. beyond rim of plate; flute edge. Line unpricked crust with a double thickness of foil. Fill with pie weights, dried beans or uncooked rice.

3. Bake until bottom is lightly browned, 20-25 minutes. Remove foil and weights; bake until light brown, 5-10 minutes longer. Cool on a wire rack.

4. In a small bowl, combine the mayonnaise, cheese, green onions and seasonings. Arrange a third of the tomatoes in crust; spread with a third of the mayonnaise mixture. Repeat the layers twice. Bake for 25 minutes. Top with bacon; bake until filling is bubbly, 5-10 minutes longer. Let stand 10 minutes before cutting.

1 PIECE: 396 cal., 32g fat (12g sat. fat), 49mg chol., 466mg sod., 22g carb. (5g sugars, 3g fiber), 7g pro.

FROM GRANDMA'S KITCHEN: It's not recommended to freeze this tomato pie because it has a high water content. Instead, wrap any leftovers and store them in the fridge for 2-3 days. You can reheat tomato pie in a 350° oven for 18-20 minutes, or in the microwave for 1-2 minutes.

PUMPKIN WITH WALNUTS & BLUE CHEESE

Don't hold off on serving pumpkin until the dinner finale. Bring it to the main event with this unique and lovely side dish. It's sure to garner you recipe requests.
—*Laurie Bock, Lynden, WA*

PREP: 20 MIN. • BAKE: 30 MIN. • MAKES: 12 SERVINGS

5 lbs. pie pumpkin, seeded, peeled and cut into 1-in. cubes
¼ cup olive oil, divided
2 tsp. salt
1 tsp. pepper
2 medium onions, chopped
⅔ cup chopped walnuts
⅔ cup crumbled blue cheese
20 fresh sage leaves, thinly sliced

1. Preheat oven to 375°. Place pumpkin in a greased 15x1x1-in. baking pan; drizzle with 2 Tbsp. oil and sprinkle with salt and pepper. Bake 30-35 minutes or until tender.

2. In a large skillet, saute onions in remaining oil until tender. Add walnuts; cook 3-5 minutes longer or until toasted.

3. Place pumpkin on a serving platter. Top with onion mixture. Sprinkle with blue cheese and sage.

1 SERVING: 154 cal., 11g fat (2g sat. fat), 6mg chol., 500mg sod., 12g carb. (4g sugars, 2g fiber), 4g pro. **DIABETIC EXCHANGES:** 2 fat, 1 starch.

KALE & FENNEL SKILLET

I love to mix different vegetables together and use a variety of herbs and spices to change things up. If you can't find apple sausage for this skillet, a good mild Italian sausage would work just fine.
—*Patricia Levenson, Santa Ana, CA*

PREP: 10 MIN. • COOK: 25 MIN. • MAKES: 6 SERVINGS

2 Tbsp. extra virgin olive oil
1 small onion, thinly sliced
1 small fennel bulb, thinly sliced
½ lb. fully cooked apple chicken sausage links or cooked Italian sausage links, halved lengthwise and sliced into half-moons
2 garlic cloves, minced
3 Tbsp. dry sherry or dry white wine
1 Tbsp. herbes de Provence
⅛ tsp. salt
⅛ tsp. pepper
1 bunch kale, trimmed and torn into bite-sized pieces

1. In a large cast-iron or other heavy skillet, heat olive oil over medium-high heat. Add onion and fennel; cook and stir until onion begins to brown, 6-8 minutes. Add the sausage, garlic, sherry and seasonings; cook until sausage starts to caramelize, 4-6 minutes.

2. Add kale; cook, covered, stirring occasionally, until kale is tender, 15-17 minutes.

NOTE: Look for herbes de Provence in the spice aisle.

¾ CUP: 167 cal., 8g fat (2g sat. fat), 27mg chol., 398mg sod., 16g carb. (6g sugars, 3g fiber), 9g pro. **DIABETIC EXCHANGES:** 2 vegetable, 1 lean meat, 1 fat.

PUMPKIN WITH
WALNUTS &
BLUE CHEESE

BAKED POTATO SOUP,
PAGE 186

GRANDMA'S FAVORITE

SOUPS & STEWS

Whether your friends and family are craving
some chunky chili, creamy chowders or beautiful
bisques, ladle up something they'll love.

MOM'S CHICKEN NOODLE SOUP

My mother was a pastor's wife, and she did a lot of cooking for potlucks. This recipe is one she created herself. The noodles aren't hard to make and taste divine.
—*Marlene Doolittle, Story City, IA*

PREP: 30 MIN. • **COOK:** 55 MIN. • **MAKES:** 6 SERVINGS

1 broiler/fryer chicken (3 to 4 lbs.), cut up
2 qt. water
1 medium onion, chopped
2 tsp. chicken bouillon granules
2 celery ribs, diced
2 medium carrots, diced
2 medium potatoes, peeled and cubed
1½ cups fresh or frozen cut green beans
1 tsp. salt
¼ tsp. pepper

NOODLES
1 cup all-purpose flour
1 large egg, lightly beaten
½ tsp. salt
1 tsp. butter, softened
¼ tsp. baking powder
2 to 3 Tbsp. 2% milk

1. In a Dutch oven, cook chicken in water; cool slightly. Remove chicken from bones; discard the bones. Skim fat from broth. Cut the chicken into bite-sized pieces; add to the broth with the next 8 ingredients. Bring to a boil. Reduce heat and simmer, uncovered, for 50-60 minutes or until vegetables are tender.

2. Meanwhile, for noodles, place flour in a small bowl and make a well in the center. Stir together remaining ingredients; pour into well. Working the mixture with your hands, form a dough ball. Knead for 5-6 minutes.

3. Cover and let rest for 10 minutes. On a floured surface, roll dough out to a square, 1/16-1/8 in. thick, and cut into ¼-in.-wide strips. Cook noodles in boiling salted water for 2-3 minutes or until done. Drain and add to soup just before serving.

FREEZE OPTION: Freeze uncooked noodles on waxed paper-lined baking sheets until firm. Transfer to freezer containers; return to freezer. Prepare soup as directed, reserving the potatoes for later. Freeze cooled soup in freezer containers. To use, partially thaw in refrigerator overnight. Place potatoes in a small saucepan; add water to cover. Simmer for 10-15 minutes or until tender. Drain. Meanwhile, cook noodles as directed; drain. Transfer soup and potatoes to a Dutch oven. Heat through. Just before serving, add the noodles.

1 CUP: 429 cal., 16g fat (5g sat. fat), 125mg chol., 1012mg sod., 36g carb. (5g sugars, 4g fiber), 34g pro.

"This was a great soup! The noodles were wonderful. I had never made my own noodles before and always wanted to try it."
—GRAMAFK7, TASTEOFHOME.COM

BLACK BEAN, CHORIZO & SWEET POTATO CHILI

Chili is one of my all-time favorite dishes. This recipe takes chili to the next level by changing up the flavors and adding a surprise.
—*Julie Merriman, Seattle, WA*

PREP: 20 MIN. • **COOK:** 6 HOURS • **MAKES:** 16 SERVINGS (4 QT.)

- 1 lb. uncooked chorizo, casings removed, or spicy bulk pork sausage
- 1 large onion, chopped
- 2 poblano peppers, finely chopped
- 2 jalapeno peppers, seeded and finely chopped
- 3 Tbsp. tomato paste
- 3 large sweet potatoes, peeled and cut into ½-in. cubes
- 4 cans (14½ oz. each) fire-roasted diced tomatoes, undrained
- 2 cans (15 oz. each) black beans, rinsed and drained
- 2 cups beef stock
- 2 Tbsp. chili powder
- 1 Tbsp. dried oregano
- 1 Tbsp. ground coriander
- 1 Tbsp. ground cumin
- 1 Tbsp. smoked paprika
- ¼ cup lime juice
  Optional: Chopped jalapenos, chopped red onion and crumbled queso fresco

1. In a large skillet, cook and stir the chorizo, onion, poblanos and jalapenos over medium heat for 8-10 minutes or until chorizo is cooked. Using a slotted spoon, transfer to a 6-qt. slow cooker.

2. Stir in tomato paste. Add potatoes, tomatoes, beans, stock and spices; stir to combine. Cover and cook on low 6-7 hours or until potatoes are tender. Stir in lime juice. If desired, top with chopped jalapenos, chopped red onion and crumbled queso fresco.

1 CUP: 263 cal., 9g fat (3g sat. fat), 25mg chol., 823mg sod., 33g carb. (11g sugars, 6g fiber), 12g pro.

FRENCH ONION
TORTELLINI SOUP

FRENCH ONION TORTELLINI SOUP

This soup is delicious, pretty and unbelievably fast to make. For a creamy variation,
I sometimes substitute cream of mushroom soup for the French onion soup.
If there are any leftovers, they taste even better the next day.
—*Marsha Farley, Bangor, ME*

TAKES: 30 MIN. • MAKES: 8 SERVINGS

1 lb. ground beef
3½ cups water
1 can (28 oz.) diced
   tomatoes, undrained
1 can (10½ oz.) condensed
   French onion soup,
   undiluted
1 pkg. (9 oz.) frozen cut
   green beans
1 pkg. (9 oz.) refrigerated
   cheese tortellini
1 medium zucchini,
   chopped
1 tsp. dried basil

In a large saucepan, cook beef over medium heat until no longer
pink; drain. Add the remaining ingredients; bring to a boil. Cook,
uncovered, 7-9 minutes or until tortellini is tender.

1 SERVING: 241 cal., 9g fat (4g sat. fat), 43mg chol., 608mg sod., 25g
carb. (7g sugars, 4g fiber), 16g pro.

HEARTY CABBAGE SOUP

I didn't have time to make my favorite cabbage rolls one day,
so I just threw together this soup, and I loved it!
—*Renee Leary, Citrus Springs, FL*

TAKES: 30 MIN. • MAKES: 6 SERVINGS

1 lb. ground beef
1 medium onion, chopped
3½ cups shredded cabbage
1 medium zucchini, halved
   and thinly sliced
1 cup sliced fresh
   mushrooms
1 carton (18.3 oz.) ready-to-
   serve sweet red pepper
   soup
1 can (10 oz.) diced
   tomatoes and green
   chiles, undrained
¼ tsp. hot pepper sauce
¼ tsp. salt
¼ tsp. pepper
¼ cup grated Parmesan
   cheese

1. In a large saucepan, cook beef and onion over medium heat
until meat is no longer pink, crumbling beef ; drain. Add cabbage,
zucchini and mushrooms; cook and stir 8 minutes longer.

2. Stir in the soup, tomatoes, pepper sauce, salt and pepper. Bring
to a boil. Reduce heat; cover and simmer for 5 minutes. Sprinkle
each serving with 2 tsp. cheese.

3. Serve immediately or cool and freeze in a freezer container.
May be frozen for up to 3 months.

4. To use frozen soup: Thaw in refrigerator overnight. Transfer
to a saucepan. Cover and cook over medium heat until heated
through. Sprinkle each serving with 2 tsp. cheese.

1 CUP: 230 cal., 11g fat (4g sat. fat), 51mg chol., 617mg sod.,
16g carb. (6g sugars, 4g fiber), 18g pro. **DIABETIC EXCHANGES:**
3 vegetable, 2 medium-fat meat.

GRANDMA'S PEA SOUP

My grandma's pea soup was a family favorite. What makes it different from any other pea soups I have tried is the addition of whole peas, spaetzle-like dumplings and sausage. Try it once and you'll be hooked.

—*Carole Talcott, Dahinda, IL*

PREP: 15 MIN. + SOAKING • **COOK:** 2½ HOURS • **MAKES:** 16 SERVINGS (4 QT.)

½ lb. dried whole peas
½ lb. dried green split peas
1 meaty ham bone
3 qt. water
1 large onion, chopped
1 medium carrot, chopped
2 celery ribs, chopped
½ cup chopped celery leaves
1 tsp. bouquet garni (mixed herbs)
1 Tbsp. minced fresh parsley
1 bay leaf
1 tsp. salt
¼ tsp. pepper
½ lb. smoked sausage, chopped, optional

SPAETZLE DUMPLINGS
1 cup all-purpose flour
1 large egg, beaten
⅓ cup water

1. Cover peas with water and soak overnight. Drain, rinse and place in a Dutch oven.

2. Add ham bone, water and remaining soup ingredients except sausage and dumplings. Bring to a boil. Reduce heat; cover and simmer 2-2½ hours.

3. Remove ham bone and skim fat. Remove meat from bone; dice. Add ham and, if desired, sausage to pan.

4. For dumplings, place flour in a small bowl. Make a depression in the center of the flour; add egg and water and stir until smooth.

5. Place a colander with ³⁄₁₆-in.-diameter holes over simmering soup; transfer dough to the colander and press through with a wooden spoon. Cook, uncovered, 10-15 minutes. Discard bay leaf.

FREEZE OPTION: Prepare soup without dumplings and freeze in serving-size portions to enjoy for months to come.

1 CUP: 155 cal., 2g fat (1g sat. fat), 20mg chol., 171mg sod., 26g carb. (2g sugars, 6g fiber), 9g pro.

"This is the best flavored pea soup I've made. I will be replacing my longtime trusted recipe with this one— yes, it's that good!"

—QUILTINGSTITCHER, TASTEOFHOME.COM

TACO TWIST SOUP

The fun, family-friendly twist in this taco soup is the spiral pasta.
I lightened this soup by substituting black beans for ground beef.
—*Colleen Zertler, Menomonie, WI*

TAKES: 30 MIN. • MAKES: 6 SERVINGS

2 tsp. olive oil
1 medium onion, chopped
2 garlic cloves, minced
3 cups vegetable broth
   or reduced-sodium
   beef broth
1 can (15 oz.) black beans,
   rinsed and drained
1 can (14½ oz.) diced
   tomatoes, undrained
1½ cups picante sauce

1 cup uncooked spiral
   pasta
1 small green pepper,
   chopped
2 tsp. chili powder
1 tsp. ground cumin
   Optional toppings:
   Shredded cheddar
   cheese, sour cream
   and cilantro

1. In a large saucepan, heat oil over medium-high heat. Add onion and garlic; cook and stir until crisp-tender, 3-4 minutes.

2. Stir in the broth, beans, tomatoes, picante sauce, pasta, green pepper and seasonings. Bring to a boil, stirring frequently. Reduce the heat; cover and simmer until pasta is tender, 10-12 minutes, stirring occasionally. Serve with optional toppings as desired.

1 CUP: 176 cal., 2g fat (0 sat. fat), 0 chol., 1044mg sod., 32g carb. (7g sugars, 5g fiber), 7g pro.

NAVY BEAN VEGETABLE SOUP

My family really likes bean soup, so I came up with this enticing version.
The leftovers are, dare I say, even better the next day!
—*Eleanor Mielke, Mitchell, SD*

PREP: 15 MIN. • COOK: 9 HOURS • MAKES: 12 SERVINGS (3 QT.)

4 medium carrots, thinly
   sliced
2 celery ribs, chopped
1 medium onion, chopped
2 cups cubed fully cooked
   ham
1½ cups dried navy beans
1 envelope vegetable
   recipe mix (Knorr)
1 envelope onion soup mix
1 bay leaf
½ tsp. pepper
8 cups water

In a 5-qt. slow cooker, combine the first 9 ingredients. Stir in water. Cover and cook on low until beans are tender, 9-10 hours. Discard bay leaf.

FREEZE OPTION: Freeze cooled soup in freezer containers. To use, partially thaw in refrigerator overnight. Heat through in a saucepan, stirring occasionally; add water or broth if necessary.

1 CUP: 157 cal., 2g fat (1g sat. fat), 12mg chol., 763mg sod., 24g carb. (4g sugars, 8g fiber), 11g pro.

GRANDMA'S SECRET
Besides just bacon and parsley, you can also top off this soup with freshly cracked pepper or sliced green onions. A hearty dollop of sour cream wouldn't hurt, either!

CREAMY BACON
MUSHROOM SOUP

CREAMY BACON MUSHROOM SOUP

I've always enjoyed cooking and recently created this rich soup. It's always a hit.
You can also garnish it with chopped green onion tops or shredded Swiss cheese.
For a creamier, smoother consistency, try pouring the soup through a strainer.
—Toby Mercer, Inman, SC

TAKES: 30 MIN. • MAKES: 8 SERVINGS (2 QT.)

10 bacon strips, diced
1 lb. sliced fresh
mushrooms
1 medium onion, chopped
3 garlic cloves, minced
1 qt. heavy whipping cream
1 can (14½ oz.)
chicken broth
1¼ cups shredded
Swiss cheese
3 Tbsp. cornstarch
½ tsp. salt
½ tsp. pepper
3 Tbsp. cold water
Minced fresh parsley,
optional

1. In a large saucepan, cook bacon over medium heat until crisp. Using a slotted spoon, remove to paper towels; drain, reserving 2 Tbsp. drippings. In the drippings, saute mushrooms and onion until tender, 5-7 minutes. Add garlic; cook 1 minute longer. Stir in cream and broth; bring mixture to a simmer. Gradually stir in cheese until melted.

2. In a small bowl, combine cornstarch, salt, pepper and water until smooth. Stir into soup. Bring to a boil; cook and stir until thickened, about 2 minutes. Garnish with the diced bacon and, if desired, parsley.

1 CUP: 592 cal., 56g fat (33g sat. fat), 193mg chol., 649mg sod., 12g carb. (3g sugars, 1g fiber), 13g pro.

CONTEST-WINNING STUFFED PEPPER SOUP

This is an excellent example of how convenience foods can be combined for a tasty entree.
Ready in minutes when I get home from work, this soup becomes part of a balanced meal with a
tossed salad, rolls or fruit. For a variation, try chicken, turkey or even venison instead of ground beef.
—Tracy Thompson, Cranesville, PA

TAKES: 30 MIN. • MAKES: 8 SERVINGS (ABOUT 2½ QT.)

1 pkg. (8.8 oz.) ready-to-
serve long grain and
wild rice
1 lb. ground beef
2 cups chopped
green pepper
1 cup chopped onion
1 jar (26 oz.) chunky
tomato pasta sauce
1 can (14½ oz.) Italian diced
tomatoes, undrained
1 can (14 oz.) beef broth

Prepare rice according to package directions. Meanwhile, in a large saucepan, cook the beef, green peppers and onion until meat is no longer pink, crumbling beef; drain. Stir in the pasta sauce, tomatoes, broth and prepared rice; heat through.

1¼ CUPS: 238 cal., 8g fat (3g sat. fat), 31mg chol., 917mg sod., 28g carb. (13g sugars, 4g fiber), 14g pro.

PASTA FAGIOLI SOUP

My husband enjoys my version of this soup so much that he stopped ordering it at restaurants. He'd rather savor the version we can have at home. It's so easy to make, yet hearty enough to be a full dinner.
—*Brenda Thomas, Springfield, MO*

TAKES: 30 MIN. • **MAKES:** 5 SERVINGS

½ lb. Italian turkey sausage links, casings removed, crumbled
1 small onion, chopped
1½ tsp. canola oil
1 garlic clove, minced
2 cups water
1 can (15½ oz.) great northern beans, rinsed and drained
1 can (14½ oz.) diced tomatoes, undrained
1 can (14½ oz.) reduced-sodium chicken broth
¾ cup uncooked elbow macaroni
¼ tsp. pepper
1 cup fresh spinach leaves, cut as desired
5 tsp. shredded Parmesan cheese

1. In a large saucepan, cook sausage over medium heat until no longer pink; drain, remove from pan and set aside. In the same pan, saute the onion in oil until tender. Add the garlic; saute for 1 minute longer.

2. Add water, beans, tomatoes, broth, macaroni and pepper; bring to a boil. Cook, uncovered, until macaroni is tender, 8-10 minutes.

3. Reduce heat to low; stir in sausage and spinach. Cook until the spinach is wilted, 2-3 minutes. Garnish with cheese.

1⅓ CUPS: 228 cal., 7g fat (1g sat. fat), 29mg chol., 841mg sod., 27g carb. (4g sugars, 6g fiber), 16g pro. **DIABETIC EXCHANGES:** 1½ starch, 1 vegetable, 1 lean meat, ½ fat.

BAKED POTATO SOUP

PICTURED ON PAGE 176

I found our favorite soup in an unexpected place—a children's cookbook! This creamy comfort food is not only delicious but it's also scaled down to make an amount that's perfect for my husband and me.
—*Linda Mumm, Davenport, IA*

TAKES: 20 MIN. • **MAKES:** 2 SERVINGS

2 medium potatoes, baked and cooled
1 can (14½ oz.) chicken broth
2 Tbsp. sour cream
⅛ tsp. pepper
¼ cup shredded cheddar cheese
1 Tbsp. crumbled cooked bacon or bacon bits
1 green onion, sliced

Peel the potatoes and cut into ½-in. cubes; place half in a blender. Add broth; cover and process until smooth. Pour into a saucepan. Stir in sour cream, pepper and remaining potatoes. Cook over low heat until heated through (do not boil). Garnish with cheese, bacon and onion.

1 CUP: 277 cal., 8g fat (5g sat. fat), 28mg chol., 1061mg sod., 41g carb. (5g sugars, 4g fiber), 11g pro.

PASTA FAGIOLI
SOUP

BROCCOLI CHEDDAR SOUP

My husband and I love this cheesy dish. It is proof that soup doesn't need to be made in big batches to be good.
—*Cheryl McRae, West Valley, UT*

TAKES: 20 MIN. • MAKES: 2 SERVINGS

¼ cup chopped onion
¼ cup butter, cubed
¼ cup all-purpose flour
¼ tsp. salt
¼ tsp. pepper
1½ cups 2% milk

¾ cup chicken broth
1 cup cooked chopped fresh or frozen broccoli
½ cup shredded cheddar cheese

1. In a small saucepan, saute onion in butter until tender. Stir in the flour, salt and pepper until blended; gradually add milk and broth. Bring to a boil; cook and stir until thickened, about 2 minutes.

2. Add broccoli. Cook and stir until heated through. Remove from the heat; stir in cheese until melted.

1 CUP: 494 cal., 37g fat (24g sat. fat), 116mg chol., 1145mg sod., 26g carb. (11g sugars, 2g fiber), 16g pro.

COCONUT SHRIMP CHOWDER

After trying a coconut soup at a Thai restaurant, I added coconut milk to my fish chowder recipe—it was perfect! The fresh, simple ingredients allow the seafood to shine.
—*Michalene Baskett, Decatur, GA*

TAKES: 30 MIN. • MAKES: 5 SERVINGS

1 medium onion, chopped
2 tsp. canola oil
¼ tsp. cayenne pepper
2 cups chicken broth
1 pkg. (10 oz.) frozen corn
¼ tsp. salt
¼ tsp. pepper
1 can (13.66 oz.) coconut milk
1 lb. uncooked medium shrimp, peeled and deveined
¼ cup lime juice
2 Tbsp. minced fresh cilantro
1 medium ripe avocado, peeled and cubed

1. In a large saucepan, saute onion in oil until tender. Add cayenne pepper. Stir in broth, corn, salt and pepper. Bring to a boil. Reduce heat; simmer, uncovered, for 5 minutes. Remove from heat and stir in coconut milk. Cool slightly.

2. In a food processor, process soup in batches until blended. Return all to pan. Add shrimp; cook and stir over medium heat for 5-6 minutes or until shrimp turn pink. Stir in lime juice and cilantro. Garnish servings with avocado.

1 CUP: 376 cal., 26g fat (16g sat. fat), 112mg chol., 633mg sod., 22g carb. (4g sugars, 5g fiber), 20g pro.

SPICY PORK & GREEN CHILI VERDE

My pork chili is brimming with poblano and sweet red peppers for a hearty kick.
Serve it with sour cream, Monterey Jack and tortilla chips.
—*Anthony Bolton, Bellevue, NE*

PREP: 40 MIN. + STANDING • **COOK:** 25 MIN. • **MAKES:** 6 SERVINGS

6 **poblano peppers**
2 **Tbsp. butter**
1½ **lbs. pork tenderloin,
    cut into 1-in. pieces**
2 **medium sweet red or
    yellow peppers, coarsely
    chopped**
1 **large sweet onion,
    coarsely chopped**
1 **jalapeno pepper, seeded
    and finely chopped**
2 **Tbsp. chili powder**
2 **garlic cloves, minced**
1 **tsp. salt**
¼ **tsp. ground nutmeg**
2 **cups chicken broth
    Optional toppings:
    Sour cream, shredded
    Monterey Jack cheese,
    crumbled tortilla chips
    and lime wedges**

1. Place poblano peppers on a foil-lined baking sheet. Broil 4 in. from heat until skins blister, about 5 minutes. With tongs, rotate the peppers a quarter turn. Broil and rotate until all sides are blistered and blackened. Immediately place peppers in a large bowl; let stand, covered, 10 minutes.

2. Peel off and discard charred skin. Remove and discard stems and seeds. Finely chop peppers.

3. In a 6-qt. stockpot, heat butter over medium heat. Brown pork in batches. Remove with a slotted spoon.

4. In same pan, add red peppers, onion and jalapeno; cook, covered, over medium heat until tender, 8-10 minutes, stirring occasionally. Stir in chili powder, garlic, salt and nutmeg. Add broth, roasted peppers and pork; bring to a boil. Reduce heat; simmer, uncovered, until pork is tender, 10-15 minutes. Serve with toppings as desired.

NOTE: Wear disposable gloves when cutting hot peppers; the oils can burn skin. Avoid touching your face.

1 CUP: 235 cal., 9g fat (4g sat. fat), 75mg chol., 913mg sod., 14g carb. (8g sugars, 4g fiber), 25g pro.

"I'm so grateful for this delicious recipe. I can't wait to make it again. It had the perfect heat, and incredible flavor from the spices."
—SUMMY, TASTEOFHOME.COM

CHUNKY VEGETARIAN CHILI

This robust chili teams rice and kidney and pinto beans with
a variety of colorful vegetables for a hearty meatless meal.
—Taste of Home *Test Kitchen*

PREP: 20 MIN. • **COOK:** 25 MIN. • **MAKES:** 11 SERVINGS (2¾ QT.)

1 medium green pepper, chopped
1 medium onion, chopped
3 garlic cloves, minced
1 Tbsp. canola oil
1 can (14½ oz.) stewed tomatoes
1 can (10 oz.) diced tomatoes and green chiles
1 can (16 oz.) kidney beans, rinsed and drained
1 can (15 oz.) pinto beans, rinsed and drained
1 can (11 oz.) whole kernel corn, drained
2½ cups water
1 cup uncooked long grain rice
1 to 2 Tbsp. chili powder
1½ tsp. ground cumin
   Salt & pepper to taste

In a Dutch oven, saute green pepper, onion and garlic in oil until tender. Stir in all remaining ingredients; bring to a boil. Reduce heat; cover and simmer until rice is cooked, stirring occasionally, 25-30 minutes. If thinner chili is desired, add more water. Taste and adjust the seasonings by adding salt and pepper if needed. Top as desired.

1 CUP: 196 cal., 2g fat (0 sat. fat), 0 chol., 424mg sod., 37g carb. (6g sugars, 6g fiber), 7g pro. **DIABETIC EXCHANGES:** 2½ starch.

"This was super easy to put together for a quick meal, very delicious and hearty. Fantastic for a cold winter day!"
—SHECOOKSALOT, TASTEOFHOME.COM

BEET BORSCHT

My mother used to make this hearty soup from her garden's bountiful crop of beets and other vegetables.
—*Ruth Andrewson, Leavenworth, WA*

PREP: 15 MIN. • **COOK:** 35 MIN. • **MAKES:** 8 SERVINGS (2 QT.)

2 cups shredded fresh beets
1 cup shredded carrots
1 cup chopped onion
2 cups water
½ tsp. salt
2 cans (14½ oz. each) beef broth
1 cup shredded cabbage
1 Tbsp. butter
1 Tbsp. lemon juice
   Optional: Sour cream and chopped chives or fresh dill sprigs

In a saucepan, bring the beets, carrots, onion, water and salt to a boil. Reduce heat; cover and simmer for 20 minutes. Add broth, cabbage and butter; simmer, uncovered, 15 minutes. Just before serving, stir in lemon juice. If desired, top each serving with sour cream and chives or dill.

1 CUP: 48 cal., 2g fat (1g sat. fat), 4mg chol., 375mg sod., 7g carb. (5g sugars, 2g fiber), 1g pro. **DIABETIC EXCHANGES:** 1 vegetable, ½ fat.

CHUNKY
VEGETARIAN
CHILI

GRANDMA'S SECRET
Separate the egg white by cracking your egg right down the middle. Then, over a bowl, tip the yolk back and forth between the shells, allowing the white to fall into the dish below.

CHIPOTLE CHICKEN
SOUP WITH
CORNMEAL
DUMPLINGS

CHIPOTLE CHICKEN SOUP WITH CORNMEAL DUMPLINGS

I combined two of my favorite recipes and came up with this filling soup that has a Tex-Mex flair. The cornmeal dumplings are the perfect finishing touch.
—*Nancy Granaman, Burlington, IA*

PREP: 20 MIN. • COOK: 30 MIN. • MAKES: 6 SERVINGS (2 QT.)

1 can (15 oz.) black beans, rinsed and drained
1 can (14½ oz.) no-salt-added stewed tomatoes, cut up
1 can (14½ oz.) reduced-sodium chicken broth
1¾ cups water
1 tsp. ground cumin
1 tsp. minced chipotle pepper in adobo sauce
2 cups cubed cooked chicken breast
1 large egg
1 large egg white
1 pkg. (8½ oz.) cornbread/muffin mix
⅓ cup reduced-fat biscuit/baking mix
1 Tbsp. fat-free milk
¼ cup minced fresh cilantro, optional

1. In a small bowl, mash half the beans. Transfer the mashed and remaining beans to a Dutch oven. Add the tomatoes, broth, water, cumin and chipotle pepper. Bring to a boil. Reduce heat; cover and simmer for 15 minutes. Add chicken.

2. In a small bowl, combine the egg, egg white, muffin mix and baking mix; stir in milk. Drop by tablespoonfuls onto simmering soup. Cover and simmer for 10-12 minutes or until a toothpick inserted in a dumpling comes out clean (do not lift the cover while simmering). Ladle soup into bowls. Sprinkle each serving with cilantro if desired.

1⅓ CUPS: 356 cal., 7g fat (2g sat. fat), 80mg chol., 808mg sod., 48g carb. (13g sugars, 5g fiber), 24g pro.

ITALIAN SAUSAGE & BEAN SOUP

The unusual blend of sausage and beans with coleslaw makes this soup the definition of complete comfort food. The recipe doubles easily, so serve a crowd and pair with a warm loaf of bread and a tossed salad.
—*Stacey Bennett, Locust Grove, VA*

TAKES: 30 MIN. • MAKES: 6 SERVINGS (2 QT.)

1 lb. bulk hot Italian sausage
2 cans (15½ oz. each) great northern beans, rinsed and drained
1 pkg. (16 oz.) coleslaw mix
1 jar (24 oz.) garlic and herb spaghetti sauce
3 cups water

In a Dutch oven, cook sausage over medium heat until no longer pink; drain. Stir in the remaining ingredients. Bring to a boil. Reduce heat; simmer, uncovered, until the flavors are blended, 16-20 minutes.

1⅓ CUPS: 416 cal., 21g fat (8g sat. fat), 53mg chol., 1411mg sod., 35g carb. (9g sugars, 12g fiber), 23g pro.

FRENCH ONION SOUP WITH PROVOLONE

I adapted a basic recipe to copy the onion soup served at my favorite restaurant.
No matter what my entree, I always ordered the soup. Now I can make it at home.
It's a meal in itself or an impressive beginning to a full-course meal.
—*Barbara Brunner, Steelton, PA*

PREP: 55 MIN. • BAKE: 10 MIN. • MAKES: 2 SERVINGS

2 medium onions, chopped
1 tsp. sugar
6 Tbsp. butter, divided
1 Tbsp. all-purpose flour
⅛ tsp. pepper
Dash ground nutmeg
2½ cups reduced-sodium beef or vegetable broth
2 Tbsp. grated Parmesan cheese
2 slices French bread (1 in. thick)
4 slices provolone cheese

1. In a large saucepan, saute onions and sugar in 3 Tbsp. butter until golden brown. Stir in the flour, pepper and nutmeg until blended. Gradually stir in broth. Bring to a boil; cook and stir for 2 minutes. Reduce heat; cover and simmer for 30 minutes. Stir in the Parmesan cheese.

2. Meanwhile, in a large skillet, melt remaining butter; add bread. Cook until golden brown on both sides. Ladle soup into 2 ovenproof bowls. Place a slice of cheese in each bowl; top with bread and remaining cheese. Bake at 375° until cheese is bubbly, about 10 minutes.

1 SERVING: 633 cal., 47g fat (30g sat. fat), 131mg chol., 1472mg sod., 34g carb. (9g sugars, 3g fiber), 19g pro.

BUTTERNUT SQUASH SOUP WITH CINNAMON

The golden color, smooth and creamy texture, and wonderful taste of
this soup make it welcome on a chilly fall day. It has a slightly tangy flavor
from the cream cheese, and the cinnamon really comes through.
—*Jackie Campbell, Stanhope, NJ*

PREP: 30 MIN. • COOK: 6¼ HOURS • MAKES: 14 SERVINGS (2½ QT.)

2 Tbsp. butter
1 medium onion, chopped
1 medium butternut squash (about 4 lbs.), peeled and cubed
3 cans (14½ oz. each) vegetable broth
1 Tbsp. brown sugar
1 Tbsp. minced fresh gingerroot
1 garlic clove, minced
1 cinnamon stick (3 in.)
1 pkg. (8 oz.) cream cheese, cubed and softened
Optional: Crystallized ginger and fresh cracked pepper

1. In a small skillet, melt butter over medium heat; add onion. Cook and stir until tender, 3-5 minutes. Transfer to a 5- or 6-qt. slow cooker; add squash. Combine broth, brown sugar, ginger, garlic and cinnamon; pour over squash. Cover and cook on low until squash is tender, 6-8 hours.

2. Cool slightly. Discard cinnamon stick. In a blender, process soup in batches until smooth. Return all to slow cooker. Whisk in cream cheese; cover and cook until cheese is melted, about 15 minutes longer. If desired, top with crystallized ginger and fresh cracked pepper.

¾ CUP: 135 cal., 7g fat (5g sat. fat), 22mg chol., 483mg sod., 17g carb. (5g sugars, 4g fiber), 2g pro. **DIABETIC EXCHANGES:** 1½ fat, 1 starch.

SPICY CHEESEBURGER SOUP

This creamy soup brings my family to the table in a hurry. I love the warming zip of cayenne, but it also tastes terrific without it if you like milder flavor. With a few simple side dishes, this soup is a full meal.

—Lisa Mast, White Cloud, MI

> PREP: 15 MIN. • COOK: 30 MIN. • MAKES: 8 SERVINGS (2 QT.)

1½ cups water
2 cups cubed peeled potatoes
2 small carrots, grated
1 small onion, chopped
¼ cup chopped green pepper
1 jalapeno pepper, seeded and chopped
1 garlic clove, minced
1 Tbsp. beef bouillon granules
½ tsp. salt
1 lb. ground beef, cooked and drained
2½ cups 2% milk, divided
3 Tbsp. all-purpose flour
8 oz. cubed Velveeta
¼ to 1 tsp. cayenne pepper, optional
½ lb. sliced bacon, cooked and crumbled

1. In a large saucepan, combine the first 9 ingredients; bring to a boil. Reduce heat; cover and simmer for 15-20 minutes or until potatoes are tender.

2. Stir in beef and 2 cups milk; heat through. Combine flour and remaining milk until smooth; gradually stir into soup. Bring to a boil; cook and stir for 2 minutes or until thickened and bubbly. Reduce heat; stir in cheese until melted.

3. Add cayenne pepper if desired. Top with the bacon just before serving.

NOTE: Wear disposable gloves when cutting hot peppers; the oils can burn skin. Avoid touching your face.

1 CUP: 351 cal., 20g fat (10g sat. fat), 81mg chol., 1063mg sod., 19g carb. (7g sugars, 1g fiber), 22g pro.

FROM GRANDMA'S KITCHEN: Buy several pounds of bacon when it's on sale. Put the strips in a single layer on jelly-roll pans and pop them in the oven to bake at 350° until crisp. Place the strips on paper towels to drain before storing them in single layers in a freezer container. Then, when you're cooking, it's easy to remove only the number of strips needed

STROGANOFF SOUP

My husband and I share a love for all kinds of soup and came up with this delicious recipe together. It really does taste like beef Stroganoff. With a crusty roll, it's a satisfying meal.
—*Karen Shiveley, Springfield, MN*

PREP: 15 MIN. • **COOK:** 40 MIN. • **MAKES:** 6 SERVINGS

½ **lb. beef top sirloin steak or beef tenderloin, cut into thin strips**
½ **cup chopped onion**
1 **Tbsp. butter**
2 **cups water**
1½ **cups 2% milk**
¼ **cup tomato paste**
2 **tsp. beef bouillon granules**
1 **can (8 oz.) mushroom stems and pieces, drained**
1 **tsp. salt**
⅛ **tsp. pepper**
1 **can (12 oz.) evaporated milk**
⅓ **cup all-purpose flour**
2 **cups cooked wide egg noodles**
½ **cup sour cream**
   Minced fresh thyme, optional

1. In a 3-qt. saucepan, cook beef and onion in butter over medium heat, until meat is almost cooked through. Stir in the water, milk, tomato paste and bouillon. Add the mushrooms, salt and pepper; bring to a boil.

2. Combine evaporated milk and flour until smooth. Gradually stir into the soup. Bring to a boil; cook and stir until thickened, 1-2 minutes. Add noodles; cook until heated through. Remove from heat; top each serving with sour cream. If desired, garnish with fresh thyme.

1 CUP: 314 cal., 13g fat (8g sat. fat), 78mg chol., 935mg sod., 28g carb. (12g sugars, 2g fiber), 17g pro.

TANGY ASPARAGUS SOUP

A dollop of creme fraiche makes this pretty soup an ideal starter for an elegant spring dinner party.
—*Jamie Concannon, Plymouth, CA*

PREP: 40 MIN. • COOK: 15 MIN. • MAKES: 7 SERVINGS

¼ cup butter, cubed
1 cup sliced shallots
2 lbs. fresh asparagus, cut into 1-in. pieces
2½ cups chicken broth
½ cup white wine or additional chicken broth
2 tsp. ground coriander
¼ tsp. pepper
1 cup shredded Parmesan cheese
¼ cup creme fraiche or sour cream
½ tsp. lemon juice
¼ tsp. grated lemon zest

1. In a large skillet over medium heat, melt butter. Add shallots; cook and stir until tender. Add asparagus; cook 1 minute longer. Stir in the broth, wine and coriander. Bring to a boil. Reduce heat; cover and simmer until the asparagus is tender, 3-5 minutes. Do not drain. Cool slightly. Place in blender; cover and process until pureed. Stir in pepper. Keep warm.

2. To make the crisps, heat a lightly greased small skillet over medium heat. Add about 2 Tbsp. cheese; cook until cheese is golden brown and bubbly, 1-2 minutes. Carefully flip the crisp; cook 30 seconds longer. Remove to waxed paper to cool. Repeat.

3. In a small bowl, combine the creme fraiche, lemon juice and lemon zest.

4. Ladle soup into cups; dollop with creme fraiche mixture. Serve with Parmesan crisps.

1 SERVING: 191 cal., 13g fat (8g sat. fat), 34mg chol., 606mg sod., 8g carb. (2g sugars, 2g fiber), 7g pro.

BEEF NOODLE SOUP

This delicious soup only takes minutes—but tastes like it simmered all day!
—*Margery Bryan, Moses Lake, WA*

TAKES: 25 MIN. • MAKES: 8 SERVINGS (2 QT.)

1 lb. ground beef
½ cup chopped onion
2 cans (14½ oz. each) Italian stewed tomatoes
2 cans (10½ oz. each) beef broth
2 cups frozen mixed vegetables or 1 can (15 oz.) mixed vegetables
1 tsp. salt
¼ tsp. pepper
1 cup uncooked medium egg noodles

In a Dutch oven, cook beef and onion over medium heat until meat is no longer pink, 5-7 minutes, crumbling beef; drain. Add the tomatoes, broth, vegetables and seasonings. Bring to a boil; add noodles. Reduce heat to medium-low; cover and cook until noodles are tender, 10-15 minutes.

1 CUP: 144 cal., 5g fat (2g sat. fat), 32mg chol., 804mg sod., 11g carb. (5g sugars, 2g fiber), 12g pro.

CREAMY SEAFOOD BISQUE

My deceptively simple bisque makes a special first course or even a casual meal with a salad or some bread. I like to top bowlfuls with shredded Parmesan cheese and green onions.
—*Wanda Allende, Orlando, FL*

PREP: 25 MIN. • **COOK:** 25 MIN. • **MAKES:** 8 SERVINGS (2½ QT.)

½ cup butter, cubed
1 medium red onion, chopped
1 cup sliced fresh mushrooms
2 garlic cloves, minced
½ cup all-purpose flour
1 tsp. salt
1 tsp. coarsely ground pepper
2 Tbsp. tomato paste
1 carton (32 oz.) chicken broth
2 cups whole baby clams, drained
½ lb. uncooked medium shrimp, peeled and deveined
2 cups lump crabmeat, drained
2 cups heavy whipping cream
½ cup shredded Parmesan cheese
2 green onions, thinly sliced

1. In a Dutch oven, heat butter over medium-high heat. Add red onion and mushrooms; saute for 4-5 minutes or until tender. Add garlic; cook 1 minute longer. Stir in the flour, salt and pepper until blended; add tomato paste. Gradually whisk in broth; bring to a boil. Reduce heat; cover and simmer for 5 minutes.

2. Add clams and shrimp; return to a boil. Reduce heat; simmer, uncovered, 5-10 minutes longer or until shrimp turn pink, stirring occasionally. Stir in crab and cream; heat through (do not boil). Serve with cheese and green onions.

1¼ CUPS: 453 cal., 36g fat (22g sat. fat), 197mg chol., 1232mg sod., 12g carb. (2g sugars, 1g fiber), 20g pro.

FROM GRANDMA'S KITCHEN: Clean mushrooms by gently rubbing the dirt off with a mushroom brush or wiping the mushrooms with a damp paper towel. If there's an excess amount of dirt, quickly rinse the mushrooms in cold water and dry immediately with a paper towel. Don't let them soak.

CHICKEN WILD RICE SOUP

This savory soup has a lot of substance, and we enjoy brimming bowls of it all winter long. The men in my family especially love it.
—*Virginia Montmarquet, Riverside, CA*

PREP: 20 MIN. • COOK: 40 MIN. • MAKES: 14 SERVINGS (3½ QT.)

- 2 qt. chicken broth
- ½ lb. fresh mushrooms, chopped
- 1 cup finely chopped celery
- 1 cup shredded carrots
- ½ cup finely chopped onion
- 1 tsp. chicken bouillon granules
- 1 tsp. dried parsley flakes
- ¼ tsp. garlic powder
- ¼ tsp. dried thyme
- ¼ cup butter, cubed
- ¼ cup all-purpose flour
- 1 can (10¾ oz.) condensed cream of mushroom soup, undiluted
- ½ cup dry white wine or additional chicken broth
- 3 cups cooked wild rice
- 2 cups cubed cooked chicken

1. In a large saucepan, combine the first 9 ingredients. Bring to a boil. Reduce heat; cover and simmer for 30 minutes.

2. In Dutch oven, melt butter; stir in flour until smooth. Gradually whisk in broth mixture. Bring to a boil; cook and stir for 2 minutes or until thickened. Whisk in soup and wine. Add rice and chicken; heat through.

1 CUP: 154 cal., 6g fat (3g sat. fat), 27mg chol., 807mg sod., 14g carb. (2g sugars, 2g fiber), 10g pro.

FROM GRANDMA'S KITCHEN: It's recommended that you avoid freezing most dairy-based soups, as the soup tastes grainy once reheated. If you'd like to freeze it, consider leaving out the can of cream of mushroom soup until you're ready to reheat and eat it.

SWEET POTATO CHILI WITH TURKEY

Swapping in ground turkey for ground beef lightens up this chili.
—*Rachel Lewis, Danville, VA*

PREP: 20 MIN. • **COOK:** 5 HOURS • **MAKES:** 6 SERVINGS (2¼ QT.)

1 **lb. ground turkey**
1 **small onion, chopped**
2 **cups chicken broth**
1 **can (15 oz.) sweet potato puree or canned pumpkin**
1 **can (4 oz.) chopped green chiles**
1 **Tbsp. chili powder**
1 **tsp. garlic powder**
1 **tsp. ground cumin**
1 **tsp. curry powder**
½ **tsp. dried oregano**
½ **tsp. salt**
1 **can (15½ oz.) great northern beans, rinsed and drained**
  Optional: Sour cream, fresh cilantro and sliced red onions

1. In a large skillet, cook turkey and onion over medium heat until turkey is no longer pink and onion is tender, 5-7 minutes, breaking up turkey into crumbles; drain. Transfer to a 3- or 4-qt. slow cooker.

2. Stir in broth, sweet potato puree, chiles and seasonings. Cook, covered, on low 4-5 hours. Stir in the beans; cook until heated through, about 1 hour. If desired, top with sour cream, cilantro and red onions.

FREEZE OPTION: Freeze cooled chili in freezer containers. To use, partially thaw in refrigerator overnight. Heat through in a saucepan, stirring occasionally; add broth if necessary.

1½ CUPS: 243 cal., 6g fat (1g sat. fat), 52mg chol., 606mg sod., 27g carb. (5g sugars, 7g fiber), 20g pro. **DIABETIC EXCHANGES:** 2 starch, 2 lean meat.

FRENCH LENTIL & CARROT SOUP

It's crazy how just a few ingredients can make such a difference. Using finely chopped rotisserie chicken in this recipe makes it perfect for a busy weeknight meal, but you can leave the chicken out if you prefer.
—*Colleen Delawder, Herndon, VA*

PREP: 15 MIN. • **COOK:** 6¼ HOURS • **MAKES:** 6 SERVINGS (2¼ QT.)

5 **large carrots, peeled and sliced**
1½ **cups dried green lentils, rinsed**
1 **shallot, finely chopped**
2 **tsp. herbes de Provence**
½ **tsp. pepper**
¼ **tsp. kosher salt**
6 **cups reduced-sodium chicken broth**
2 **cups cubed rotisserie chicken**
¼ **cup heavy whipping cream**

1. Combine the first 7 ingredients in a 5- or 6-qt. slow cooker; cover. Cook on low 6-8 hours or until lentils are tender.

2. Stir in chicken and cream. Cover and continue cooking until heated through, about 15 minutes.

1½ CUPS: 338 cal., 8g fat (3g sat. fat), 53mg chol., 738mg sod., 39g carb. (5g sugars, 7g fiber), 29g pro. **DIABETIC EXCHANGES:** 3 lean meat, 2 starch, 1 vegetable.

FROM GRANDMA'S KITCHEN: Remember to check the label when buying herbes de Provence; some contain lavender and some don't. The lavender adds an unusual flavor that complements both carrots and lentils.

STONE SOUP

We enjoyed concocting this version of the folktale classic. It's packed with veggies and chicken. Reenact the legend by asking guests to bring an ingredient to add to the hearty soup.
—Taste of Home *Test Kitchen*

PREP: 15 MIN. • **COOK:** 40 MIN. • **MAKES:** 12 SERVINGS

4 **cans (14½ oz. each) chicken broth**
4 **medium red potatoes, cut into eighths**
1 **yellow summer squash, chopped**
2 **medium carrots, chopped**
1 **medium onion, chopped**
2 **celery ribs, chopped**
1 **tsp. dried thyme**
½ **tsp. pepper**
4 **cups cubed cooked chicken**
1 **cup frozen cut green beans**
½ **cup quick-cooking barley**
1 **can (14½ oz.) diced tomatoes, undrained**
4 **cups salad croutons**
1 **cup shredded Parmesan cheese**

1. In a Dutch oven, combine the first 8 ingredients. Bring to a boil. Reduce heat; cover and simmer until vegetables are crisp-tender, 10-15 minutes.

2. Stir in the chicken, beans and barley. Bring to a boil. Reduce heat; cover and simmer until vegetables and barley are tender, 10-12 minutes. Add tomatoes; heat through. Serve with croutons and cheese.

1 CUP: 260 cal., 8g fat (3g sat. fat), 47mg chol., 868mg sod., 26g carb. (4g sugars, 4g fiber), 21g pro.

FROM GRANDMA'S KITCHEN: You can easily omit a veggie or two and add more of another to make up the difference. Or, try swapping in different vegetables such as zucchini, frozen peas or lima beans.

AMISH CHICKEN CORN SOUP

Creamed corn and butter make my chicken noodle soup homey and rich. This recipe makes a big batch, but the soup freezes well for future meals.
—Beverly Hoffman, Sandy Lake, PA

PREP: 15 MIN. • **COOK:** 50 MIN. • **MAKES:** 12 SERVINGS (ABOUT 4 QT.)

1 **medium onion, chopped**
2 **celery ribs, chopped**
1 **cup shredded carrots**
2 **lbs. boneless skinless chicken breasts, cubed**
3 **chicken bouillon cubes**
1 **tsp. salt**
¼ **tsp. pepper**
12 **cups water**
2 **cups uncooked egg noodles**
2 **cans (14¾ oz. each) cream-style corn**
¼ **cup butter**

1. Place first 8 ingredients in a Dutch oven; bring slowly to a boil. Reduce heat; simmer, uncovered, until chicken is no longer pink and vegetables are tender, about 30 minutes.

2. Stir in noodles, corn and butter. Cook, uncovered, until noodles are tender, about 10 minutes, stirring occasionally.

1⅓ CUPS: 201 cal., 6g fat (3g sat. fat), 57mg chol., 697mg sod., 19g carb. (3g sugars, 2g fiber), 18g pro. **DIABETIC EXCHANGES:** 2 lean meat, 1 starch, 1 fat.

STONE SOUP

ROASTED
RED PEPPERS
SOUP

ROASTED RED PEPPERS SOUP

If you like cream of tomato soup, try making it with purchased roasted red peppers instead. Using jarred roasted red peppers makes it extra easy, and pureeing the soup in a blender gives it a nice smooth texture.
—Taste of Home *Test Kitchen*

PREP: 10 MIN. • COOK: 25 MIN. • MAKES: 6 SERVINGS

2 tsp. butter
1 large sweet onion, chopped
2 garlic cloves, minced
2 jars (15½ oz. each) roasted sweet red peppers, drained
2 cups vegetable broth
½ tsp. dried basil
¼ tsp. salt
1 cup half-and-half cream
   Optional: Fresh basil leaves and additional half-and-half cream

1. In a saucepan, melt butter over medium heat; add onion. Cook and stir until tender, 3-5 minutes. Add the garlic; cook 1 minute longer. Stir in red peppers, broth, basil and salt. Bring to a boil. Reduce heat; cover and simmer 20 minutes. Cool slightly.

2. In a blender, cover and process soup in batches until smooth. Remove 1 cup to a small bowl; stir in cream. Return remaining puree to pan. Stir in the cream mixture; heat through (do not boil). If desired, garnish with additional cream and basil.

1 CUP: 135 cal., 6g fat (3g sat. fat), 23mg chol., 753mg sod., 21g carb. (9g sugars, 1g fiber), 2g pro.

POTATO, SAUSAGE & KALE SOUP

I let my young son pick out seed packets and he chose kale, which grew like crazy. This hearty soup helped make good use of it, and it rivals some of our restaurant favorites.
—Michelle Babbie, Malone, NY

TAKES: 30 MIN. • MAKES: 4 SERVINGS

½ lb. bulk pork sausage
1 medium onion, finely chopped
2 tsp. chicken bouillon granules
½ tsp. garlic powder
½ tsp. pepper
2 medium red potatoes, cut into ½-in. cubes
2 cups sliced fresh kale
3 cups 2% milk
1 cup heavy whipping cream
1 Tbsp. cornstarch
¼ cup cold water
   Crumbled cooked bacon, optional

1. In a large saucepan, cook sausage and onion over medium heat 4-6 minutes or until sausage is no longer pink and onion is tender, breaking up sausage into crumbles; drain.

2. Stir in the bouillon and seasonings. Add the potatoes, kale, milk and cream; bring to a boil. Reduce heat; simmer, covered, 10-15 minutes or until potatoes are tender.

3. In a small bowl, mix cornstarch and water until smooth; stir into soup. Return to a boil, stirring constantly; cook and stir 1-2 minutes or until thickened. If desired, top with bacon.

1½ CUPS: 504 cal., 38g fat (20g sat. fat), 128mg chol., 881mg sod., 26g carb. (12g sugars, 2g fiber), 15g pro.

PORK & BOK CHOY UDON SOUP

While traveling in Thailand, my husband sampled a local version of this tasty soup from street vendors. We have tried many variations, and this comes the closest to his recollection. We double the recipe so we have lots of leftovers.
—*Donna Noecker, Tulalip, WA*

TAKES: 25 MIN. • MAKES: 6 SERVINGS (2¼ QT).

- 6 oz. dried Japanese udon noodles or fettuccine
- 1 small bunch bok choy, coarsely chopped
- 1 pork tenderloin (1 lb.), cut into ¼-in. slices
- 6 cups reduced-sodium chicken broth
- 3 Tbsp. reduced-sodium soy sauce
- 4 tsp. minced fresh gingerroot
- 3 garlic cloves, minced
  Optional: Thinly sliced green onions and Sriracha chili sauce

1. Cook noodles according to package directions; drain and rinse with water. Meanwhile, in a Dutch oven, combine bok choy, pork, broth, soy sauce, ginger and garlic; bring just to a boil. Reduce heat; gently simmer, uncovered, 5-7 minutes or just until bok choy and pork are tender.

2. Add noodles to soup. Serve immediately. If desired, sprinkle with green onions and serve with chili sauce.

1½ CUPS: 225 cal., 4g fat (1g sat. fat), 42mg chol., 1309mg sod., 24g carb. (5g sugars, 3g fiber), 25g pro.

LENTIL-TOMATO SOUP

Double the recipe and share this fabulous soup with friends and neighbors on cold winter nights. I serve it with cornbread for dunking.
—*Michelle Curtis, Baker City, OR*

PREP: 15 MIN. • COOK: 30 MIN. • MAKES: 6 SERVINGS

- 4½ cups water
- 4 medium carrots, sliced
- 1 medium onion, chopped
- ⅔ cup dried brown lentils, rinsed
- 1 can (6 oz.) tomato paste
- 2 Tbsp. minced fresh parsley
- 1 Tbsp. brown sugar
- 1 Tbsp. white vinegar
- 1 tsp. garlic salt
- ½ tsp. dried thyme
- ¼ tsp. dill weed
- ¼ tsp. dried tarragon
- ¼ tsp. pepper

In a large saucepan, combine the water, carrots, onion and lentils; bring to a boil. Reduce the heat; cover and simmer for 20-25 minutes or until vegetables and lentils are tender. Stir in the remaining ingredients; return to a boil. Reduce heat; simmer, uncovered, for 5 minutes to allow flavors to blend.

¾ CUP: 138 cal., 0 fat (0 sat. fat), 0 chol., 351mg sod., 27g carb. (9g sugars, 9g fiber), 8g pro. DIABETIC EXCHANGES: 1 starch, 1 vegetable, 1 lean meat.

FOR SAUSAGE VARIATION: Stir in ½ lb. chopped fully cooked turkey sausage; heat through.

SHORTCUT MINESTRONE

This soup is hearty and makes a comforting lunch or dinner on a brisk day. The spaghetti sauce provides rich flavor without a long simmering time. I further cut the prep time by using my food processor to chop the vegetables.
—*Barbara Jellison, Bellevue, WA*

PREP: 20 MIN. • **COOK:** 15 MIN. • **MAKES:** 10 SERVINGS (2½ QT.)

- 4 bacon strips, diced
- 1 large onion, chopped
- 3 medium carrots, chopped
- 3 garlic cloves, minced
- 1 jar (28 oz.) spaghetti sauce
- 4 cups beef broth
- 1 can (16 oz.) kidney beans, rinsed and drained
- 1 can (15 oz.) garbanzo beans or chickpeas, rinsed and drained
- ⅔ cup uncooked small shell pasta
- 2 tsp. brown sugar
- ½ tsp. dried basil
- ½ tsp. dried oregano
- 1 cup frozen cut green beans
  Grated Parmesan cheese, optional

1. In a Dutch oven or soup kettle, cook bacon over medium heat until crisp. Using a slotted spoon, remove to paper towels. Drain, reserving 2 Tbsp. drippings; set the bacon aside. In the drippings, saute onion and carrots until tender, 3-4 minutes. Add the garlic; cook 2 minutes longer.

2. Stir in the spaghetti sauce, broth and beans. Bring to a boil. Add the pasta, brown sugar, basil and oregano. Cook, uncovered, until the pasta is tender, 8-10 minutes, stirring occasionally. Add green beans; cook until heated through, about 5 minutes longer. Garnish with reserved bacon and Parmesan cheese if desired.

1 CUP: 188 cal., 3g fat (1g sat. fat), 2mg chol., 560mg sod., 31g carb. (0 sugars, 7g fiber), 10g pro. **DIABETIC EXCHANGES:** 2 starch, ½ meat.

FROM GRANDMA'S KITCHEN: Replace the shell pasta with any other pasta shape you love, such as farfalle, fusilli, ditalini, cavatappi or whatever small pasta you have in the pantry.

MAGIC BROWNIE
BARS, PAGE 227

GRANDMA'S FAVORITE

COOKIES, BROWNIES & BARS

Take a note from Grandma and bake up several batches of these mouthwatering treats—it will be hard to stop after having just one!

DOUBLE-LAYER CHEESECAKE BARS

Can't choose between chocolate or vanilla cheesecake?
Have both when you make this bar recipe with two distinct layers.
—*Andrea Price, Grafton, WI*

PREP: 35 MIN. • BAKE: 30 MIN. + CHILLING • MAKES: 2 DOZEN

1 **pkg. yellow cake mix (regular size)**
¼ **cup canola oil**
3 **large eggs, divided use**
1¼ **cups milk chocolate chips, divided**
3 **pkg. (8 oz. each) cream cheese, softened**
½ **cup sugar**
½ **cup sour cream**
½ **cup heavy whipping cream**
1 **tsp. vanilla extract**

1. Preheat oven to 350°. Reserve 1 cup dry cake mix for filling. In a large bowl, combine oil, 1 egg and remaining cake mix; stir until blended. Stir in ½ cup chocolate chips. Press onto the bottom of a greased 13x9-in. baking pan. Bake until set, 10-12 minutes.

2. Meanwhile, in a large bowl, beat cream cheese and sugar until smooth. Beat in sour cream, heavy cream, vanilla and reserved cake mix. Add the remaining 2 eggs; beat on low speed just until blended. Remove 2 cups for chocolate topping; pour remaining batter over crust.

3. For topping, melt remaining ¾ cup chocolate chips. Stir into reserved cream cheese mixture; spoon over filling. Bake until center is almost set, 30-35 minutes. Cool 1 hour on a wire rack. Refrigerate at least 4 hours before serving. Refrigerate leftovers.

1 BAR: 292 cal., 19g fat (10g sat. fat), 61mg chol., 248mg sod., 28g carb. (19g sugars, 1g fiber), 4g pro.

LAVENDER LEMON BARS

Hints of lavender and lemon zest in the crust make these treats a favorite.
—*Judith Hilinski, Cuyahoga Falls, OH*

PREP: 20 MIN. • BAKE: 20 MIN. • MAKES: 2 DOZEN

¾ **cup butter, softened**
½ **cup confectioners' sugar**
2 **cups all-purpose flour**
½ **cup ground almonds**
2 **tsp. dried lavender flowers**
2 **tsp. grated lemon zest**

TOPPING
1¾ **cups sugar**
⅓ **cup all-purpose flour**
½ **tsp. baking soda**
4 **large eggs**
⅓ **cup lemon juice**
Confectioners' sugar

1. Preheat oven to 350°. In a small bowl, cream the butter and confectioners' sugar. Add flour, almonds, lavender and lemon zest; beat until crumbly. Pat into an ungreased 13x9-in. baking dish. Bake 15 minutes or until edges are golden brown.

2. Meanwhile, in another small bowl, combine sugar, flour, baking soda, eggs and lemon juice; beat until frothy. Pour over hot crust. Return to oven and bake for 20-25 minutes or until light golden brown. Cool on a wire rack. Cut into bars; dust with confectioners' sugar. Refrigerate leftovers.

NOTE: Look for dried lavender flowers in spice shops. If using lavender from the garden, make sure it hasn't been treated with chemicals.

1 BAR: 185 cal., 8g fat (4g sat. fat), 51mg chol., 95mg sod., 27g carb. (17g sugars, 1g fiber), 3g pro.

GRANDMA'S SECRET

Use a hot wet knife to get clean-cut pieces of cheesecake bars. Just make sure that you take the time to clean the knife between slices.

DOUBLE-LAYER
CHEESECAKE BARS

PEANUT BUTTER
BROWNIE BITES

PEANUT BUTTER BROWNIE BITES

I used to make these brownie bites with a cherry in the center. Then I discovered that my granddaughter Lily is big on peanut butter, so I switched it up. Now she loves to help me make them.
—*Donna McGinnis, Taylor Ridge, IL*

PREP: 20 MIN. • BAKE: 20 MIN. + COOLING • MAKES: 3½ DOZEN

1 pkg. fudge brownie mix
(13x9-in. pan size)

FROSTING
½ cup creamy peanut butter
3 oz. cream cheese, softened
2 cups confectioners' sugar
4 tsp. 2% milk
1 tsp. vanilla extract
Chopped salted peanuts, optional

1. Preheat oven to 350°. Line 42 mini-muffin cups with paper or foil liners.

2. Prepare brownie mix batter according to package directions. Fill prepared cups two-thirds full. Bake until a toothpick inserted in center comes out clean, 18-22 minutes (do not overbake).

3. Place pans on wire racks. Using the end of a wooden spoon handle, make a ½-in.-deep indentation in the center of each brownie. Cool for 10 minutes before removing from pans.

4. For frosting, in a large bowl, beat the peanut butter and cream cheese until blended. Gradually beat in confectioners' sugar, milk and vanilla until smooth. Spoon or pipe frosting into indentations. If desired, sprinkle with chopped peanuts. Refrigerate leftovers.

1 BROWNIE BITE: 134 cal., 7g fat (1g sat. fat), 11mg chol., 71mg sod., 16g carb. (12g sugars, 0 fiber), 2g pro.

OAT-RAGEOUS CHOCOLATE CHIP COOKIES

My aunt gave me this recipe, and my family thinks these cookies are delicious.
We enjoy all kinds of cookies and with this recipe. We can combine
three of our favorites—oatmeal, peanut butter and chocolate chip—in one!
—*Jaymie Noble, Kalamazoo, MI*

PREP: 25 MIN. • BAKE: 10 MIN./BATCH • MAKES: 3 DOZEN

½ cup butter, softened
½ cup creamy peanut butter
½ cup sugar
⅓ cup packed brown sugar
1 large egg, room temperature
½ tsp. vanilla extract
1 cup all-purpose flour
½ cup quick-cooking oats
1 tsp. baking soda
¼ tsp. salt
1 cup semisweet chocolate chips

In a bowl, cream butter, peanut butter and sugars; beat in egg and vanilla. Combine flour, oats, baking soda and salt. Add to creamed mixture and mix well. Stir in chocolate chips. Drop by rounded tablespoonfuls onto ungreased baking sheets. Bake at 350° for 10-12 minutes or until lightly browned.

1 COOKIE: 104 cal., 6g fat (3g sat. fat), 12mg chol., 90mg sod., 12g carb. (8g sugars, 1g fiber), 2g pro.

BEST DATE BARS

These wholesome bar cookies freeze well. Simply cool them in the pan,
cut into squares and then store in freezer containers.
—Dorothy DeLeske, Scottsdale, AZ

PREP: 25 MIN. • BAKE: 35 MIN. • MAKES: 40 BARS

2½ cups pitted dates, cut up
¼ cup sugar
1½ cups water
⅓ cup coarsely chopped
   walnuts, optional
1¼ cups all-purpose flour
½ tsp. salt
½ tsp. baking soda
1½ cups quick-cooking oats
1 cup packed brown sugar
½ cup butter, softened
1 Tbsp. water

1. In a saucepan, combine dates, sugar and water. Cook, stirring frequently, until very thick. Stir in walnuts if desired; cool.

2. Sift the flour, salt and baking soda together in a large bowl; add oats and brown sugar. Cut in butter until mixture is crumbly. Sprinkle water over mixture; stir lightly. Pat half into a greased 13x9-in. baking pan. Spread with the date mixture; cover with remaining oat mixture and pat lightly.

3. Bake at 350° for 35-40 minutes or until lightly browned. Cool on a wire rack. Cut into bars.

1 BAR: 97 cal., 3g fat (2g sat. fat), 6mg chol., 65mg sod., 19g carb. (12g sugars, 1g fiber), 1g pro.

FROM GRANDMA'S KITCHEN: There are two main kinds of dates that are readily available, medjool or deglet noor dates. While it's really a personal preference, medjool dates are naturally sweeter than deglet noor dates, and may be better for these bars.

CHOCOLATY S'MORES BARS

One night my husband had some friends over to play poker and he requested these s'mores bars.
They polished off the pan and asked for more! I shared the recipe, and now their families make them, too.
—Rebecca Shipp, Beebe, AR

PREP: 15 MIN. + COOLING • MAKES: 1½ DOZEN

¼ cup butter, cubed
1 pkg. (10 oz.) large
   marshmallows
1 pkg. (12 oz.) Golden
   Grahams cereal
⅓ cup milk chocolate chips,
   melted

1. In a large saucepan, melt the butter over low heat. Add marshmallows; cook and stir until blended. Remove from heat. Stir in cereal until coated.

2. Press into a greased 13x9-in. pan using a buttered spatula. Drizzle with melted chocolate. Cool completely before cutting. Store in an airtight container.

1 BAR: 159 cal., 4g fat (2g sat. fat), 7mg chol., 197mg sod., 30g carb. (17g sugars, 1g fiber), 1g pro.

FROM GRANDMA'S KITCHEN: Use a butter wrapper to press the cereal into the pan; it helps keep your hands from getting sticky!

CRUNCHY APRICOT-COCONUT BALLS

My mom gave me this no-bake cookie recipe years ago when she had them on her Christmas buffet. I can't believe how simple they are to make.
—*Jane Whittaker, Pensacola, FL*

TAKES: 30 MIN. • MAKES: 2 DOZEN

1¼ cups sweetened shredded coconut
1 cup dried apricots, finely chopped
⅔ cup chopped pecans
½ cup fat-free sweetened condensed milk
½ cup confectioners' sugar

1. In a small bowl, combine coconut, apricots and pecans. Add condensed milk; mix well (mixture will be sticky).

2. Shape into 1¼-in. balls and roll in confectioners' sugar. Store in an airtight container in the refrigerator.

1 BALL: 87 cal., 4g fat (2g sat. fat), 1mg chol., 19mg sod., 12g carb. (10g sugars, 1g fiber), 1g pro.

MANGO GETAWAY BARS

I've always enjoyed the flavor of mango, so I created this recipe to feature the sweet tropical fruit.
—*Patricia Harmon, Baden, PA*

PREP: 25 MIN. • BAKE: 25 MIN. • MAKES: 3 DOZEN

½ cup macadamia nuts
2¼ cups all-purpose flour, divided
½ cup confectioners' sugar
½ tsp. salt
1 cup cold butter, cubed
1 medium mango, peeled and chopped
½ cup orange marmalade
½ cup sugar
4 large eggs
1 tsp. grated lemon zest
1 cup sweetened shredded coconut

1. Place nuts in a food processor; cover and process until finely chopped. Add 2 cups flour, confectioners' sugar and salt; cover and process until blended. Add butter; pulse just until mixture is crumbly. Press into an ungreased 13x9-in. baking pan. Bake at 350° for 15-20 minutes or until lightly browned.

2. In a clean food processor, combine the mango and orange marmalade; cover and process until smooth. Add sugar and remaining flour; process until combined. Add eggs and lemon zest; process just until combined. Pour over crust. Sprinkle with coconut.

3. Bake until golden brown around the edges, 23-28 minutes. Cool on a wire rack. Cut into bars. Refrigerate leftovers.

1 BAR: 139 cal., 8g fat (4g sat. fat), 37mg chol., 91mg sod., 16g carb. (9g sugars, 1g fiber), 2g pro.

GRANDMA'S
CHRISTMAS SPICE
CUTOUTS

GRANDMA'S CHRISTMAS SPICE CUTOUTS

My great-grandmother made these, and the tradition was passed down in the family—
without a written recipe! My mother would always start them the day after Thanksgiving,
which was exciting for us kids, as we knew Christmas wasn't far off.
—*Elaine Phelps, Cornell, WI*

PREP: 1 HOUR 20 MIN. + CHILLING • BAKE: 10 MIN./BATCH • MAKES: ABOUT 7 DOZEN

2 cups molasses
2 cups dark corn syrup
½ cup shortening, melted
2 Tbsp. white vinegar
1 Tbsp. cold water
10 cups all-purpose flour
1 tsp. baking soda
1 tsp. powdered star anise
¼ tsp. ground cloves
⅛ tsp. ground cinnamon
⅛ tsp. ground nutmeg
Dash salt

1. Combine the first 5 ingredients. Whisk together remaining ingredients; add to molasses mixture and mix well. Refrigerate, covered, 3 hours or overnight.

2. Preheat oven to 375°. On a lightly floured surface, roll out dough to ⅛-in. thickness. Cut into desired shapes with floured 2-in. cookie cutters; place 1 in. apart on greased baking sheets. Bake until set, 10-12 minutes. Remove to wire racks to cool.

1 COOKIE: 109 cal., 1g fat (0 sat. fat), 0 chol., 47mg sod., 23g carb. (12g sugars, 0 fiber), 2g pro. DIABETIC EXCHANGES: 1½ starch.

ICED ORANGE CUTOUTS

I put a tablespoon of orange zest in both the dough and icing to make
these crispy cookies nice and bright, like little rays of sunshine.
—*Wendy Montecalvo, Pleasantville, NJ*

PREP: 45 MIN. + CHILLING • BAKE: 10 MIN./BATCH + COOLING • MAKES: ABOUT 4 DOZEN

2½ cups all-purpose flour
⅓ cup sugar
1 to 2 Tbsp. grated
    orange zest
1 cup cold butter, cubed
2 to 4 Tbsp. ice water

ICING
3 cups confectioners' sugar
¼ cup orange juice
1 Tbsp. grated orange zest

1. Whisk flour, sugar and orange zest; cut in butter until crumbly. Gradually add ice water, tossing with a fork until the dough holds together when pressed. Knead gently until dough forms. Divide dough in half; shape each into a disk. Wrap and refrigerate 1 hour.

2. Preheat oven to 350°. On a lightly floured surface, gently roll dough to ⅛-in. thickness. Cut with a floured 2¼-in. scalloped or plain round cookie cutter. Place 1 in. apart on ungreased baking sheets. Bake until the bottoms are light brown, 10-12 minutes. Remove from pans to wire racks to cool completely.

3. For icing, mix the confectioners' sugar, orange juice and zest until smooth. Spread over cookies. Let stand at room temperature until set.

1 COOKIE: 89 cal., 4g fat (2g sat. fat), 10mg chol., 30mg sod., 13g carb. (9g sugars, 0 fiber), 1g pro.

BANANA SPLIT CAKE BARS

Summer isn't summer without a banana split or two, and these
fun bars bring that same delicious flavor in potluck-perfect form.
—*Jasey McBurnett, Rock Springs, WY*

PREP: 25 MIN. • **BAKE:** 25 MIN. + COOLING • **MAKES:** 2 DOZEN

½ cup butter, softened

1½ cups sugar

2 large eggs, room
temperature

1½ cups mashed ripe
bananas (about 3 large)

1 cup sour cream

2 tsp. vanilla extract

2 cups all-purpose flour

1 tsp. baking soda

¾ tsp. salt

2 jars (10 oz. each)
maraschino cherries,
drained and chopped

2 cups semisweet
chocolate chips

1 pkg. (10 oz.) miniature
marshmallows
Optional: Chopped salted
peanuts and banana
slices or dried banana
chips

1. Preheat oven to 375°. Grease a 15x10x1-in. baking pan.

2. In a large bowl, beat butter and sugar until crumbly, about
2 minutes. Add eggs; mix well. Beat in bananas, sour cream
and vanilla. In another bowl, whisk flour, baking soda and salt;
gradually add to butter mixture. Transfer to prepared pan.

3. Bake until a toothpick inserted in center comes out clean,
18-20 minutes. Top the cake with cherries, chocolate chips,
marshmallows and, if desired, peanuts. Bake until chips are
slightly melted and marshmallows puff, 3-5 minutes longer.
Cool completely in pan on a wire rack; cut into bars. If desired,
top with banana slices or banana chips before serving.

1 BAR: 294 cal., 11g fat (6g sat. fat), 28mg chol., 177mg sod.,
52g carb. (38g sugars, 1g fiber), 3g pro.

FROM GRANDMA'S KITCHEN: Plan to eat these topping-laden bars
with a fork to scoop up all the goodness that falls off.

JELLY-TOPPED SUGAR COOKIES

On busy days, I appreciate this fast-to-fix drop sugar cookie.
Top each cookie with your favorite flavor of jam or jelly.
—*June Quinn, Kalamazoo, MI*

PREP: 20 MIN. • **COOK:** 10 MIN./BATCH • **MAKES:** ABOUT 3½ DOZEN

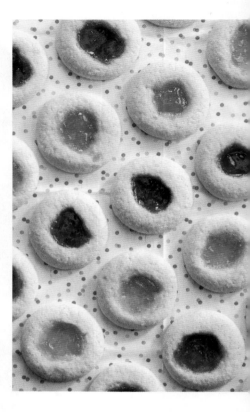

¾ cup plus 3 Tbsp.
   sugar, divided
¾ cup canola oil
2 large eggs
2 tsp. vanilla extract
1 tsp. lemon extract

1 tsp. grated lemon zest
2 cups all-purpose flour
2 tsp. baking powder
½ tsp. salt
1 cup jam or jelly

1. Preheat oven to 400°. In a large bowl, beat ¾ cup sugar and oil until blended. Beat in eggs, extracts and lemon zest. Combine the flour, baking powder and salt; gradually add to sugar mixture and mix well.

2. Drop tablespoonfuls of dough 2 in. apart onto ungreased baking sheets. Sprinkle with remaining 3 Tbsp. sugar. Press a deep indentation in the center of each cookie with the back of a rounded teaspoon.

3. Place ½ tsp. jelly in the center of each cookie. Bake until set, 6-8 minutes. Remove to wire racks to cool.

1 COOKIE: 97 cal., 4g fat (0 sat. fat), 9mg chol., 58mg sod., 14g carb. (8g sugars, 0 fiber), 1g pro.

FROM GRANDMA'S KITCHEN: Jam and jelly cookie fillings tend to loosen up a bit as they thaw after being frozen, so it's best for these cookies to be made fresh and enjoyed right away.

PUMPKIN BARS WITH BROWNED BUTTER FROSTING

I based this recipe on one my grandmother used to make, so sweet memories are baked into every bar. When making the frosting, carefully watch the butter and remove it from the heat as soon as it starts to brown. Do not use margarine.
—Mary Wilhelm, Sparta, WI

PREP: 30 MIN. • BAKE: 20 MIN. + COOLING • MAKES: 2 DOZEN

1½ cups sugar
1 cup canned pumpkin
½ cup orange juice
½ cup canola oil
2 large eggs
2 tsp. grated orange zest
2 cups all-purpose flour
2 tsp. baking powder
2 tsp. pumpkin pie spice
1 tsp. baking soda
¼ tsp. salt

FROSTING
⅔ cup butter, cubed
4 cups confectioners' sugar
1 tsp. vanilla extract
4 to 6 Tbsp. 2% milk

1. Preheat oven to 350°. Grease a 15x10x1-in. baking pan. In a large bowl, beat first 6 ingredients until well blended. In another bowl, whisk the flour, baking powder, pie spice, baking soda and salt; gradually beat into pumpkin mixture.

2. Transfer to prepared pan. Bake for 18-22 minutes or until a toothpick inserted in center comes out clean. Cool completely in pan on a wire rack.

3. In a small heavy saucepan, melt butter over medium heat. Heat 5-7 minutes or until golden brown, stirring constantly. Transfer to a large bowl. Gradually beat in confectioners' sugar, vanilla and enough milk to reach desired consistency. Spread over top; let stand until set. Cut into bars.

1 BAR: 265 cal., 10g fat (4g sat. fat), 29mg chol., 166mg sod., 42g carb. (33g sugars, 1g fiber), 2g pro.

GOLDEN M&M'S BARS

Our family loves to go on drives, and I often bring these bars along for snacking in the car.
—Martha Haseman, Hinckley, IL

PREP: 15 MIN. • BAKE: 25 MIN. • MAKES: 2 DOZEN

½ cup butter, softened
¾ cup sugar
¾ cup packed brown sugar
2 tsp. vanilla extract
2 large eggs, room temperature
1½ cups all-purpose flour
1 tsp. baking powder
½ tsp. salt
1 cup white baking chips
1¾ cups plain M&M's, divided

1. Preheat oven to 350°. In a large bowl, cream butter, sugars and vanilla until light and fluffy, 5-7 minutes. Beat in eggs, 1 at a time. Whisk together the flour, baking powder and salt; gradually add to the creamed mixture. Stir in baking chips and 1 cup M&M's.

2. Spread evenly into a greased 13x9-in. baking pan. Sprinkle with the remaining ¾ cup M&M's. Bake until golden brown and a toothpick inserted in the center comes out with moist crumbs, 25-30 minutes. Cool on a wire rack. Cut into bars.

1 BAR: 233 cal., 10g fat (6g sat. fat), 29mg chol., 123mg sod., 34g carb. (27g sugars, 1g fiber), 2g pro.

PISTACHIO BUTTONS

This cookie recipe makes a big batch, which comes in handy
during the holidays. The green center adds a festive touch.
—*Nella Parker, Hersey, MI*

PREP: 30 MIN. + CHILLING • **BAKE:** 10 MIN./BATCH • **MAKES:** ABOUT 10 DOZEN

½ **cup butter, softened**
¾ **cup sugar**
1 **large egg, room temperature**
1 **tsp. almond extract**
¼ **tsp. vanilla extract**
2 **cups all-purpose flour**
1 **tsp. baking powder**
½ **tsp. salt**
1 **oz. unsweetened chocolate, melted**
⅓ **cup finely chopped pistachios**
5 **drops green food coloring, optional**

1. Cream butter and sugar until light and fluffy, 5-7 minutes. Beat in egg and extracts. In another bowl, whisk together flour, baking powder and salt; gradually beat into creamed mixture.

2. Divide dough in half. Mix melted chocolate into 1 portion; mix pistachios and, if desired, food coloring into remaining portion. Divide each dough into 4 portions.

3. On a lightly floured surface, roll 1 chocolate portion into an 8x3-in. rectangle. Roll 1 green portion into an 8-in. log; place on chocolate rectangle 1 in. from a long side. Roll chocolate dough around green log; pinch seam to seal. Wrap in waxed paper. Repeat with remaining dough. Refrigerate until firm, about 1 hour.

4. Preheat oven to 350°. Unwrap and cut dough into ¼-in. slices. Place 2 in. apart on lightly greased baking sheets. Bake until set, 8-10 minutes. Remove from pans to wire racks to cool.

1 COOKIE: 23 cal., 1g fat (1g sat. fat), 4mg chol., 22mg sod., 3g carb. (1g sugars, 0 fiber), 0 pro.

"This cookie was very easy to make and very good. It's something different and festive to add to my cookie trays this year."
—LESLIW122858, TASTEOFHOME.COM

CARAMEL PECAN SHORTBREAD

My grandchildren look for Grandma's candy bar cookies every Christmas.
I recommend doubling the recipe for these sweet treats because they go so fast.
—*Dorothy Buiter, Worth, IL*

PREP: 30 MIN. + CHILLING • **BAKE:** 15 MIN./BATCH + COOLING • **MAKES:** ABOUT 4 DOZEN

¾ **cup butter, softened**
¾ **cup confectioners' sugar**
2 **Tbsp. evaporated milk**
1 **tsp. vanilla extract**
2 **cups all-purpose flour**
¼ **tsp. salt**

FILLING
28 **caramels**
6 **Tbsp. evaporated milk**
2 **Tbsp. butter**
½ **cup confectioners' sugar**
¾ **cup finely chopped pecans**

ICING
1 **cup semisweet chocolate chips**
3 **Tbsp. evaporated milk**
2 **Tbsp. butter**
½ **cup confectioners' sugar**
½ **tsp. vanilla extract**
Pecan halves

1. In a large bowl, cream butter and confectioners' sugar until light and fluffy, 3-4 minutes. Beat in milk and vanilla. Combine flour and salt; gradually add to the creamed mixture. Cover and refrigerate for 1 hour or until easy to handle.

2. On a lightly floured surface, roll out dough to ¼-in. thickness. Cut into 2x1-in. strips. Place 1 in. apart on greased baking sheets.

3. Bake at 325° for 12-14 minutes or until lightly browned. Remove to wire racks to cool completely.

4. For filling, combine the caramels and milk in a large saucepan. Cook and stir over medium-low heat until caramels are melted and smooth. Remove from the heat; stir in the butter, sugar and pecans. Cool for 5 minutes. Spread 1 tsp. over each cookie.

5. For icing, in a microwave-safe bowl, melt chips and milk; stir until smooth. Stir in butter, confectioners' sugar and vanilla until smooth. Cool for 5 minutes.

6. Spread 1 tsp. icing on each cookie; top each with a pecan half. Let stand until set. Store in an airtight container.

1 COOKIE: 126 cal., 7g fat (3g sat. fat), 12mg chol., 61mg sod., 16g carb. (10g sugars, 1g fiber), 1g pro.

"I have to hide these in order to keep them for Christmas Day! It's a delicious recipe, and so easy to make."
—TKARINAS, TASTEOFHOME.COM

CARAMEL SNICKERDOODLE BARS

What did I do when I couldn't decide between two of my favorite desserts? I combined them!
This snickerdoodle-blondie hybrid is even better with my other favorite ingredient: caramel.
—*Niki Plourde, Gardner, MA*

PREP: 30 MIN. + CHILLING • BAKE: 25 MIN. + COOLING • MAKES: 4 DOZEN

1 cup butter, softened
2 cups packed brown sugar
2 large eggs, room temperature
2 tsp. vanilla extract
2½ cups all-purpose flour
2 tsp. baking powder
1 tsp. salt
¼ cup sugar
3 tsp. ground cinnamon
2 cans (13.4 oz. each) dulce de leche
12 oz. white baking chocolate, chopped
⅓ cup heavy whipping cream
1 Tbsp. light corn syrup

1. Preheat oven to 350°. Line a 13x9-in. baking pan with parchment, letting ends extend 1 in. over the sides.

2. In a large bowl, cream butter and brown sugar until light and fluffy, 3-4 minutes; beat in the eggs and vanilla. In another bowl, whisk flour, baking powder and salt; gradually beat into creamed mixture. Spread onto bottom of prepared pan.

3. In a small bowl, mix sugar and cinnamon; sprinkle 2 Tbsp. mixture over batter. Bake for 25-30 minutes or until the edges are light brown. Cool completely in pan on a wire rack.

4. Spread dulce de leche over crust. In a small saucepan, combine white baking chocolate, cream and corn syrup; cook and stir over low heat until smooth. Cool slightly. Spread over dulce de leche. Sprinkle with remaining cinnamon sugar. Refrigerate, covered, at least 1 hour.

5. Lifting with parchment, remove from pan. Cut into bars. Refrigerate leftovers.

NOTE: This recipe was tested with Nestle La Lechera dulce de leche; look for it in the international foods section. If using Eagle Brand dulce de leche (caramel flavored sauce), thicken according to package directions before using.

1 BAR: 197 cal., 8g fat (5g sat. fat), 27mg chol., 137mg sod., 28g carb. (23g sugars, 0 fiber), 2g pro.

FROM GRANDMA'S KITCHEN: To help the dulce de leche layer set up a bit, pop it into the fridge for 30 minutes before adding the white chocolate layer.

MAGIC BROWNIE BARS

One of my all-time favorite treats as a kid was magic cookie bars.
This recipe combines all the same classic flavors in a brownie!
—*Mandy Rivers, Lexington, SC*

PREP: 15 MIN. • BAKE: 35 MIN. + COOLING • MAKES: 3 DOZEN

1 **pkg. (17½ oz.) brownie mix**	1 **cup chopped pecans, optional**
1 **pkg. (11 oz.) butterscotch chips**	1 **can (14 oz.) sweetened condensed milk**
2 **cups sweetened shredded coconut**	

1. Preheat oven to 350°. Line a 13x9-in. baking pan with foil, letting ends extend up sides; grease foil.

2. Prepare brownie mix batter according to package directions. Transfer to prepared pan. Top with butterscotch chips, coconut and, if desired, pecans. Drizzle with milk. Bake until topping is light golden, 35-40 minutes.

3. Cool completely in pan on a wire rack. Lifting with foil, remove brownies from pan. Cut into bars. Store in an airtight container.

1 BAR: 200 cal., 10g fat (5g sat. fat), 14mg chol., 91mg sod., 25g carb. (21g sugars, 1g fiber), 3g pro.

SALTED NUT SQUARES

A favorite of young and old, this recipe came from my sister-in-law. It's
simple to prepare and delicious. There's no need to keep it warm or cold,
so it's perfect for the potluck that has you traveling longer distances.
—*Kathy Tremel, Earling, IA*

PREP: 15 MIN. + CHILLING • MAKES: 32 SQUARES

3 **cups salted peanuts without skins, divided**
2 **Tbsp. plus 1½ tsp. butter**
2 **cups peanut butter chips**
1 **can (14 oz.) sweetened condensed milk**
2 **cups miniature marshmallows**

1. Place half of the peanuts in an ungreased 11x7-in. dish; set aside. In a large saucepan, melt butter and peanut butter chips over low heat. Add the milk and marshmallows; cook and stir until melted.

2. Pour over peanuts. Sprinkle with the remaining peanuts. Cover and refrigerate until chilled. Cut into squares.

1 SQUARE: 194 cal., 12g fat (4g sat. fat), 7mg chol., 95mg sod., 16g carb. (13g sugars, 2g fiber), 7g pro.

RED VELVET
PEPPERMINT
THUMBPRINTS

RED VELVET PEPPERMINT THUMBPRINTS

I love red velvet cookies and cakes. In this pretty thumbprint cookie, I added my favorite holiday ingredient: peppermint. It's a fun seasonal twist!
—*Priscilla Yee, Concord, CA*

PREP: 30 MIN. • BAKE: 10 MIN./BATCH + COOLING • MAKES: ABOUT 4 DOZEN

1 cup butter, softened
1 cup sugar
1 large egg, room temperature
4 tsp. red food coloring
1 tsp. peppermint extract
2½ cups all-purpose flour
3 Tbsp. baking cocoa
1 tsp. baking powder
¼ tsp. salt
2 cups white baking chips
2 tsp. canola oil
¼ cup crushed peppermint candies

1. Preheat oven to 350°. In a large bowl, cream butter and sugar until light and fluffy, 5-7 minutes. Beat in egg, food coloring and extract. In another bowl, whisk flour, cocoa, baking powder and salt; gradually beat into creamed mixture.

2. Shape dough into 1-in. balls. Place 1 in. apart on ungreased baking sheets. Press a deep indentation in center of each with the end of a wooden spoon handle.

3. Bake 9-11 minutes or until set. Remove from pans to wire racks to cool completely.

4. In a microwave, melt baking chips with oil; stir until smooth. Spoon a scant teaspoon filling into each cookie. Drizzle the tops with remaining mixture. Sprinkle with peppermint candies. Let stand until set.

1 COOKIE: 118 cal., 7g fat (4g sat. fat), 16mg chol., 63mg sod., 14g carb. (9g sugars, 0 fiber), 1g pro.

BUTTERSCOTCH-TOFFEE CHEESECAKE BARS

I'd been making lemon cheesecake bars for years and wanted a new flavor combo. Using the original bar as a starting point, I decided to try a butterscotch and toffee version. The results were great!
—*Pamela Shank, Parkersburg, WV*

PREP: 15 MIN. • BAKE: 30 MIN. + CHILLING • MAKES: 2 DOZEN

1 pkg. yellow cake mix (regular size)
1 pkg. (3.4 oz.) instant butterscotch pudding mix
⅓ cup canola oil
2 large eggs, divided use
1 pkg. (8 oz.) cream cheese, softened
⅓ cup sugar
1 cup brickle toffee bits, divided
½ cup butterscotch chips

1. Preheat oven to 350°. In a large bowl, combine the cake mix, pudding mix, oil and 1 egg; mix until crumbly. Reserve 1 cup for topping. Press the remaining mixture into an ungreased 13x9-in. baking pan. Bake 10 minutes. Cool completely on a wire rack.

2. In a small bowl, beat cream cheese and sugar until smooth. Add remaining egg; beat on low speed just until combined. Fold in ½ cup toffee bits. Spread over crust. Sprinkle with reserved crumb mixture. Bake for 15-20 minutes or until filling is set.

3. Sprinkle with butterscotch chips and remaining ½ cup toffee bits. Return to oven; bake 1 minute longer. Cool on a wire rack 1 hour. Refrigerate 2 hours or until cold. Cut into bars.

1 BAR: 257 cal., 13g fat (6g sat. fat), 31mg chol., 297mg sod., 34g carb. (22g sugars, 0 fiber), 2g pro.

CARAMEL CHIP BISCOTTI

The combination of caramel and chocolate in these delicate Italian biscuits is to die for. It's divine dunked in coffee or a sweet wine, or even enjoyed on its own.
—*Tami Kuehl, Loup City, NE*

PREP: 30 MIN. • BAKE: 30 MIN. + COOLING • MAKES: 2 DOZEN

½ cup butter, softened
1 cup sugar
2 large eggs, room temperature
1 tsp. vanilla extract
2½ cups all-purpose flour
1½ tsp. baking powder
¼ tsp. salt
1 cup Kraft caramel bits
1 cup semisweet chocolate chips
3 oz. white candy coating, melted

1. Preheat oven to 325°. Cream the butter and sugar until light and fluffy, 5-7 minutes; beat in the eggs and vanilla. In another bowl, whisk together flour, baking powder and salt; gradually beat into creamed mixture (dough will be stiff). Stir in caramel bits and chocolate chips.

2. Divide the dough into 3 portions. On parchment-lined baking sheets, shape each portion into a 7x3-in. rectangle. Bake until a toothpick inserted in center comes out clean, 20-25 minutes. Cool on pans on wire racks 5 minutes.

3. On a cutting board, use a serrated knife to cut each rectangle crosswise into 8 slices. Place slices on baking sheets, cut side down. Bake until crisp, 10-12 minutes per side. Remove from pans to wire racks; cool completely.

4. Drizzle melted candy coating over tops; let stand until set. Store between pieces of waxed paper in airtight containers.

1 COOKIE: 206 cal., 8g fat (5g sat. fat), 26mg chol., 115mg sod., 32g carb. (21g sugars, 1g fiber), 2g pro.

FROM GRANDMA'S KITCHEN: Instead of the semisweet chocolate, you can try other flavors of baking chips, such as butterscotch, dark chocolate, milk chocolate, espresso or peanut butter chips.

SURPRISE MERINGUES

My crisp, delicate cookies are light as a feather. Miniature chocolate chips and chopped nuts are a delightful and yummy surprise in every bite. This fun cookie is a fitting finale to a big meal.

—Gloria Grant, Sterling, IL

PREP: 15 MIN. • BAKE: 40 MIN./BATCH + COOLING • MAKES: 4 DOZEN

3 large egg whites
1 tsp. vanilla extract
⅛ tsp. cream of tartar
⅛ tsp. salt
¾ cup sugar

1 cup miniature semisweet chocolate chips
¼ cup chopped pecans or walnuts

1. Place egg whites in a large bowl; let stand for 30 minutes. Add the vanilla, cream of tartar and salt; beat on medium speed until soft peaks form. Gradually add sugar, 1 Tbsp. at a time, beating on high until stiff glossy peaks form and sugar is dissolved, about 6 minutes. Fold in chocolate chips and nuts.

2. Drop by rounded teaspoonfuls 2 in. apart onto parchment-lined baking sheets. Bake at 250° for 40-45 minutes or until firm to the touch. Turn the oven off; leave meringues in oven for 1½ hours. Remove to wire racks. Store in an airtight container.

1 MERINGUE: 70 cal., 3g fat (1g sat. fat), 0 chol., 20mg sod., 11g carb. (10g sugars, 1g fiber), 1g pro.

TOFFEE MERINGUES: Substitute milk chocolate English toffee bits for the chocolate chips.

PEPPERMINT MERINGUES: Omit vanilla extract, chocolate chips and nuts. Finely crush 2 peppermint candy canes; sprinkle over meringues just before baking.

MERINGUE KISSES: Omit chocolate chips and nuts. Drop meringue by tablespoonfuls onto parchment-lined baking sheets. Press a chocolate kiss into the center of each and cover with meringue, using a knife. Bake at 275° for 30-35 minutes or until firm to the touch. Immediately remove to a wire rack to cool.

BUTTERY SPRITZ COOKIES

This tender spritz cookie recipe is very eye-catching on my Christmas cookie tray.
The dough is easy to work with, so it's fun to make these into a variety of festive shapes.
—*Beverly Launius, Sandwich, IL*

PREP: 20 MIN. • BAKE: 10 MIN./BATCH + COOLING • MAKES: ABOUT 7½ DOZEN

1 cup butter, softened
2¼ cups confectioners' sugar, divided
½ tsp. salt
1 large egg, room temperature
1 tsp. vanilla extract
½ tsp. almond extract
2½ cups all-purpose flour
2 to 3 Tbsp. water
Colored sugar and sprinkles
Melted semisweet chocolate, optional

1. Preheat oven to 375°. In a large bowl, cream butter, 1¼ cups confectioners' sugar and salt until light and fluffy, 3-4 minutes. Beat in the egg and extracts. Gradually beat the flour into the creamed mixture.

2. Using a cookie press fitted with a disk of your choice, press the dough 2 in. apart onto ungreased baking sheets. Bake until set, 6-8 minutes (do not brown). Remove cookies to wire racks to cool completely.

3. In a small bowl, mix remaining 1 cup confectioners' sugar and enough water to reach desired consistency. Dip cookies in glaze; sprinkle with colored sugar and sprinkles. Let stand until set. Or, if desired, dip in melted chocolate, decorate and let stand until set.

1 COOKIE: 43 cal., 2g fat (1g sat. fat), 7mg chol., 30mg sod., 6g carb. (3g sugars, 0 fiber), 0 pro.

FROM GRANDMA'S KITCHEN: For a fun pop of extra color, try dyeing the dough your favorite color with a few drops of the right food coloring.

GREAT-GRANDMA'S OATMEAL COOKIES

This yummy cookie—a favorite of my husband's—goes back to my great-grandmother.
At Christmastime, we use colored sugar for a festive touch.
—*Mary Ann Konechne, Kimball, SD*

PREP: 35 MIN. • BAKE: 15 MIN./BATCH • MAKES: 12 DOZEN

1½ cups shortening
2 cups sugar
4 large eggs, room
   temperature
4 tsp. water
4 cups all-purpose flour
2 tsp. baking soda
2 tsp. ground cinnamon
½ tsp. salt
4 cups quick-cooking oats
2 cups chopped raisins
1 cup chopped walnuts
   Additional sugar or
   colored sugar

1. Preheat oven to 350°. Cream shortening and sugar until light and fluffy, 5-7 minutes. Add eggs, 1 at a time, beating well after each addition. Beat in the water. In another bowl, whisk together flour, baking soda, cinnamon and salt; add to creamed mixture and mix well. Stir in oats, raisins and walnuts.

2. On a surface sprinkled with additional sugar, roll the dough to ¼-in. thickness. Cut with a floured 2½-in. cookie cutter into desired shapes. Place 2 in. apart on greased baking sheets. Bake until set, 12-15 minutes. Remove to wire racks to cool.

1 COOKIE: 63 cal., 3g fat (1g sat. fat), 5mg chol., 28mg sod., 9g carb. (4g sugars, 0 fiber), 1g pro.

FROM GRANDMA'S KITCHEN: If you want to add a sweet icing, mix 1 cup confectioners' sugar with ¼ tsp. cinnamon and 5-6 tsp. water to make a quick glaze.

CONFETTI CAKE BATTER COOKIES

Mom and I took up cake decorating. Funfetti was our favorite cake, so we used the mix to make cutout cookies. Plain or decorated, they're a fave at parties.
—*Danielle DeMarco, Basking Ridge, NJ*

PREP: 15 MIN. + CHILLING • BAKE: 10 MIN./BATCH + COOLING • MAKES: ABOUT 2 DOZEN

½ cup butter, softened
2 large eggs, room
   temperature
1 tsp. vanilla extract
1 pkg. Funfetti cake mix

1. In a large bowl, beat butter, eggs and vanilla until combined. Beat in cake mix. Refrigerate, covered, 2 hours or until firm enough to roll.

2. Preheat oven to 350°. On a well-floured surface, roll dough to ¼-in. thickness. Cut with a floured 2½-in. cookie cutter. Place 1 in. apart on ungreased baking sheets. Bake until set, 8-10 minutes. Remove from pans to wire racks to cool completely. Decorate as desired.

FREEZE OPTION: Transfer dough to an airtight container; freeze. To use, thaw dough in the refrigerator until soft enough to roll. Prepare and bake cookies as directed; decorate as desired.

1 COOKIE: 102 cal., 5g fat (3g sat. fat), 22mg chol., 144mg sod., 13g carb. (7g sugars, 0 fiber), 1g pro.

GREAT-GRANDMA'S
OATMEAL COOKIES

HONEY BUN CAKE,
PAGE 253

GRANDMA'S FAVORITE

CAKES & PIES

Get family and friends excited for the final course by
serving up some slices of sweetness. They pair best
with good company—and maybe a scoop of ice cream!

BERRY COOL CREAM & PRETZEL PIE

This cool no-bake strawberry pie is the perfect cure for your sweet tooth this summer. Made with pantry staples and as easy as pie to create, it's become one of my family's most requested warm-weather treats.
—*Shauna Havey, Roy, UT*

PREP: 45 MIN. + CHILLING • **MAKES:** 16 SERVINGS

4   cups miniature pretzels
6   Tbsp. butter, melted
¼   cup sugar
¾   cup boiling water
1   pkg. (6 oz.) strawberry gelatin
¼   cup lemon juice
1   lb. fresh strawberries, hulled, divided
2   cups heavy whipping cream, divided
1   jar (7 oz.) marshmallow creme
⅔   cup whipped cream cheese
⅔   cup sweetened condensed milk

1. Place pretzels in a food processor; pulse until chopped. Add butter and sugar; pulse until combined. Reserve ⅓ cup pretzel mixture for topping. Press remaining mixture onto bottom of a greased 9-in. springform pan. Refrigerate 30 minutes.

2. Meanwhile, in a bowl, add boiling water to the gelatin; stir for 2 minutes to completely dissolve. Stir in the lemon juice. Refrigerate 30 minutes, stirring occasionally.

3. Chop half the strawberries; slice remaining berries and reserve for topping. In a large bowl, beat 1 cup heavy cream until stiff peaks form. Beat the marshmallow creme, cream cheese and sweetened condensed milk into cooled gelatin mixture until blended. Gently fold in chopped strawberries and whipped cream. Pour into crust.

4. Refrigerate, covered, until firm, 4-6 hours. Beat remaining 1 cup heavy cream until stiff peaks form; spread over pie. Top with reserved strawberries and pretzel mixture.

1 PIECE: 350 cal., 19g fat (12g sat. fat), 56mg chol., 284mg sod., 39g carb. (30g sugars, 1g fiber), 4g pro.

*"This pie is totally tasty as is and no-bake is always great.
I will make it again!"*
—MARILYNN, TASTEOFHOME.COM

SUGAR CREAM PIE

I absolutely love creamy sugar pie, especially the one that my grandma made for me. Here in Indiana, we serve it warm or chilled.
—*Laura Kipper, Westfield, IN*

PREP: 40 MIN. + CHILLING • **BAKE:** 15 MIN. + CHILLING • **MAKES:** 8 SERVINGS

Dough for single-crust pie
1 cup sugar
¼ cup cornstarch
2 cups 2% milk
½ cup butter, cubed
1 tsp. vanilla extract
¼ tsp. ground cinnamon

1. Preheat oven to 450°. On a lightly floured surface, roll dough to a ⅛-in.-thick circle; transfer to a 9-in. pie plate. Trim crust to ½ in. beyond rim of plate; flute edge. Refrigerate 30 minutes.

2. Line unpricked crust with a double thickness of foil. Fill with pie weights, dried beans or uncooked rice. Bake on a lower oven rack until edge is light golden brown, 15-20 minutes. Remove foil and weights; bake until bottom is golden brown, 3-6 minutes longer. Cool on a wire rack. Reduce oven setting to 375°.

3. Meanwhile, in a large saucepan, combine the sugar and cornstarch; stir in milk until smooth. Bring to a boil. Reduce heat; cook and stir 2 minutes or until thickened and bubbly. Remove from heat; stir in the butter and vanilla. Transfer to crust; sprinkle with cinnamon. Bake until golden brown, 15-20 minutes. Cool on a wire rack; refrigerate until chilled.

DOUGH FOR SINGLE-CRUST PIE (9 IN.): Combine 1¼ cups all-purpose flour and ¼ tsp. salt; cut in ½ cup cold butter until crumbly. Gradually add 3-5 Tbsp. ice water, tossing with a fork until the dough holds together when pressed. Shape into a disk; wrap and refrigerate for 1 hour.

1 PIECE: 418 cal., 24g fat (15g sat. fat), 66mg chol., 275mg sod., 47g carb. (28g sugars, 1g fiber), 4g pro.

FROM GRANDMA'S KITCHEN: Need a Thanksgiving pie? Add ⅛ tsp. each of cloves, nutmeg and ginger when adding the cinnamon. Your home will smell heavenly!

PERFECT RHUBARB PIE

Nothing hides the tangy rhubarb in this lovely pie, which has just the right balance of sweet and tart.
—*Ellen Benninger, Greenville, PA*

PREP: 20 MIN. + STANDING • **BAKE:** 55 MIN. + COOLING • **MAKES:** 8 SERVINGS

4 cups sliced fresh or frozen rhubarb, thawed
4 cups boiling water
1½ cups sugar
3 Tbsp. all-purpose flour
1 tsp. quick-cooking tapioca
1 large egg, room temperature
2 tsp. cold water
Dough for double-crust pie
1 Tbsp. butter

1. Place rhubarb in a colander; pour boiling water over rhubarb and allow to drain. In a large bowl, mix sugar, flour and tapioca. Add the drained rhubarb; toss to coat. Let stand 15 minutes. In a small bowl, whisk egg and cold water; stir into rhubarb mixture.

2. Preheat oven to 400°. On a lightly floured surface, roll half of dough to a ⅛-in.-thick circle; transfer to a 9-in. pie plate. Trim even with rim. Add filling; dot with butter. Roll remaining dough to a ⅛-in.-thick circle. Place over filling. Trim, seal and flute edge. Cut slits in top. Bake 15 minutes.

3. Reduce oven setting to 350°. Bake until crust is golden brown and filling is bubbly, 40-50 minutes longer. Cool on a wire rack.

NOTE: If using frozen rhubarb, measure rhubarb while still frozen, then thaw completely. Drain in a colander, but do not press liquid out.

DOUGH FOR DOUBLE-CRUST PIE (9 IN.): Combine 2½ cups all-purpose flour and ½ tsp. salt; cut in 1 cup cold butter until crumbly. Gradually add ⅓-⅔ cup ice water, tossing with a fork until dough holds together when pressed. Divide dough in half. Shape each into a disk; wrap and refrigerate 1 hour.

1 PIECE: 432 cal., 16g fat (7g sat. fat), 40mg chol., 225mg sod., 69g carb. (40g sugars, 1g fiber), 4g pro.

FROM GRANDMA'S KITCHEN: If you like a thicker filling, bump your tapioca up from a teaspoon to a tablespoon. The pie will cut like a dream!

FANCY FUSS-FREE TORTE

Thanks to frozen pound cake and a can of pie filling, this torte is easy to make. If layers slide, keep them in place with toothpicks around the edges as you build. Just remove before serving.
—*Joan Causey, Greenwood, AR*

TAKES: 15 MIN. • MAKES: 10 SERVINGS

1 loaf (10¾ oz.) frozen pound cake, thawed
1 can (21 oz.) cherry pie filling or flavor of your choice
1 carton (8 oz.) frozen whipped topping, thawed
½ cup chopped pecans

Using a long serrated knife, cut the cake horizontally into 3 layers. Place bottom cake layer on a serving plate; top with half of the pie filling. Repeat layers. Top with remaining cake layer. Frost top and sides of cake with whipped topping. Sprinkle with pecans.

1 PIECE: 287 cal., 13g fat (7g sat. fat), 44mg chol., 122mg sod., 38g carb. (25g sugars, 1g fiber), 3g pro.

GRANDMA MEG'S RAISIN PIE

The wonderful flavor of this old-fashioned pie will take you back in taste and time to Grandma's kitchen.
—*Pat Sisk, South Eglin, IL*

PREP: 20 MIN. • BAKE: 40 MIN. + COOLING • MAKES: 8 SERVINGS

¾ cup sugar
2 Tbsp. cornstarch
¼ tsp. salt
1 cup water
½ cup dark corn syrup
1½ cups raisins
1 Tbsp. lemon juice
2 tsp. butter
Dough for a double-crust pie (p. 242)

1. In a saucepan, combine sugar, cornstarch and salt. Stir in water and corn syrup until blended. Add the raisins. Bring to a boil over medium heat; cook and stir for 2 minutes or thickened. Remove from the heat; stir in lemon juice and butter (filling will be thin).

2. On a lightly floured surface, roll half the dough to a ⅛-in.-thick circle; transfer to 9-in. pie plate. Trim even with rim. Add filling. Roll out remaining dough to ⅛-in.-thick circle; place over filling. Trim, seal and flute edge. Cut slits in top.

3. Bake at 425° for 10 minutes. Reduce heat to 375°; bake 30 minutes longer or until crust is golden brown. Cool on a wire rack.

1 PIECE: 477 cal., 16g fat (7g sat. fat), 15mg chol., 328mg sod., 84g carb. (45g sugars, 1g fiber), 3g pro.

GINGER-STREUSEL PUMPKIN PIE

I love to bake and have spent a lot of time making goodies for my family and friends. The streusel topping gives this pie a special touch your family will love.
—*Sonia Parvu, Sherrill, NY*

PREP: 25 MIN. • **BAKE:** 55 MIN. + COOLING • **MAKES:** 8 SERVINGS

- **1** sheet refrigerated pie crust
- **3** large eggs
- **1** can (15 oz.) solid-pack pumpkin
- **1½** cups heavy whipping cream
- **½** cup sugar
- **¼** cup packed brown sugar
- **1½** tsp. ground cinnamon
- **½** tsp. salt
- **¼** tsp. ground allspice
- **¼** tsp. ground nutmeg
- **¼** tsp. ground cloves

STREUSEL
- **1** cup all-purpose flour
- **½** cup packed brown sugar
- **½** cup cold butter, cubed
- **½** cup chopped walnuts
- **⅓** cup finely chopped crystallized ginger

1. Preheat oven to 350°. On a lightly floured surface, unroll crust. Transfer to a 9-in. pie plate and trim to ½ in. beyond edge of plate; flute edge.

2. In a large bowl, whisk the eggs, pumpkin, cream, sugars, cinnamon, salt, allspice, nutmeg and cloves. Pour into crust. Bake 40 minutes.

3. In a small bowl, combine flour and brown sugar; cut in butter until crumbly. Stir in walnuts and ginger. Gently sprinkle over the filling.

4. Bake 15-25 minutes longer or until a knife inserted in the center comes out clean. Cool on a wire rack. Refrigerate leftovers.

1 PIECE: 684 cal., 42g fat (21g sat. fat), 176mg chol., 388mg sod., 73g carb. (39g sugars, 3g fiber), 9g pro.

EASY PINEAPPLE UPSIDE-DOWN CAKE

Here's a traditional dessert that's been updated with packaged items for convenience. It has the same fabulous flavor as any from-scratch version.
—*Karen Ann Bland, Gove, KS*

PREP: 10 MIN. • **BAKE:** 45 MIN. • **MAKES:** 15 SERVINGS

¼ **cup butter, melted**
1 **can (20 oz.) sliced pineapple**
10 **pecan halves**
1 **jar (12 oz.) apricot preserves**
1 **pkg. yellow cake mix (regular size)**

1. Pour butter into a well-greased 13x9-in. baking dish. Drain pineapple, reserving ¼ cup juice. Arrange pineapple slices in the prepared pan; place a pecan half in the center of each slice. Combine the apricot preserves and reserved pineapple juice; spoon over pineapple slices.

2. Prepare cake batter according to package directions; pour over pineapple.

3. Bake at 350° for 45-50 minutes or until a toothpick inserted in the center comes out clean. Immediately invert onto a large serving platter. Cool slightly; serve warm.

1 PIECE: 252 cal., 7g fat (3g sat. fat), 8mg chol., 260mg sod., 47g carb. (33g sugars, 1g fiber), 2g pro.

BERRY NUT TARTS

Cranberries are a delicious addition to this spin on individual pecan pies. Folks have a hard time eating only one.
—*Lena Ehlert, Vancouver, BC*

PREP: 25 MIN. + CHILLING • **BAKE:** 25 MIN. + COOLING • **MAKES:** ABOUT 1 DOZEN

½ **cup butter, softened**
3 **oz. cream cheese, softened**
1 **cup all-purpose flour**

FILLING
1½ **cups packed brown sugar**
2 **Tbsp. butter, melted**
2 **large eggs, lightly beaten**
2 **tsp. vanilla extract**
⅔ **cup finely chopped cranberries**
⅓ **cup chopped pecans**

1. In a small bowl, beat butter and cream cheese until creamy; gradually add flour and mix well. Cover and refrigerate 1 hour or until easy to handle.

2. Cut dough into 12 portions. Press onto the bottom and all the way up the sides of greased muffin cups. In a large bowl, combine the brown sugar, butter, eggs and vanilla. Stir in the cranberries and pecans. Spoon into prepared crusts.

3. Bake at 350° until edges are golden brown, 25-30 minutes. Cool for 5 minutes before removing from pan to a wire rack to cool completely. Store in the refrigerator.

1 TART: 289 cal., 15g fat (8g sat. fat), 69mg chol., 139mg sod., 36g carb. (28g sugars, 1g fiber), 3g pro.

COCONUT FUDGE CAKE

A big piece of this delectable cake is a chocolate and coconut devotee's dream.
You should see my husband, children and grandkids smile when I serve it.
—*Johnnie McLeod, Bastrop, LA*

PREP: 40 MIN. • **BAKE:** 1 HOUR + COOLING • **MAKES:** 16 SERVINGS

1 cup buttermilk
1 cup canola oil
1 cup brewed coffee, chilled
2 large eggs, room temperature
1 tsp. vanilla extract
3 cups all-purpose flour
2 cups sugar
¾ cup baking cocoa
2 tsp. baking powder
1½ tsp. baking soda
1½ tsp. salt
½ cup chopped pecans

FILLING
2 Tbsp. all-purpose flour, divided
1 pkg. (8 oz.) cream cheese, softened
¼ cup sugar
1 large egg, room temperature
1 tsp. vanilla extract
1 cup semisweet chocolate chips
½ cup sweetened shredded coconut

CHOCOLATE GLAZE
1 cup confectioners' sugar
3 Tbsp. baking cocoa
2 to 3 Tbsp. hot water
2 Tbsp. butter, melted
2 tsp. vanilla extract

1. Preheat oven to 350°. Grease and flour a 10-in. fluted tube pan. In a large bowl, combine buttermilk, oil, coffee, eggs and vanilla. Combine flour, sugar, cocoa, baking powder, baking soda and salt; add to the buttermilk mixture, beating just until combined. Fold in the pecans.

2. Pour half of the batter into prepared pan; sprinkle with 1 Tbsp. flour. In a small bowl, beat cream cheese, sugar, egg and vanilla until smooth. Toss chocolate chips and coconut with remaining 1 Tbsp. flour; fold into cream cheese mixture. Spoon over batter to within ½ in. of edges; top with remaining batter.

3. Bake until a toothpick inserted in the center comes out clean, 60-70 minutes. Cool 20-25 minutes before removing from pan to a wire rack to cool completely.

4. In a small bowl, combine glaze ingredients until smooth. Drizzle over cake.

1 PIECE: 540 cal., 29g fat (8g sat. fat), 54mg chol., 508mg sod., 68g carb. (44g sugars, 3g fiber), 7g pro.

FROM GRANDMA'S KITCHEN: Tossing the chocolate chips and coconut with flour helps to keep them from sinking to the bottom of the pan. To remove cakes easily, use solid shortening to grease plain and fluted tube pans.

GRAPEFRUIT YOGURT CAKE

We eat grapefruit for breakfast and in winter fruit salads—
why not for dessert? Here's a sweet-tart cake that's easy,
delicious and one of a kind. It's healthier too!
—*Maiah Miller, Montclair, VA*

PREP: 10 MIN. • **BAKE:** 25 MIN. + COOLING • **MAKES:** 12 SERVINGS

1½ **cups all-purpose flour**
2 **tsp. baking powder**
¼ **tsp. salt**
3 **large eggs, room temperature**
1 **cup fat-free plain yogurt**
⅓ **cup sugar**
5 **Tbsp. grated grapefruit zest**
¼ **cup agave nectar or honey**

½ **tsp. vanilla extract**
¼ **cup canola oil**

GLAZE
½ **cup confectioners' sugar**
2 **to 3 tsp. grapefruit juice**
   Optional: Grapefruit wheels and fresh mint leaves

1. Preheat oven to 350°. Whisk together flour, baking powder and salt. Combine next 7 ingredients. Gradually stir the flour mixture into yogurt mixture, then pour into a 9-in. round baking pan coated with cooking spray. Bake until a toothpick inserted in center of cake comes out clean, 25-30 minutes. Cool.

2. For glaze, mix confectioners' sugar with enough grapefruit juice to reach desired consistency; drizzle the glaze over top, allowing some to flow over sides. Top cake with grapefruit and mint if desired.

FREEZE OPTION: Omit glaze. Securely wrap cooled cake and freeze. To use, thaw at room temperature. Prepare glaze; top as directed.

1 PIECE: 187 cal., 6g fat (1g sat. fat), 47mg chol., 159mg sod., 30g carb. (17g sugars, 1g fiber), 4g pro. **DIABETIC EXCHANGES:** 2 starch, 1 fat.

FROM GRANDMA'S KITCHEN: Any citrus works well in this cake. If grapefruit isn't your thing, use lemon, orange or lime zest and juice.

OLD-FASHIONED JAM CAKE

I remember my Aunt Murna telling me she made this cake often when she was a young girl. Through the years, she made improvements to it, and her cake become a real family favorite. It has been a popular staple at our reunions.
—*Janet Robinson, Lawrenceburg, KY*

PREP: 25 MIN. + STANDING • BAKE: 40 MIN. + COOLING • MAKES: 16 SERVINGS

1 cup raisins
1 can (8 oz.) crushed pineapple, undrained
1 cup butter, softened
1 cup sugar
4 large eggs, room temperature
3 cups all-purpose flour
⅓ cup baking cocoa
1 tsp. baking soda
1 tsp. ground cinnamon
1 tsp. ground nutmeg
½ tsp. ground cloves
1 jar (12 oz.) or 1 cup blackberry jam
⅔ cup buttermilk
1 cup chopped pecans

CARAMEL ICING

1 cup butter, cubed
2 cups packed brown sugar
½ cup 2% milk
3½ to 4 cups confectioners' sugar

1. In a small bowl, combine raisins and pineapple; let stand for at least 30 minutes.

2. In a large bowl, cream butter and sugar until light and fluffy, 5-7 minutes. Add the eggs, 1 at a time, beating well after each addition. Combine dry ingredients; gradually add to creamed mixture alternately with jam and buttermilk, beating well after each addition. Stir in raisin mixture and nuts.

3. Spread into 2 greased and floured 9-in. round baking pans. Bake at 350° for 40-45 minutes or until a toothpick inserted in the center comes out clean. Cool for 10 minutes before removing from pans to wire racks to cool completely.

4. For icing, in a large saucepan, melt the butter over medium heat. Stir in the sugar and milk. Bring to a boil. Remove from the heat; cool until just warm. Pour into a large bowl; beat in enough confectioners' sugar to achieve a spreading consistency. Spread frosting between layers and over the top and side of cake.

1 PIECE: 702 cal., 30g fat (15g sat. fat), 116mg chol., 353mg sod., 107g carb. (86g sugars, 2g fiber), 6g pro.

CARROT SHEET CAKE

We sold pieces of this to-die-for carrot cake at an art show.
Before long, we sold all 10 cakes we had made!
—*Dottie Cosgrove, South El Monte, CA*

PREP: 20 MIN. • **BAKE:** 35 MIN. + COOLING • **MAKES:** 30 SERVINGS

4 large eggs, room
  temperature
1 cup canola oil
2 cups sugar
2 cups all-purpose flour
2 tsp. baking soda
¼ tsp. baking powder
2 tsp. ground cinnamon
½ tsp. salt
3 cups shredded carrots
⅔ cup chopped walnuts

FROSTING

1 pkg. (8 oz.) cream cheese,
  softened
½ cup butter, softened
1 tsp. vanilla extract
4 cups confectioners' sugar
⅔ cup chopped walnuts

1. Preheat oven to 350°. In a bowl, beat eggs, oil and sugar until smooth. Combine flour, baking soda, baking powder, cinnamon and salt; add to the egg mixture and beat well. Stir in the carrots and walnuts. Pour into a greased 15x10x1-in. baking pan. Bake until a toothpick inserted in the center comes out clean, about 35 minutes. Cool on a wire rack.

2. For frosting, beat cream cheese, butter and vanilla in a bowl until smooth; beat in confectioners' sugar. Spread over cake. Sprinkle with nuts. Decorate as desired. Store in the refrigerator.

1 PIECE: 311 cal., 17g fat (5g sat. fat), 45mg chol., 193mg sod., 38g carb. (29g sugars, 1g fiber), 4g pro.

SHOOFLY CHOCOLATE PIE

If you like traditional shoofly pie, the chocolate version is even better!
I sometimes serve it with vanilla ice cream, but it's just as good on its own.
—*Gwen Brounce Widdowson, Fleetwood, PA*

PREP: 20 MIN. • **BAKE:** 45 MIN. + COOLING • **MAKES:** 8 SERVINGS

Pastry for single-crust
  pie (p. 241)
½ cup semisweet chocolate
  chips
1½ cups all-purpose flour
½ cup packed brown sugar
3 Tbsp. butter-flavored
  shortening
1 tsp. baking soda
1½ cups water
1 large egg, room
  temperature,
  lightly beaten
1 cup molasses

1. Roll out dough to fit a 9-in. deep-dish pie plate or cast-iron skillet. Trim to ½ in. beyond rim of plate; flute edge. Sprinkle chocolate chips into crust; set aside.

2. In a large bowl, combine flour and brown sugar; cut in shortening until crumbly. Set aside 1 cup for topping. Add baking soda, water, egg and molasses to remaining crumb mixture and mix well. Pour over the chips. Sprinkle with reserved crumb mixture.

3. Bake at 350° until a knife inserted in the center comes out clean, 45-55 minutes. Let stand on a wire rack for 15 minutes before cutting. Serve warm.

1 PIECE: 526 cal., 20g fat (10g sat. fat), 53mg chol., 341mg sod., 83g carb. (49g sugars, 2g fiber), 6g pro.

GRANDMA'S SECRET

Whenever you're making a frosted cake and want a clean finished product, use an offset spatula. It allows you to get professional-looking, smooth frosting.

CARROT SHEET CAKE

CARAMEL-PECAN
CHEESECAKE PIE

CARAMEL-PECAN CHEESECAKE PIE

In fall or any time of year, this nutty, rich and delicious pecan pie recipe is one I am proud to serve. While it seems very special, this caramel pecan cheesecake is a snap to make.
—*Becky Ruff, McGregor, IA*

PREP: 15 MIN. • **BAKE:** 35 MIN. + CHILLING • **MAKES:** 8 SERVINGS

1 **sheet refrigerated pie crust**
1 **pkg. (8 oz.) cream cheese, softened**
½ **cup sugar**
4 **large eggs, room temperature, divided use**
1 **tsp. vanilla extract**
1¼ **cups chopped pecans**
1 **jar (12¼ oz.) fat-free caramel ice cream topping**
Additional fat-free caramel ice cream topping, optional

1. Preheat the oven to 375°. Line a 9-in. deep-dish pie plate or cast-iron skillet with crust. Trim and flute the edge. In a small bowl, beat cream cheese, sugar, 1 egg and vanilla until smooth. Spread into crust; sprinkle with pecans.

2. In a small bowl, whisk remaining eggs; gradually whisk in caramel topping until blended. Pour slowly over pecans.

3. Bake for 35-40 minutes or until lightly browned (loosely cover edge with foil after 20 minutes if pie browns too quickly). Cool on a wire rack 1 hour. Refrigerate 4 hours or overnight before slicing. If desired, garnish with additional caramel ice cream topping.

1 PIECE: 502 cal., 33g fat (11g sat. fat), 142mg chol., 277mg sod., 45g carb. (26g sugars, 2g fiber), 8g pro.

HONEY BUN CAKE

PICTURED ON PAGE 236

I take along recipe cards to hand out when I bring this moist, fluffy cake to school socials and the like. It always goes quickly.
—*Kathy Mayo, Winston-Salem, NC*

PREP: 20 MIN. • **BAKE:** 35 MIN. • **MAKES:** 20 SERVINGS

1 **pkg. yellow or white cake mix (regular size)**
4 **large egg whites**
1 **cup sour cream**
⅔ **cup unsweetened applesauce**
½ **cup packed brown sugar**
2 **tsp. ground cinnamon**
1½ **cups confectioners' sugar**
2 **Tbsp. 2% milk**
1 **tsp. vanilla extract**

1. Preheat oven to 325°. In a large bowl, combine dry cake mix, egg whites, sour cream and applesauce. Beat on low speed until moistened. Beat on medium for 2 minutes.

2. Pour half into a greased 13x9-in. baking pan. Combine brown sugar and cinnamon; sprinkle over batter. Cover with remaining batter; cut through with a knife to swirl. Bake until a toothpick comes out clean, 35-40 minutes. Cool on a wire rack.

3. For glaze, combine confectioners' sugar, milk and vanilla until smooth; drizzle over warm cake.

1 PIECE: 185 cal., 3g fat (2g sat. fat), 9mg chol., 204mg sod., 38g carb. (27g sugars, 0 fiber), 2g pro.

PRUNE CAKE WITH GLAZE

This cake recipe was given to me years ago by a friend, who got it from her mother.
I'm 82 years old; I've been married 57 years, and I still enjoy baking this cake for my husband.
—*Laura Olson, Mesa, AZ*

PREP: 15 MIN. • **BAKE:** 45 MIN. • **MAKES:** 16 SERVINGS

1½ cups sugar
2 cups all-purpose flour
1 tsp. baking soda
1 tsp. ground nutmeg
1 tsp. ground cinnamon
1 tsp. salt
1 cup canola oil
3 large eggs, beaten
½ cup buttermilk
1 tsp. vanilla extract
1 cup chopped pitted dried plums (prunes), cooked
1 cup chopped nuts

TOPPING

½ cup butter, cubed
⅓ cup buttermilk
1 tsp. vanilla extract
½ tsp. baking soda
¾ cup sugar

1. Preheat the oven to 350°. In a large bowl, combine the first 6 ingredients. Add oil, eggs, buttermilk and vanilla; mix well. Fold in prunes and nuts. Pour into an ungreased 13x9-in. baking pan. Bake until toothpick comes out clean, about 45 minutes.
2. Meanwhile, combine all topping ingredients in a saucepan. Bring to a boil and boil for 2 minutes. Pour over hot cake. Leave in pan to cool.

1 PIECE: 437 cal., 25g fat (6g sat. fat), 51mg chol., 351mg sod., 48g carb. (32g sugars, 2g fiber), 5g pro.

FROM GRANDMA'S KITCHEN: To cook prunes, combine 2 cups water per pound of dried prunes in a saucepan; bring to a boil, then remove from the heat and let cool.

CHERRY DREAM CAKE

I serve this because it's so festive and easy. No one will know
your secret is adding a package of gelatin to a boxed cake mix!
—*Margaret McNeil, Germantown, TN*

PREP: 15 MIN. + CHILLING • **BAKE:** 30 MIN. + COOLING • **MAKES:** 20 SERVINGS

1 pkg. white cake mix (regular size)
1 pkg. (3 oz.) cherry gelatin
1½ cups boiling water
1 pkg. (8 oz.) cream cheese, softened
2 cups frozen whipped topping
1 can (21 oz.) cherry pie filling

1. Prepare cake mix according to package directions, using a greased 13x9-in. baking pan. Bake at 350° for 30-35 minutes or until a toothpick comes out clean.

2. Dissolve gelatin in boiling water. Cool cake on a wire rack 3-5 minutes. Poke holes in cake with a meat fork or wooden skewer; gradually pour gelatin over cake. Cool for 15 minutes. Cover and refrigerate for 30 minutes.

3. In a large bowl, beat cream cheese until fluffy. Fold in whipped topping. Carefully spread over cake. Top with pie filling. Cover and refrigerate for at least 2 hours before serving.

1 PIECE: 245 cal., 11g fat (5g sat. fat), 39mg chol., 242mg sod., 34g carb. (22g sugars, 1g fiber), 3g pro.

MINI BLUEBERRY BUNDT CAKES
PICTURED ON COVER

These pretty little blueberry cakes are topped with a yummy lemon-flavored glaze. This recipe makes 12 tiny cakes, so one batch gives you plenty of sweet treats to share with friends.
—*Cathy Isaak, Rivers, MB*

PREP: 20 MIN. • **BAKE:** 30 MIN. + COOLING • **MAKES:** 1 DOZEN

1 **cup butter, softened**
2 **cups sugar**
4 **large eggs, room temperature**
2 **tsp. vanilla extract**
4 **cups all-purpose flour**
1 **tsp. baking powder**
1 **tsp. salt**

1 **cup 2% milk**
4 **cups fresh blueberries**

LEMON ICING
2 **cups confectioners' sugar**
2 **Tbsp. 2% milk**
4 **tsp. lemon juice**

1. Preheat oven to 350°. In a large bowl, cream butter and sugar until light and fluffy, 5-7 minutes. Beat in the eggs and vanilla. In another bowl, combine the flour, baking powder and salt; add to creamed mixture alternately with milk, beating well after each addition. Fold in blueberries.

2. Scoop into 12 greased 4-in. fluted tube pans. Place pans on a large baking sheet. Bake until a toothpick inserted in the center comes out clean, 30-35 minutes. Cool for 10 minutes before removing from tube pans to wire racks to cool completely.

3. For icing, in a small bowl, combine the confectioners' sugar, milk and lemon juice; drizzle over cakes. If desired, garnish with additional blueberries.

NOTE: If using frozen blueberries, use without thawing to avoid discoloring the batter.

1 MINI CAKE: 560 cal., 18g fat (11g sat. fat), 105mg chol., 395mg sod., 94g carb. (59g sugars, 2g fiber), 8g pro.

GRANDMA RILEY'S BANANA CAKE

This favorite recipe has been passed down through my husband's family. His grandmother wrote this out for me shortly after we were married. She copied it from a recipe that her mother had written out for her many years before. These handwritten treasures in my recipe box bring back so many fond memories.
—*Jamie Dunn, Milwaukee, WI*

PREP: 15 MIN. • **BAKE:** 25 MIN. + COOLING • **MAKES:** 12 SERVINGS

1½ **cups sugar**
½ **cup shortening**
2 **large eggs, room temperature**
1 **tsp. vanilla**
½ **cup buttermilk**
3 **mashed ripe bananas**
2 **cups flour**
1 **tsp. baking soda**
1 **tsp. baking powder**
½ **tsp. salt**

FROSTING
½ **cup butter, softened**
2½ **cups confectioners' sugar**
3 **Tbsp. 2% milk**
1 **tsp. vanilla**
Dash of salt

1. Cream sugar and shortening together; add eggs and vanilla. Mix in buttermilk and mashed bananas.

2. In a separate bowl, combine flour, soda, baking powder and salt; add to the banana mixture and mix until ingredients are combined. Spoon into a greased 13x9-in. baking pan or two 9-in. round cake pans.

3. Bake at 350° for 25-30 minutes or until toothpick inserted into center comes out clean. Cool cake for 30 minutes before frosting.

4. For frosting, mix butter, confectioners' sugar and milk until smooth; add vanilla and salt. If frosting is too thick, add more milk 1 tsp. at a time until reaching desired consistency. Spread on warm banana cake.

NOTE: For each cup of buttermilk, you can use 1 Tbsp. of white vinegar or lemon juice plus enough milk to measure 1 cup. Stir, then let stand 5 minutes. You can also use 1 cup of plain yogurt or 1¾ tsp. cream of tartar plus 1 cup milk.

1 PIECE: 458 cal., 17g fat (7g sat. fat), 52mg chol., 351mg sod., 74g carb. (54g sugars, 1g fiber), 4g pro.

HONEY CRAN-RASPBERRY PIE

This is my son Michael's recipe. It was passed down to him when he got married in 2002. The pie is quite tart, but it pairs well with a favorite vanilla ice cream or a dollop of whipped cream.
—*Beverly Batty, Forest Lake, MN*

PREP: 30 MIN. + CHILLING • **BAKE:** 45 MIN. + COOLING • **MAKES:** 8 SERVINGS

1 **large egg**
3 **to 4 Tbsp. ice water**
1 **Tbsp. cider vinegar**
2 **cups all-purpose flour**
¾ **tsp. salt**
½ **cup butter-flavored shortening**
¼ **cup lard**
1¼ **cups plus 2 Tbsp. sugar, divided**
5 **Tbsp. quick-cooking tapioca**
3 **cups fresh or frozen cranberries, halved**
2½ **cups fresh or frozen unsweetened raspberries, thawed**
⅓ **cup honey**
1 **tsp. almond extract**
½ **tsp. ground cinnamon Dairy-free vanilla ice cream, optional**

1. In a small bowl, whisk egg, 3 Tbsp. ice water and vinegar until blended. In a large bowl, mix flour and salt; cut in shortening and lard until crumbly. Gradually add egg mixture, tossing with a fork, until the dough holds together when pressed. If mixture is too dry, slowly add more ice water, a teaspoon at a time, just until the mixture comes together.

2. Divide the dough in half. Shape each into a disk; wrap and refrigerate 1 hour or overnight.

3. On a lightly floured surface, roll 1 portion of dough to a ⅛-in.-thick circle; transfer to a 9-in. deep-dish pie plate. Trim crust even with rim. Refrigerate for 30 minutes. Meanwhile, preheat oven to 425°. In a large bowl, mix 1¼ cups sugar and tapioca. Add the cranberries, raspberries, honey and almond extract; toss to coat evenly. Let stand 15 minutes.

4. Pour filling into pie plate. Roll remaining dough to a ⅛-in.-thick circle. Place over filling. Trim, seal and flute edge. Cut slits in top. Combine cinnamon and remaining 2 Tbsp. sugar; sprinkle over top. Place pie on a baking sheet; bake 10 minutes.

5. Reduce oven setting to 350°. Bake until crust is golden brown and filling is bubbly, 35-40 minutes. Cool the pie on a wire rack. If desired, serve with ice cream.

1 PIECE: 532 cal., 20g fat (6g sat. fat), 29mg chol., 233mg sod., 86g carb. (49g sugars, 5g fiber), 5g pro.

TO MAKE SUGARED CRANBERRIES: Heat 3 Tbsp. light corn syrup in microwave until warm; gently toss with 1 cup fresh or frozen cranberries, allowing excess syrup to drip off. Toss in ⅓ cup sugar to coat. Place on waxed paper; let stand until set, about 1 hour.

GINGER PLUM TART

Sweet cravings, begone: This free-form plum tart is done
in only 35 minutes. Plus, it's extra-awesome when served warm.
—Taste of Home *Test Kitchen*

PREP: 15 MIN. • BAKE: 20 MIN. + COOLING • MAKES: 8 SERVINGS

1 **sheet refrigerated pie crust**
3½ **cups sliced fresh plums (about 10 medium)**
3 **Tbsp. plus 1 tsp. coarse sugar, divided**
1 **Tbsp. cornstarch**
2 **tsp. finely chopped crystallized ginger**
1 **large egg white**
1 **Tbsp. water**

1. Preheat oven to 400°. On a work surface, unroll crust. Roll to a 12-in. circle. Transfer to a parchment-lined baking sheet.

2. In a large bowl, toss plums with 3 Tbsp. sugar and cornstarch. Arrange the plums on crust to within 2 in. of edge; sprinkle with ginger. Fold crust edge over plums, pleating as you go.

3. In a small bowl, whisk egg white and water; brush over folded crust. Sprinkle with remaining sugar.

4. Bake until crust is golden brown, 20-25 minutes. Cool in pan on a wire rack. Serve warm or at room temperature.

1 PIECE: 190 cal., 7g fat (3g sat. fat), 5mg chol., 108mg sod., 30g carb. (14g sugars, 1g fiber), 2g pro. **DIABETIC EXCHANGES:** 1½ starch, 1 fat, ½ fruit.

CLASSIC SWEET POTATO PIE

This simple but special deep-dish pie provides a down-home finish to hearty autumn meals served at home. Pecans and pumpkin pie spice make this a comforting seasonal classic.
—Paul Azzone, Shoreham, NY

PREP: 25 MIN. • BAKE: 45 MIN. + COOLING • MAKES: 8 SERVINGS

1⅔ **cups pie crust mix**
¼ **cup finely chopped pecans**
3 **to 4 Tbsp. cold water**
3 **large eggs, room temperature**
2 **cans (15 oz. each) sweet potatoes, drained**
1 **can (14 oz.) sweetened condensed milk**
1½ **to 2 tsp. pumpkin pie spice**
1 **tsp. vanilla extract**
½ **tsp. salt**
  Optional: Whipped cream and additional chopped pecans, toasted

1. In a small bowl, combine pie crust mix and pecans. Gradually add water, tossing with a fork until dough forms a ball. Roll out to fit a 9-in. deep-dish pie plate or cast-iron skillet. Transfer crust to pie plate. Flute edge; set aside.

2. In a food processor, combine the eggs, sweet potatoes, milk, pumpkin pie spice, vanilla and salt; blend until smooth. Pour into the crust.

3. Bake at 425° for 15 minutes. Reduce the heat to 350°; bake for 30-35 minutes longer or until a knife inserted in the center comes out clean. Cool on a wire rack. Garnish with whipped cream and toasted pecans if desired.

1 PIECE: 417 cal., 17g fat (6g sat. fat), 96mg chol., 436mg sod., 59g carb. (42g sugars, 3g fiber), 9g pro.

GINGER PLUM TART

GRANDMA'S SECRET
If you don't like plums, or they're not in-season where you live, you can also swap in apples, pears or peaches for this tart! Just make sure you choose a fruit that pairs well with ginger.

PATCHWORK QUILT CAKE

This cake has a great homemade flavor and tender crumb.
Be sure to pile on the buttery frosting, which adds a burst of vanilla.
—*Aria Thornton, Milwaukee, WI*

PREP: 55 MIN. • **BAKE:** 40 MIN. + COOLING • **MAKES:** 15 SERVINGS

⅔ cup butter, softened
1¾ cups sugar
1 Tbsp. vanilla extract
2 large eggs, room
   temperature
2½ cups all-purpose flour
2½ tsp. baking powder
½ tsp. salt
1¼ cups 2% milk

FROSTING
1 cup butter, softened
3 cups confectioners' sugar
4 tsp. vanilla extract
3 to 4 Tbsp. heavy
   whipping cream
   Assorted fresh berries

1. Preheat oven to 350°. Grease a 13x9-in. baking dish.

2. Cream butter and sugar until light and fluffy, 5-7 minutes. Add vanilla and eggs, 1 at at time, beating well. In another bowl, whisk together flour, baking powder and salt; beat into creamed mixture alternately with milk. Transfer to prepared dish.

3. Bake until a toothpick inserted in the center comes out clean, 40-45 minutes. Place on a wire rack; cool completely.

4. For frosting, beat butter until creamy; gradually beat in confectioners' sugar until smooth and light in color, about 3 minutes. Beat in vanilla and 3 Tbsp. cream until light and fluffy, about 2 minutes; thin with additional cream if desired. Spread over cake. Before serving, top with the berries in a patchwork quilt pattern.

1 PIECE: 477 cal., 23g fat (14g sat. fat), 84mg chol., 342mg sod., 65g carb. (48g sugars, 1g fiber), 4g pro.

CREAM-FILLED CUPCAKES

These chocolate cupcakes have a fun filling and shiny chocolate frosting
that make them extra special. They always disappear in a flash!
—Kathy Kittell, Lenexa, KS

PREP: 20 MIN. • BAKE: 15 MIN. + COOLING • MAKES: 2 DOZEN

1 pkg. devil's food cake mix
(regular size)
2 tsp. hot water
¼ tsp. salt
1 jar (7 oz.) marshmallow
creme
½ cup shortening
⅓ cup confectioners' sugar
½ tsp. vanilla extract

GANACHE FROSTING
1 cup semisweet
chocolate chips
¾ cup heavy
whipping cream

1. Prepare and bake the cake batter according to package directions, using 24 paper-lined muffin cups. Cool 5 minutes before removing from pans to wire racks to cool completely.

2. For filling, in a small bowl, combine water and salt until salt is dissolved. Cool. In a small bowl, beat the marshmallow creme, shortening, confectioners' sugar and vanilla until light and fluffy; beat in the salt mixture.

3. Cut a small hole in the corner of a pastry bag; insert round pastry tip. Fill the bag with cream filling. Push tip through top of each cupcake to fill center.

4. Place chocolate chips in a small bowl. In a small saucepan, bring cream just to a boil. Pour over chocolate; whisk until smooth. Cool, stirring occasionally, to room temperature or until ganache reaches a dipping consistency.

5. Dip cupcake tops in ganache; chill for 20 minutes or until set. Store in the refrigerator.

1 CUPCAKE: 262 cal., 15g fat (5g sat. fat), 32mg chol., 223mg sod., 29g carb. (20g sugars, 1g fiber), 2g pro.

LEMON CHESS PIE

This luscious, lemony pie cuts beautifully and has a smooth texture. It's one of my favorites.
—Hannah LaRue Rider, East Point, KY

PREP: 15 MIN. • BAKE: 35 MIN. + CHILLING • MAKES: 8 SERVINGS

1 sheet refrigerated
pie crust
4 large eggs, room
temperature
1½ cups sugar
½ cup lemon juice
¼ cup butter, melted
1 Tbsp. cornmeal
2 tsp. all-purpose flour
⅛ tsp. salt
Confectioners' sugar,
optional

1. Preheat oven to 350°. Unroll crust into a 9-in. pie plate; flute edge. In a large bowl, beat eggs for 3 minutes. Gradually add sugar; beat until mixture becomes thick and lemon-colored, about 2 minutes. Beat in lemon juice, butter, cornmeal, flour and salt.

2. Pour into crust. Bake until a knife inserted in the center comes out clean, 35-40 minutes. Cool on a wire rack 1 hour. Refrigerate at least for 3 hours before serving. If desired, garnish pie with confectioners' sugar.

1 PIECE: 363 cal., 15g fat (7g sat. fat), 113mg chol., 219mg sod., 54g carb. (39g sugars, 0 fiber), 4g pro.

GRANDMA'S MOLASSES FRUITCAKE

This dense, dark, moist fruitcake was my grandmother's recipe.
The flavor just gets better and better as it sits in the fridge, so be sure to make it ahead!
—*Debbie Harmon, Lavina, MT*

PREP: 25 MIN. + CHILLING • BAKE: 1¼ HOURS + COOLING • MAKES: 3 LOAVES (16 PIECES EACH)

3¼ cups dried currants
2⅔ cups raisins
1 cup chopped walnuts
⅔ cup chopped candied citron or candied lemon peel
4 cups all-purpose flour, divided
1 cup butter, softened
2 cups packed brown sugar
4 large eggs, room temperature
1 cup molasses
1 tsp. baking soda
1 tsp. each ground cinnamon, nutmeg and cloves
1 cup strong brewed coffee

1. Preheat oven to 300°. Grease and flour three 9x5-in. loaf pans. Line bottoms with waxed paper; grease and flour the paper. Combine currants, raisins, walnuts, candied citron and ¼ cup flour. Toss to coat; set aside.

2. Cream the butter and brown sugar until light and fluffy, 5-7 minutes. Add eggs, 1 at a time, beating well after each addition. Beat in molasses. In another bowl, whisk baking soda, cinnamon, nutmeg, cloves and remaining flour; add to creamed mixture alternately with coffee. Stir into currant mixture and mix well.

3. Transfer to prepared pans. Bake until a toothpick inserted in the center comes out clean, 1¼-1½ hours. Cool in pans 10 minutes before removing to wire racks to cool completely. Wrap tightly and store in the refrigerator for at least 2 days to blend flavors. Slice and bring to room temperature before serving. Refrigerate leftovers.

1 PIECE: 210 cal., 6g fat (3g sat. fat), 26mg chol., 79mg sod., 39g carb. (28g sugars, 2g fiber), 3g pro.

TO SOAK FRUITCAKES IN ALCOHOL: Using a toothpick, poke holes on all sides of fruitcakes until well perforated. Pour about 1 cup of desired alcohol such as brandy, rum or whiskey into a bowl. Brush some of the alcohol over all sides of fruitcakes. Cut three 36x17-in. pieces of cheesecloth. Let each piece soak in the bowl of alcohol; gently squeezing out some of the excess. Place each fruitcake on a piece of cheesecloth and tightly wrap the cheesecloth around fruitcake. Wrap each loaf tightly in foil and place in the refrigerator. Remove foil and brush each cheesecloth-covered loaf with an additional 2-3 Tbsp. of alcohol once a week for up to one month.

GRANDMA'S
MOLASSES
FRUITCAKE

ELEGANT FRESH BERRY TART

This elegant tart was my first original creation. If other fresh
fruits are used, adjust simple syrup flavor to match.
—*Denise Nakamoto, Elk Grove, CA*

PREP: 45 MIN. + CHILLING • **BAKE:** 10 MIN. + COOLING • **MAKES:** 10 SERVINGS

½ **cup butter, softened**
⅓ **cup sugar**
½ **tsp. grated orange zest**
¼ **tsp. orange extract**
⅛ **tsp. vanilla extract**
1 **cup all-purpose flour**

FILLING
1 **pkg. (8 oz.) cream cheese, softened**
¼ **cup sugar**
½ **tsp. lemon juice**

SYRUP
2 **Tbsp. water**
1½ **tsp. sugar**
1½ **tsp. red raspberry or strawberry preserves**
⅛ **tsp. lemon juice**

TOPPING
¾ **cup fresh strawberries, sliced**
½ **cup fresh raspberries**
½ **cup fresh blueberries**
2 **medium kiwifruit, peeled and sliced**

1. Preheat oven to 375°. Cream butter and sugar until light and fluffy, 5-7 minutes. Add orange zest and extracts; gradually add flour until mixture forms a ball. Press into a greased 9-in. fluted tart pan with a removable bottom. Bake for 10-12 minutes or until golden brown. Cool on a wire rack.

2. For filling, beat cream cheese, sugar and lemon juice until smooth; spread over crust. Cover and refrigerate until set, about 30 minutes.

3. Meanwhile, for syrup, bring the water, sugar, preserves and lemon juice to a boil in a small saucepan. Reduce heat; simmer, uncovered, for 10 minutes. Set aside to cool.

4. Combine strawberries, raspberries, blueberries and kiwi; toss with syrup to glaze. Arrange fruit as desired over filling. Cover and refrigerate at least 1 hour before serving.

1 PIECE: 277 cal., 17g fat (10g sat. fat), 47mg chol., 145mg sod., 29g carb. (17g sugars, 2g fiber), 3g pro.

"I love this tart! I have made it several times using different fruits. It turns out equally good."
—AJN-OH, TASTEOFHOME.COM

LEMON-BLUEBERRY POUND CAKE

Pair a slice of this moist cake with a scoop of vanilla ice cream. It's a staple at our family barbecues.
—*Rebecca Little, Park Ridge, IL*

PREP: 25 MIN. • **BAKE:** 55 MIN. + COOLING • **MAKES:** 12 SERVINGS

⅓ **cup butter, softened**
4 **oz. cream cheese, softened**
2 **cups sugar**
3 **large eggs, room temperature**
1 **large egg white, room temperature**
1 **Tbsp. grated lemon zest**
2 **tsp. vanilla extract**
2 **cups fresh or frozen unsweetened blueberries**
3 **cups all-purpose flour, divided**
1 **tsp. baking powder**
½ **tsp. baking soda**
½ **tsp. salt**
1 **cup lemon yogurt**

GLAZE
1¼ **cups confectioners' sugar**
2 **Tbsp. lemon juice**

1. Preheat oven to 350°. Grease and flour a 10-in. fluted tube pan. In a large bowl, cream the butter, cream cheese and sugar until blended. Add eggs and egg white, 1 at a time, beating well after each addition. Beat in lemon zest and vanilla.

2. Toss blueberries with 2 Tbsp. flour. In another bowl, mix the remaining flour with baking powder, baking soda and salt; add to creamed mixture alternately with yogurt, beating after each addition just until combined. Fold in blueberry mixture.

3. Transfer batter to prepared pan. Bake 55-60 minutes or until a toothpick inserted in center comes out clean. Cool in pan for 10 minutes before removing to wire rack; cool completely.

4. In a small bowl, mix confectioners' sugar and lemon juice until smooth. Drizzle over cake.

NOTE: To remove cakes easily, use solid shortening to grease plain and fluted tube pans.

1 PIECE: 434 cal., 10g fat (6g sat. fat), 78mg chol., 281mg sod., 80g carb. (54g sugars, 1g fiber), 7g pro.

FROM GRANDMA'S KITCHEN: To prevent the blueberries from sinking in your lemon-blueberry pound cake (or other cakes!), toss the blueberries in a little flour before them adding into the batter.

WATERMELON CUPCAKES

My granddaughter and I bake together each week. She was inspired by all of her mommy's flavored syrups, so we came up with this watermelon cupcake. If you have watermelon syrup, it can replace some of the lemon-lime soda in the cake batter and frosting, but the gelatin adds a lot of watermelon flavor on its own. If you are not going to pipe the frosting, you can reduce the amount of frosting by half.
—Elizabeth Bramkamp, Gig Harbor, WA

PREP: 30 MIN. • BAKE: 20 MIN. + COOLING • MAKES: 2 DOZEN

1 pkg. white cake mix (regular size)
1 cup lemon-lime soda
3 large egg whites, room temperature
¼ cup canola oil
1 pkg. (3 oz.) watermelon gelatin
2 drops watermelon oil, optional

FROSTING
2 cups butter, softened
6 cups confectioners' sugar
1 pkg. (3 oz.) watermelon gelatin
5 to 6 Tbsp. lemon-lime soda
15 drops red food coloring
3 Tbsp. miniature semisweet chocolate chips

1. Preheat oven to 350°. Line 24 muffin cups with paper liners. In a large bowl, combine cake mix, soda, egg whites, canola oil, gelatin and, if desired, the watermelon oil; beat on low speed for 30 seconds. Beat on medium speed for 2 minutes. Transfer to prepared pans. Bake until a toothpick inserted in the center comes out clean, 18-21 minutes. Cool in pans 10 minutes before removing to wire racks to cool completely.

2. For frosting, in a large bowl, combine butter, confectioners' sugar, gelatin, soda and food coloring; beat until smooth. Frost cupcakes. Sprinkle with chocolate chips. Store in the refrigerator.

1 CUPCAKE: 385 cal., 19g fat (11g sat. fat), 41mg chol., 282mg sod., 54g carb. (46g sugars, 1g fiber), 2g pro.

FAVORITE PUMPKIN CAKE ROLL

Keep this cake roll in the freezer for a quick dessert for family or unexpected guests, to take to a gathering, or to give as a yummy gift.
—*Erica Berchtold, Freeport, IL*

PREP: 30 MIN. • **BAKE:** 15 MIN. + FREEZING • **MAKES:** 10 SERVINGS

3 **large eggs, separated, room temperature**
1 **cup sugar, divided**
⅔ **cup canned pumpkin**
¾ **cup all-purpose flour**
1 **tsp. baking soda**
½ **tsp. ground cinnamon**
⅛ **tsp. salt**

FILLING
8 **oz. cream cheese, softened**
2 **Tbsp. butter, softened**
1 **cup confectioners' sugar**
¾ **tsp. vanilla extract**
Additional confectioners' sugar, optional

1. Line a 15x10x1-in. baking pan with waxed paper; grease the paper and set aside. In a large bowl, beat the egg yolks on high speed until thick and lemon-colored. Gradually add ½ cup sugar and pumpkin, beating on high until sugar is almost dissolved.

2. In a small bowl, beat the egg whites until soft peaks form. Gradually add remaining ½ cup sugar, beating until stiff peaks form. Fold into egg yolk mixture. Combine the flour, baking soda, cinnamon and salt; gently fold into pumpkin mixture. Spread into prepared pan.

3. Bake at 375° until cake springs back when lightly touched, 12-15 minutes. Cool for 5 minutes. Turn cake onto a kitchen towel dusted with confectioners' sugar. Gently peel off waxed paper. Roll up cake in the towel jelly-roll style, starting with a short side. Cool completely on a wire rack.

4. In a small bowl, beat the cream cheese, butter, confectioners' sugar and vanilla until smooth. Unroll cake; spread filling evenly to within ½ in. of edges. Roll up again, without towel. Cover and freeze until firm. May be frozen for up to 3 months. Remove from the freezer 15 minutes before cutting. If desired, dust with the confectioners' sugar.

1 PIECE: 285 cal., 12g fat (7g sat. fat), 94mg chol., 261mg sod., 41g carb. (32g sugars, 1g fiber), 5g pro.

FROM GRANDMA'S KITCHEN: Cracks are the bane of all cake rolls, but they aren't inevitable! The most important thing you can do to prevent cracks is to roll the sponge cake while it's still hot out of the oven. The heat and moisture still in the cake will help keep the sponge intact. Another cause of cracks is if your cake is overbaked. Timing is key—since the cake layer is so thin, you have to remove it from the oven just as it's done.

GRANDMA ZAUNER'S DOBOSH TORTE

This rich torte is very special and makes an ideal dessert at the holidays.

—Kathy Wells, Brodhead, WI

PREP: 30 MIN. • BAKE: 15 MIN. + COOLING • MAKES: 16 SERVINGS

6 **large eggs, separated**
1 **cup sugar, divided**
2 **tsp. vanilla extract**
  Pinch salt
1 **cup cake flour**

FROSTING

1 **cup butter, softened**
2 **cups confectioners' sugar**
4 **oz. semisweet chocolate, melted**
3 **Tbsp. whole milk**
1 **tsp. vanilla extract**
1 **cup heavy whipping cream**
  Grated chocolate, optional

1. Let eggs stand at room temperature for 30 minutes. Line 2 greased 9-in. round baking pans with waxed paper and grease and flour the waxed paper; set aside.

2. In a large bowl, beat egg yolks for 2 minutes. Add ¾ cup sugar and beat for 3 minutes until mixture is thick and pale yellow and falls in a ribbon from beaters. Beat in vanilla.

3. In another large bowl, beat egg whites and salt on medium speed until soft peaks form. Gradually beat in remaining sugar, 1 Tbsp. at a time, on high until stiff peaks form. Fold flour into egg yolk a third at a time. Stir in a third of the whites. Fold in the remaining whites. Spread into prepared pans.

4. Bake at 350° for 15-18 minutes or until cake springs back when lightly touched. Cool for 10 minutes before removing from pan to wire racks to cool completely.

5. For frosting, in a large bowl, beat the butter, confectioners' sugar, chocolate, milk and vanilla until smooth. In a chilled small bowl, beat cream until stiff peaks form; fold into the chocolate mixture.

6. To assemble, split each cake into 2 horizontal layers. Spread 1 cup frosting on 1 layer. Repeat using all layers. Frost the top and side of cake with remaining frosting. Sprinkle with grated chocolate if desired. Store in the refrigerator.

1 PIECE: 330 cal., 19g fat (11g sat. fat), 131mg chol., 156mg sod., 36g carb. (28g sugars, 0 fiber), 4g pro.

TAPIOCA PUDDING,
PAGE 294

GRANDMA'S FAVORITE
DESSERTS

Nothing quite beats the blues like a bowl of cozy
bread pudding, a cup of rich creme brulee or
a cut of your grandma's famous cobbler!

BREAD PUDDING WITH
WHITE CHOCOLATE SAUCE

A delectable white chocolate sauce is the crowning touch on servings
of this comforting cinnamon bread pudding.
—*Kathy Rundle, Fond du Lac, WI*

PREP: 30 MIN. + STANDING • BAKE: 55 MIN. • MAKES: 12 SERVINGS (1½ CUPS SAUCE)

16 slices cinnamon bread,
     crusts removed, cubed
 1 cup dried cranberries
 ¾ cup white baking chips
 ¾ cup chopped pecans
 ¼ cup butter, melted
 6 large eggs, lightly beaten
 4 cups 2% milk
 ¾ cup plus 1 Tbsp.
     sugar, divided
 1 tsp. vanilla extract
 ¼ tsp. ground cinnamon
 ¼ tsp. ground allspice

SAUCE
 ⅔ cup heavy
     whipping cream
 2 Tbsp. butter
 8 oz. white baking
     chocolate, chopped

1. Preheat oven to 375°. In a greased 13x9-in. baking dish, layer half of the bread cubes, cranberries, baking chips and pecans. Repeat layers. Drizzle with butter.

2. In a large bowl, whisk the eggs, milk, ¾ cup sugar, vanilla, cinnamon and allspice until blended; pour over bread mixture. Let stand 15-30 minutes.

3. Sprinkle with remaining sugar. Bake, uncovered, until a knife inserted in the center comes out clean, 55-65 minutes. Cover loosely with foil during the last 15 minutes if the top browns too quickly.

4. In a small saucepan, bring cream and butter to a boil. Add chocolate and remove from the heat (do not stir). Let stand for 5 minutes; whisk until smooth. Serve with warm bread pudding.

1 PIECE: 495 cal., 29g fat (13g sat. fat), 153mg chol., 300mg sod., 54g carb. (31g sugars, 4g fiber), 12g pro.

FROM GRANDMA'S KITCHEN: Other stale bread or leftover bread you have on hand, such as brioche, French bread or challah, will work in this recipe too. You might, however, need to adjust the spices and add more cinnamon.

CLASSIC CREME BRULEE

My favorite dessert is creme brulee, so I quickly learned how to successfully make this on my own. Recently I was at a party where the guests finished off their own desserts by broiling the sugar on their portions with a small torch. What a clever idea!

—*Joylyn Trickel, Helendale, CA*

PREP: 30 MIN. • **BAKE:** 25 MIN. + CHILLING • **MAKES:** 8 SERVINGS

4   **cups heavy whipping cream**
9   **large egg yolks**

¾   **cup sugar**
1   **tsp. vanilla extract**
    Brown sugar

1. In a large saucepan, combine the cream, egg yolks and sugar. Cook and stir over medium heat until mixture reaches 160° or is thick enough to coat the back of a metal spoon. Stir in vanilla.

2. Transfer to eight 6-oz. ramekins or custard cups. Place cups in a baking pan; add 1 in. boiling water to pan. Bake, uncovered, at 325° until centers are just set (mixture will jiggle), 25-30 minutes. Remove ramekins from water bath; cool 10 minutes. Cover and refrigerate for at least 4 hours.

3. One hour before serving, place custards on a baking sheet. Sprinkle each with 1-2 tsp. brown sugar. Broil 8 in. from heat until sugar is caramelized, 4-7 minutes. Refrigerate leftovers.

1 SERVING: 551 cal., 50g fat (29g sat. fat), 402mg chol., 53mg sod., 22g carb. (22g sugars, 0 fiber), 6g pro.

FROM GRANDMA'S KITCHEN: Feel free to use a blowtorch instead. We suggest working slowly, as well as keeping the ramekins on a baking sheet to protect your countertops.

NUTTY COOKIES &
CREAM DESSERT

NUTTY COOKIES & CREAM DESSERT

Flavors of hot fudge, caramel, chocolate cookies and ice cream all combine in every mouthful of this fabulous frozen dessert. No matter how big the meal, folks will find room for this treat!
—*Cheryl Melerski, Harborcreek, PA*

PREP: 25 MIN. + FREEZING • MAKES: 15 SERVINGS

1 pkg. (14.3 oz.) Oreo cookies, crushed
½ cup butter, melted
½ gallon cookies and cream ice cream, softened
1½ cups salted peanuts, coarsely chopped
⅔ cup hot fudge ice cream topping
⅔ cup caramel ice cream topping
1 carton (8 oz.) frozen whipped topping, thawed

1. In a large bowl, combine cookie crumbs and butter; set aside 1 cup. Press remaining crumbs into an ungreased 13x9-in. dish. Spread with ice cream. Layer with peanuts, ice cream toppings and whipped topping; sprinkle with reserved crumbs. Cover and freeze until firm.

2. Remove from the freezer 15 minutes before serving.

1 PIECE: 559 cal., 31g fat (13g sat. fat), 43mg chol., 409mg sod., 66g carb. (34g sugars, 3g fiber), 8g pro.

CONTEST-WINNING STRAWBERRY PRETZEL DESSERT

I love the sweet-salty flavor of this pretty layered dessert. Sliced strawberries and gelatin top a smooth cream cheese filling and crispy pretzel crust. I think it's best when eaten within a day of being made.
—*Wendy Weaver, Leetonia, OH*

PREP: 15 MIN. + CHILLING • MAKES: 2 SERVINGS

⅓ cup crushed pretzels
2 Tbsp. butter, softened
2 oz. cream cheese, softened
¼ cup sugar
¾ cup whipped topping
2 Tbsp. plus 1½ tsp. strawberry gelatin
½ cup boiling water
1 cup sliced fresh strawberries
Optional: Whipped topping and pretzel twists

1. Preheat oven to 375°. In a large bowl, combine pretzels and butter. Press onto the bottom of 2 greased 10-oz. custard cups. Bake until set, 6-8 minutes. Cool on a wire rack.

2. In a small bowl, combine the cream cheese and sugar until smooth. Fold in whipped topping. Spoon over crust. Refrigerate for 30 minutes.

3. Meanwhile, in a small bowl, dissolve gelatin in boiling water. Cover and refrigerate for 20 minutes or until slightly thickened. Fold in strawberries. Carefully spoon over filling. Cover and refrigerate at least 3 hours. If desired, top with whipped topping and pretzel twists.

1 SERVING: 516 cal., 27g fat (18g sat. fat), 62mg chol., 458mg sod., 64g carb. (47g sugars, 2g fiber), 6g pro.

MAMA'S MILLION-DOLLAR FUDGE

My mother-in-law gave me her signature fudge recipe one Christmas, and I was hooked. No other version I've tried comes close to its rich, smooth chocolate taste.
—*Gloria Heidner, Elk River, MN*

PREP: 25 MIN. + COOLING • **MAKES:** ABOUT 5½ LBS.

4 tsp. plus ½ cup butter, divided
2 jars (7 oz. each) marshmallow creme
2 cups chopped walnuts
2 cups semisweet chocolate chips
12 oz. German sweet chocolate, chopped
1 can (12 oz.) evaporated milk
4½ cups sugar
Pinch salt

1. Line a 13x9-in. pan with foil and grease the foil with 4 tsp. butter; set aside.

2. In a large bowl, place the marshmallow creme, walnuts, chocolate chips and chopped sweet chocolate in the order listed; top with the remaining butter. Set aside.

3. In a heavy saucepan, combine milk, sugar and salt. Cook over low heat, stirring constantly, until mixture reaches 235° (soft-ball stage). Pour over the mixture in bowl and stir. Immediately spread into prepared pan. Cool completely.

4. Using foil, lift the fudge out of pan. Discard foil; cut fudge into 1-in. squares. Store in airtight containers.

1 PIECE: 167 cal., 7g fat (3g sat. fat), 7mg chol., 30mg sod., 26g carb. (24g sugars, 1g fiber), 2g pro.

OLD-FASHIONED RICE CUSTARD

I don't remember where or how I found this dessert. When I took it to a family reunion many years ago, however, a great-uncle was sure I'd used my great-grandmother's recipe! I like to have it warm after dinner. Then, the next morning, I'll enjoy the cold leftovers for my breakfast.
—*Shirley Leister, West Chester, PA*

PREP: 50 MIN. • **BAKE:** 50 MIN. • **MAKES:** 8 SERVINGS

½ cup uncooked long grain rice
4 cups 2% milk, divided
¼ cup butter, cubed
¾ cup sugar
3 large eggs
1 tsp. vanilla extract
¼ tsp. salt
½ tsp. ground nutmeg

1. In a large saucepan, bring the rice and 2 cups milk to a boil. Reduce the heat; cover and simmer for 15-18 minutes or until liquid is absorbed and rice is tender. Stir in butter. Cool slightly.

2. In a large bowl, beat the sugar, eggs, vanilla, salt and remaining milk; stir into the rice mixture.

3. Pour into a lightly greased 2-qt. baking dish; sprinkle with nutmeg. Bake at 350° for 50 minutes or until knife inserted in the center comes out clean. Refrigerate leftovers.

1 CUP: 256 cal., 10g fat (6g sat. fat), 95mg chol., 209mg sod., 34g carb. (25g sugars, 0 fiber), 7g pro.

GRANDMA'S CHRISTMAS BRITTLE

Whenever my grandmother was in the kitchen, everything
had to be just so to guarantee her time-tested results.
Watching her make this brittle is one of my favorite memories,
and I'm glad I can pass on this delicious recipe.
—*Karen Grenzow, Sumas, WA*

PREP: 15 MIN. • **COOK:** 15 MIN. + COOLING • **MAKES:** ABOUT 2½ LBS.

3 **cups sugar**
½ **cup light corn syrup**
1 **cup water**
¼ **cup butter, cubed**
1 **tsp. salt**

1 **jar (16 oz.) unsalted
dry roasted peanuts**
1½ **tsp. baking soda**
1 **tsp. water**
1 **tsp. vanilla extract**

1. Grease 2 baking sheets and keep warm in a 200° oven.
In a large saucepan, combine sugar, corn syrup and 1 cup
water. Cook over medium heat, stirring constantly, until a
candy thermometer reaches 240° (soft-ball stage). Stir in
butter, salt and peanuts. Continue heating, stirring constantly,
until mixture reaches 300°. Remove saucepan from heat.

2. Combine the baking soda, 1 tsp. water and vanilla. Stir baking
soda mixture into the saucepan. Quickly pour half the mixture
over each baking sheet. Spread with a buttered metal spatula to
a ¼-in. thickness. Cool completely. Break into pieces. Store in an
airtight container.

NOTE: We recommend that you test your candy thermometer
before each use by bringing water to a boil; the thermometer
should read 212°. Adjust your recipe temperature up or down
based on your test.

1 OZ.: 292 cal., 14g fat (3g sat. fat), 6mg chol., 247mg sod., 41g carb.
(34g sugars, 2g fiber), 5g pro.

FROM GRANDMA'S KITCHEN: If you want to replace the corn syrup,
use golden syrup since it has identical properties and will work just
as well. Other sweeteners might not work because they crystallize,
so double-check before making any swaps.

RHUBARB DUMPLINGS

When I served these delectable dumplings at a family gathering, I got lots of compliments.
The melt-in-your-mouth goodies are perfect for parties!
—*Elsie Shell, Topeka, IN*

PREP: 25 MIN. • BAKE: 35 MIN. • MAKES: 12 SERVINGS

SAUCE
- 1½ **cups sugar**
- 1 **Tbsp. all-purpose flour**
- ½ **tsp. ground cinnamon**
- ¼ **tsp. salt**
- 1½ **cups water**
- ⅓ **cup butter**
- 1 **tsp. vanilla extract**
  Red food coloring, optional

DOUGH
- 2 **cups all-purpose flour**
- 2 **Tbsp. sugar**
- 2 **tsp. baking powder**
- ¼ **tsp. salt**
- 2½ **Tbsp. cold butter**
- ¾ **cup 2% milk**

FILLING
- 2 **Tbsp. butter, softened**
- 2 **cups finely chopped fresh or frozen rhubarb**
- ½ **cup sugar**
- ½ **tsp. ground cinnamon**

1. In a saucepan, combine sugar, flour, cinnamon and salt. Stir in water; add butter. Bring to a boil; cook and stir 1 minute. Remove from heat. Add vanilla and, if desired, enough food coloring to tint sauce a deep pink. Set aside.

2. For dough, in a medium bowl, combine flour, sugar, baking powder and salt. Cut in butter until mixture resembles coarse crumbs. Add milk and mix quickly. (Do not overmix.) Gather the dough into a ball and roll out on a floured surface into a 12x9-in. rectangle.

3. Spread with softened butter; arrange rhubarb on top. Combine sugar and cinnamon; sprinkle over rhubarb. Roll up from a long side and place on a cutting board, seam side down. Cut roll into 12 slices. Arrange slices cut side up in a greased 13x9-in. baking dish. Pour the sauce over. Bake at 350° for 35-40 minutes or until golden brown.

1 PIECE: 312 cal., 10g fat (6g sat. fat), 27mg chol., 269mg sod., 54g carb. (36g sugars, 1g fiber), 3g pro.

"We absolutely love this recipe. I have been making it every year since it first appeared in Taste of Home *back in 1993. I cut the recipe out and used it every time, but it's getting tattered so now I'm printing off a new copy. It's such a family favorite."*
—GRAMMIEGREAT, TASTEOFHOME.COM

CHEESECAKE CROWNS

These elegant dessert pastries are so easy to make, but no one will believe it!
I've served the fruit-filled crowns at brunch as well as after dinner.
—*Brenda Westra, Kalamazoo, MI*

PREP: 30 MIN. • BAKE: 20 MIN. + CHILLING • MAKES: 1 DOZEN

3 **sheets frozen puff pastry, thawed**
½ **cup all-purpose flour**
½ **cup finely chopped pecans**
¼ **cup packed brown sugar**
½ **tsp. ground cinnamon**
¼ **cup cold butter**
3 **pkg. (8 oz. each) cream cheese, softened**
1 **cup sugar**
3 **large eggs, room temperature, lightly beaten**
6 **tsp. vanilla extract**
¼ **cup confectioners' sugar**
1½ **to 2 tsp. water**
　 Optional: Fresh berries and apricot jam

1. Preheat oven to 400°. Unfold pastry; cut each into 4 squares. Gently press squares into greased jumbo muffin cups, pulling corners up and out of cups; press corners down onto muffin pan.

2. In a small bowl, combine the flour, pecans, brown sugar and cinnamon. Cut in butter until crumbly. Sprinkle about 1 Tbsp. into each muffin cup. In a large bowl, beat cream cheese and sugar until smooth. Beat in eggs on low speed just until combined. Stir in vanilla. Spoon into pastry cups.

3. Bake until filling is almost set and pastry is golden brown, 20-25 minutes. Cool completely on wire racks. Refrigerate, uncovered, for 1 hour or until set.

4. For glaze, in a small bowl, combine confectioners' sugar and enough water to achieve a drizzling consistency. If desired, toss berries with apricot jam to coat; place on top of pastries. Drizzle with glaze. Refrigerate leftovers.

1 PASTRY: 699 cal., 44g fat (18g sat. fat), 114mg chol., 431mg sod., 66g carb. (26g sugars, 5g fiber), 11g pro.

GRANDMA BUELAH'S APPLE DUMPLINGS

Grandma had a reputation for being a talented musician, an avid card player and a marvelous cook!
I always make a double batch of her dumplings for my husband and our four children.
—*Jenny Hughson, Mitchell, NE*

PREP: 15 MIN. • BAKE: 45 MIN. • MAKES: 6 SERVINGS

2 **sheets refrigerated pie crust**
6 **small tart apples, peeled and cored**
⅓ **cup sugar**
2 **Tbsp. half-and-half cream**
¾ **cup maple or maple-flavored syrup, warmed**

1. Unroll the crusts and roll together to one 18x12-in. rectangle. Cut into six 6-in. squares. Place an apple on each crust square. Combine sugar and cream and spoon into apple center. Moisten edges of crust; fold up the corners to center and pinch to seal.

2. Place in an ungreased 13x9-in. baking pan. Bake at 450° for 15 minutes. Reduce the heat to 350° and bake 30 minutes longer or until golden brown, basting twice with syrup. Serve warm.

1 SERVING: 537 cal., 20g fat (8g sat. fat), 16mg chol., 273mg sod., 89g carb. (53g sugars, 2g fiber), 3g pro.

CHEESECAKE CROWNS

GRANDMA'S SECRET

If you don't want to top these treats off with fresh berries, you can also serve them with mini chocolate chips, caramel sauce or crushed candy, depending on your tastes.

DESSERTS

TRADITIONAL POPCORN BALLS

Having an old-fashioned popcorn ball will make you feel like a kid again. You'll find that one batch of this goes a long way.
—*Cathy Karges, Hazen, ND*

TAKES: 20 MIN. • **MAKES:** 20 SERVINGS

7 qt. popped popcorn	¼ tsp. salt
1 cup sugar	3 Tbsp. butter
1 cup light corn syrup	1 tsp. vanilla extract
¼ cup water	Food coloring, optional

1. Place popcorn in a large baking pan; keep warm in a 200° oven.

2. In a heavy saucepan, combine the sugar, corn syrup, water and salt. Cook over medium heat until a candy thermometer reads 235° (soft-ball stage).

3. Remove from the heat. Add butter, vanilla and, if desired, food coloring; stir until butter is melted. Immediately pour over popcorn and stir until evenly coated.

4. When the mixture is cool enough to handle, quickly shape into 3-in. balls, dipping hands in cold water to prevent sticking.

1 POPCORN BALL: 177 cal., 6g fat (2g sat. fat), 5mg chol., 203mg sod., 31g carb. (18g sugars, 2g fiber), 1g pro.

FROM GRANDMA'S KITCHEN: Try adding any of your favorite candies, like M&M's minis or chopped Snickers, before forming the popcorn mixture into balls. Mix in crushed Oreo cookies and drizzle with white chocolate for a cookies and cream version, or make a salty-sweet combo by adding chopped salted peanuts. You can even decorate the popcorn balls to resemble festive objects like ornament popcorn balls or popcorn jack-o'-lanterns.

CONTEST-WINNING BUTTER PECAN ICE CREAM

This rich, buttery ice cream sure beats store-bought versions. And with its pretty color and plentiful pecan crunch, it's nice enough to serve guests at a summer party.
—Jenny White, Glen, MS

PREP: 45 MIN. + CHILLING • PROCESS: 20 MIN. + FREEZING • MAKES: 1 QT.

- ½ cup chopped pecans
- 1 Tbsp. butter
- 1½ cups half-and-half cream
- ¾ cup packed brown sugar
- 2 large eggs, lightly beaten
- ½ cup heavy whipping cream
- 1 tsp. vanilla extract

1. In a small skillet, toast pecans in butter for 5-6 minutes or until lightly browned. Cool.

2. In a heavy saucepan, heat half-and-half to 175°; stir in the brown sugar until dissolved. Whisk a small amount of hot cream mixture into the eggs; return all to the pan, whisking constantly. Cook and stir over low heat until mixture reaches at least 160° and coats the back of a metal spoon.

3. Remove from the heat. Cool quickly by placing pan in a bowl of ice water; stir for 2 minutes. Stir in whipping cream and vanilla. Press plastic wrap onto the surface of custard. Refrigerate for several hours or overnight. Stir in toasted pecans.

4. Fill the cylinder of ice cream freezer; freeze according to the manufacturer's directions. Allow to ripen in ice cream freezer or firm up in the refrigerator freezer for 2-4 hours before serving.

½ CUP: 269 cal., 17g fat (8g sat. fat), 90mg chol., 62mg sod., 23g carb. (22g sugars, 1g fiber), 4g pro.

BANANA PUDDING PARFAIT

When served in a pretty glass bowl, the results of this beautifully layered creamy concoction make for a fancy yet fuss-free dessert.
—Edna Perry, Rice, TX

PREP: 15 MIN. + CHILLING • MAKES: 12 SERVINGS

- 1 pkg. (8 oz.) cream cheese, softened
- 1 can (14 oz.) sweetened condensed milk
- 1 cup cold 2% milk
- 1 pkg. (3.4 oz.) instant vanilla pudding mix
- 1 carton (8 oz.) frozen whipped topping, thawed
- 52 vanilla wafers
- 4 medium firm bananas, sliced

In a large bowl, beat cream cheese until smooth. Beat in condensed milk; set aside. In another bowl, whisk milk and pudding mix; add to cream cheese mixture. Fold in whipped topping. Place a third of the vanilla wafers in a 2½-qt. glass bowl. Top with a third of the bananas and pudding mixture. Repeat layers twice. Cover and refrigerate at least 4 hours or overnight. If desired, garnish with additional whipped topping, bananas and wafers.

¾ CUP: 376 cal., 16g fat (10g sat. fat), 35mg chol., 225mg sod., 52g carb. (41g sugars, 1g fiber), 5g pro.

PINEAPPLE-STRAWBERRY-KIWI PAVLOVA

My sister learned to prepare this dessert from her Australian mother-in-law and then taught my mother. To avoid a sticky pavlova, make sure all the sugar is dissolved when you beat it into the egg whites.
—*Kathy Spang, Manheim, PA*

PREP: 25 MIN. • BAKE: 45 MIN. + COOLING • MAKES: 8 SERVINGS

4 **large egg whites**
1 **tsp. vanilla extract**
1 **tsp. white vinegar**
1 **cup sugar**
1 **carton (8 oz.) frozen whipped topping, thawed**
2 **cups sliced fresh strawberries**
2 **cups cubed fresh pineapple**
2 **medium kiwifruit, peeled and sliced**

1. Place egg whites in a large bowl; let stand at room temperature for 30 minutes.

2. Beat the egg whites, vanilla and vinegar on medium speed until soft peaks form. Gradually beat in sugar, 1 Tbsp. at a time, on high until stiff peaks form and sugar is dissolved.

3. Spoon meringue onto a parchment-lined baking sheet. Using the back of a spoon, shape into a 9-in. circle.

4. Bake at 225° for 45-55 minutes or until set and dry. Turn oven off and do not open door. Let meringue dry in oven for 1 hour.

5. Just before serving, top meringue with whipped topping and fruit. Refrigerate leftovers.

1 PIECE: 229 cal., 5g fat (5g sat. fat), 0 chol., 29mg sod., 42g carb. (36g sugars, 2g fiber), 3g pro.

ICE CREAM SANDWICH CAKE

It takes 10 minutes tops to prepare this cool treat, but it tastes as though you spent a lot of time creating it.
—*Cathie Valentine, Graniteville, SC*

PREP: 10 MIN. + FREEZING • MAKES: 18 SERVINGS

10½ **ice cream sandwiches**
1 **jar (12 oz.) caramel ice cream topping**
1 **carton (12 oz.) frozen whipped topping, thawed**
¼ **cup chocolate syrup**
2 **Symphony candy bars with almonds and toffee (4¼ oz. each), chopped Maraschino cherries, optional**

Arrange 9 ice cream sandwiches in a single layer in an ungreased 13x9-in. dish. Cut the remaining sandwiches to fill in the spaces in the dish. Spread with caramel and whipped toppings. Drizzle with chocolate syrup. Sprinkle with the chopped candy bar. Cover and freeze for at least 45 minutes before serving. If desired, garnish with cherries.

1 PIECE: 254 cal., 11g fat (7g sat. fat), 13mg chol., 105mg sod., 36g carb. (17g sugars, 1g fiber), 3g pro.

ROASTED GRAPE & SWEET CHEESE PHYLLO GALETTE

Faced with an abundant crop of grapes, I had to come up with a creative way to use them. It's fun to work with phyllo dough, and it bakes up golden and flaky. In this recipe, a layer of orange-kissed cream cheese is topped with roasted grapes. Then a bit of honey is drizzled on, and a sprinkle of coarse sugar is added to finish it off. You can use berries for this too.
—*Kallee Krong-McCreery, Escondido, CA*

PREP: 25 MIN. • BAKE: 35 MIN. + COOLING • MAKES: 10 SERVINGS

- 1 **pkg. (8 oz.) cream cheese, softened**
- 2 **Tbsp. orange marmalade**
- 1 **tsp. sugar**
- 8 **sheets phyllo dough (14x9-in. size)**
- 4 **Tbsp. butter, melted**
- 1 **cup seedless grapes**
- 1 **Tbsp. honey**
- 2 **tsp. coarse sugar**

1. Preheat oven to 350°. In a large bowl, beat cream cheese, marmalade and sugar until smooth. Set aside.

2. Place 1 sheet of phyllo on a parchment-lined baking sheet; brush with butter. Layer with remaining phyllo sheets, brushing each layer. (Keep remaining phyllo covered with a damp towel to prevent it from drying out.) Spread cream cheese mixture over phyllo to within 2 in. of edges. Arrange grapes over cream cheese.

3. Fold edges of phyllo over filling, leaving the center uncovered. Brush folded phyllo with any remaining butter; drizzle with honey and sprinkle with coarse sugar. Bake for 35-40 minutes or until phyllo is golden brown. Transfer to a wire rack to cool completely. Refrigerate leftovers.

1 PIECE: 177 cal., 13g fat (8g sat. fat), 35mg chol., 148mg sod., 15g carb. (9g sugars, 0 fiber), 2g pro.

EASY
TRUFFLES

EASY TRUFFLES

You may be tempted to save this recipe for a special occasion since these smooth, creamy chocolates are divine. But with just a few ingredients, they're easy to make anytime.
—Taste of Home *Test Kitchen*

PREP: 25 MIN. + CHILLING • COOK: 5 MIN. • MAKES: ABOUT 6 DOZEN

3 **cups semisweet chocolate chips**
1 **can (14 oz.) sweetened condensed milk**
1 **Tbsp. vanilla extract**
   Toasted, finely chopped nuts or assorted jimmies

1. Place the chocolate chips and milk in a microwave-safe bowl; microwave on high for 3 minutes, stirring halfway through. Stir in vanilla. Refrigerate, covered, until firm enough to shape, about 3 hours.

2. Shape into 1-in. balls; roll in nuts or jimmies. Place in a 15x10x1-in. pan; refrigerate until firm, about 1 hour.

1 TRUFFLE: 52 cal., 3g fat (2g sat. fat), 2mg chol., 8mg sod., 7g carb. (7g sugars, 0 fiber), 1g pro.

CREAM PUFF DESSERT

Instead of making individual cream puffs, make this rich dessert with a cream puff base and sweet toppings.
—Lisa Nash, Blaine, MN

PREP: 20 MIN. + CHILLING • BAKE: 30 MIN. + COOLING • MAKES: 12 SERVINGS

1 **cup water**
½ **cup butter**
1 **cup all-purpose flour**
4 **large eggs, room temperature**

FILLING
1 **pkg. (8 oz.) cream cheese, softened**
3½ **cups cold 2% milk**
2 **pkg. (3.9 oz. each) instant chocolate pudding mix**

TOPPING
1 **carton (8 oz.) frozen whipped topping, thawed**
¼ **cup chocolate ice cream topping**
¼ **cup caramel ice cream topping**
⅓ **cup chopped almonds**

1. In a large saucepan, bring the water and butter to a boil over medium heat. Add flour all at once; stir until a smooth ball forms. Remove from the heat; let stand for 5 minutes. Add the eggs, 1 at a time, beating well after each addition. Continue beating until mixture is smooth and shiny.

2. Spread into a greased 13x9-in. baking dish. Bake at 400° for 30-35 minutes or until puffed and golden brown. Remove to a wire rack to cool completely.

3. For filling, beat the cream cheese, milk and pudding mix in a large bowl until smooth. Spread over puff; refrigerate for 20 minutes.

4. Spread with whipped topping; refrigerate until serving. Drizzle with the chocolate and caramel toppings; sprinkle with almonds. Refrigerate leftovers.

1 PIECE: 381 cal., 23g fat (14g sat. fat), 122mg chol., 354mg sod., 34g carb. (20g sugars, 1g fiber), 8g pro.

RAINBOW SHERBET DESSERT

Macaroons, pecans and layers of fruity sherbet combine in this beautiful, special dessert.
Try garnishing with fresh strawberries and just listen to folks ooh and aah when you bring it in!
—*Kathryn Dunn, Axton, VA*

PREP: 30 MIN. + FREEZING • **MAKES:** 12 SERVINGS

12 **macaroon cookies, crumbled**
2 **cups heavy whipping cream**
3 **Tbsp. confectioners' sugar**
1 **tsp. vanilla extract**
¾ **cup chopped pecans, toasted**
1 **pint each raspberry, lime and orange sherbet, softened**

1. Preheat oven to 350°. Sprinkle cookie crumbs onto an ungreased baking sheet. Bake 5-8 minutes or until golden brown. Cool completely.

2. In a large bowl, beat cream until it begins to thicken. Add confectioners' sugar and vanilla; beat until stiff peaks form. Combine cookie crumbs and pecans; fold in whipped cream. Spread half of cream mixture onto the bottom of an ungreased 9-in. springform pan. Freeze 30 minutes.

3. Gently spread the raspberry sherbet over cream layer; freeze until set, about 30 minutes. Repeat with the lime and orange sherbet. Spread with the remaining cream mixture. Cover and freeze until firm. Remove from the freezer 10 minutes before serving. Remove side of pan.

1 PIECE: 387 cal., 26g fat (13g sat. fat), 54mg chol., 38mg sod., 37g carb. (30g sugars, 4g fiber), 3g pro.

FROM GRANDMA'S KITCHEN: Allow plenty of time to assemble this dessert, as the key to clean layers is letting each layer chill and harden thoroughly before adding the next layer. We suggest 30 minutes per layer in the freezer, but you could go even longer if you wish. Use an offset spatula to gently spread the sherbet evenly, and clean off the spatula after each layer.

OLD-FASHIONED HARD CANDY

A dusting of confectioners' sugar gives a frosty look to this old-fashioned holiday candy. The color is beautiful, and people are surprised by the wonderful watermelon flavor.
—*Amy Short, Milton, WV*

PREP: 10 MIN. • COOK: 30 MIN. + COOLING • MAKES: 2 LBS.

3¾ cups sugar
1½ cups light corn syrup
1 cup water
2 to 3 drops red food coloring or color of your choice
¼ tsp. watermelon flavoring or flavoring of your choice
½ cup confectioners' sugar

1. Butter two 15x10x1-in. pans. Set aside. In a large heavy saucepan, combine the sugar, corn syrup, water and food coloring. Cook and stir over medium heat until the sugar is dissolved. Bring to a boil. Cook, without stirring, until a candy thermometer reads 300° (hard-crack stage).

2. Remove from the heat; stir in flavoring. Immediately pour into prepared pans. Cool completely. Dust with confectioners' sugar; break into pieces. Store in airtight containers.

NOTE: We recommend that you test your candy thermometer before each use by bringing water to a boil; the thermometer should read 212°. Adjust your recipe temperature up or down based on your test.

1 OZ.: 146 cal., 0 fat (0 sat. fat), 0 chol., 11mg sod., 38g carb. (38g sugars, 0 fiber), 0 pro.

PEANUT BUTTER MILKSHAKES

You've got milk, peanut butter and probably vanilla ice cream, too. Using just a few ingredients, you can whip up this peanut butter milkshake recipe in seconds.
—*Joyce Turley, Slaughters, KY*

TAKES: 5 MIN. • MAKES: 3 SERVINGS

1 cup whole milk
2 cups vanilla ice cream
½ cup peanut butter
2 Tbsp. sugar

In a blender, combine all ingredients; cover and process for 30 seconds or until smooth. Stir if necessary. Pour into chilled glasses. Serve immediately.

1 CUP: 519 cal., 34g fat (12g sat. fat), 47mg chol., 287mg sod., 43g carb. (35g sugars, 3g fiber), 15g pro.

STRAWBERRY BLISS

STRAWBERRY BLISS

You'll love this homemade puff pastry crust topped with a soft-set pudding layer that has a hint of strawberry flavor. This dessert needs to chill for at least an hour, so it's a fabulous make-ahead dish.
—*Candace Richter, Stevens Point, WI*

PREP: 30 MIN. • **BAKE:** 20 MIN. + CHILLING • **MAKES:** 12 SERVINGS

1 **cup water**
½ **cup butter, cubed**
1 **cup all-purpose flour**
4 **large eggs, room temperature**
1 **pkg. (8 oz.) cream cheese, softened**
½ **cup sugar**
5 **Tbsp. seedless strawberry jam**
3 **cups cold whole milk**
1 **pkg. (5.1 oz.) instant vanilla pudding mix**
½ **cup heavy whipping cream**
3 **cups quartered fresh strawberries**

1. Preheat oven to 400°. In a large saucepan, bring the water and butter to a rolling boil. Add flour all at once and beat until blended. Cook over medium heat, stirring vigorously until the mixture pulls away from sides of pan and forms a ball. Remove from the heat; let stand 5 minutes.

2. Add eggs, 1 at a time, beating well after each addition. Continue beating until mixture is smooth and shiny.

3. Spread into a greased 15x10x1-in. baking pan. Bake for 20-25 minutes or until puffed and golden brown (surface will be uneven). Cool completely in pan on a wire rack.

4. In a large bowl, beat the cream cheese, sugar and jam until smooth. Beat in milk and pudding mix until smooth. In a small bowl, beat the cream until stiff peaks form; fold into pudding mixture. Spread over crust. Refrigerate at least 1 hour.

5. Just before serving, top with strawberries.

1 PIECE: 377 cal., 22g fat (13g sat. fat), 131mg chol., 332mg sod., 40g carb. (27g sugars, 1g fiber), 7g pro.

SOFT & CHEWY CARAMELS

I made these caramels with my children, and now I enjoy making them with our eight grandchildren too.
—*Darlene Edinger, Turtle Lake, ND*

PREP: 5 MIN. • **COOK:** 30 MIN. + COOLING • **MAKES:** 2 LBS. (108 PIECES)

2 **tsp. plus 1 cup butter, divided**
2 **cups sugar**
1 **cup light corn syrup**
2 **cups half-and-half cream, divided**
1 **tsp. vanilla extract**

1. Line a 13x9-in. pan with foil; grease foil with 2 tsp. butter. Cube remaining butter. In a Dutch oven, combine sugar, corn syrup and 1 cup cream. Bring to a boil over medium heat, stirring constantly. Slowly stir in the remaining cream. Cook over medium heat until a candy thermometer reads 250° (hard-ball stage), stirring mixture frequently. Remove from the heat; stir in cubed butter and vanilla until well mixed, about 5 minutes.

2. Pour into prepared pan. Cool completely. Remove foil from pan; cut the candy into 1-in. squares. Wrap individually in waxed paper; twist ends.

1 PIECE: 45 cal., 2g fat (1g sat. fat), 7mg chol., 18mg sod., 6g carb. (6g sugars, 0 fiber), 0 pro.

CHOCOLATE ECLAIRS

With creamy filling and thick, decadent frosting, these eclairs are extra special.
Now you can indulge in classic bakery treats without leaving the house!
—*Jessica Campbell, Viola, WI*

PREP: 45 MIN. • BAKE: 35 MIN. + COOLING • MAKES: 9 SERVINGS

1 cup water
½ cup butter, cubed
¼ tsp. salt
1 cup all-purpose flour
4 large eggs, room
temperature

FILLING
2½ cups cold 2% milk
1 pkg. (5.1 oz.) instant
vanilla pudding mix
1 cup heavy whipping
cream
¼ cup confectioners' sugar
1 tsp. vanilla extract

FROSTING
2 oz. semisweet chocolate
2 Tbsp. butter
1¼ cups confectioners' sugar
2 to 3 Tbsp. hot water

1. Preheat oven to 400°. In a large saucepan, bring water, butter and salt to a boil. Add the flour all at once and stir until a smooth ball forms. Remove from the heat; let stand 5 minutes. Add eggs, 1 at a time, beating well after each addition. Continue beating until mixture is smooth and shiny.

2. Using a tablespoon or a pastry tube with a #10 or large round tip, form the dough into nine 4x1½-in. strips on a greased baking sheet. Bake 35-40 minutes or until puffed and golden. Place on a wire rack. Immediately split eclairs open; remove tops and set aside. Discard soft dough from inside. Cool eclairs.

3. In a large bowl, beat milk and pudding mix according to package directions. In another bowl, whip cream until soft peaks form. Beat in the confectioners' sugar and vanilla; fold into pudding. Fill eclairs (chill any remaining filling for another use). Replace tops.

4. For frosting, in a microwave, melt the chocolate and butter; stir until smooth. Stir in the confectioners' sugar and enough hot water to achieve a smooth consistency. Cool slightly. Frost eclairs. Store in refrigerator.

1 ECLAIR: 483 cal., 28g fat (17g sat. fat), 174mg chol., 492mg sod., 52g carb. (37g sugars, 1g fiber), 7g pro.

FROM GRANDMA'S KITCHEN: The common cause for eclair collapse is too much moisture in the batter. After adding the flour to the butter, water and salt mixture in the pot, heat and stir vigorously for several minutes until the mixture forms a firm, dry ball and there is an even, thin coating of batter on the inside of the pan. Don't rush this—it's almost better for the dough to overcook than undercook. Let the dough rest in the pot for a full 5 minutes before adding the eggs. Additionally, while the choux pastries are baking, resist the temptation to open the door of the oven. Opening the door allows necessary steam from the puffed shells to escape.

TAPIOCA PUDDING

The best thing about this creamy, old-fashioned pudding is that it's made the night before. That's a real plus when cooking for a crowd.
—*Bernice Hartje, Cavalier, ND*

PREP: 10 MIN. + CHILLING • COOK: 5 MIN. • MAKES: 60 SERVINGS

- 4 pkg. (3 oz. each) tapioca pudding mix
- 8 cups whole milk
- 1 carton (16 oz.) frozen whipped topping, thawed
- 2 cans (15¾ oz. each) lemon pie filling
- 4 cans (15 oz. each) fruit cocktail, drained
- 4 cans (15 oz. each) mandarin oranges, drained
- 1 can (20 oz.) crushed pineapple, drained
- 1 pkg. (10½ oz.) pastel or plain miniature marshmallows

In a Dutch oven, cook the pudding and milk according to package directions. Transfer to a large bowl and refrigerate until chilled. In another bowl, fold whipped topping into pie filling. Gently stir in the remaining ingredients. Fold in pudding. Refrigerate overnight.

½ CUP: 142 cal., 3g fat (2g sat. fat), 3mg chol., 71mg sod., 29g carb. (24g sugars, 1g fiber), 1g pro.

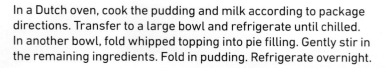

CIRCUS PEANUT GELATIN

Circus peanuts are one of the most popular candies in my hometown's old-fashioned candy shop. When I saw this circus peanut gelatin recipe, I knew just where to buy them. Kids love the cool, fruity taste, and older folks enjoy the trip down memory lane.
—*Ruthanne Mengel, DeMotte, IN*

PREP: 10 MIN. + CHILLING • MAKES: 15 SERVINGS

- 47 circus peanut candies, divided
- 1 cup boiling water, divided
- 2 pkg. (3 oz. each) orange gelatin
- 2 cans (8 oz. each) crushed pineapple, undrained
- 1 carton (8 oz.) frozen whipped topping, thawed

1. Cut 32 candies into small pieces; place in a microwave-safe bowl. Add ¼ cup boiling water. Cover and microwave on high for 45 seconds. Stir. Microwave 45 seconds longer. Stir until smooth. In a large bowl, dissolve gelatin in remaining boiling water. Stir in candy mixture and pineapple. Refrigerate until partially set.

2. Fold in whipped topping. Pour into a greased 13x9-in. dish. Refrigerate until firm. Cut into 15 squares; top each square with a remaining circus peanut.

1 PIECE: 186 cal., 3g fat (3g sat. fat), 0 chol., 26mg sod., 39g carb. (38g sugars, 0 fiber), 1g pro.

FRUITY BROWNIE PIZZA

I start with a basic brownie mix to create this luscious treat that's sure to impress company. Sometimes I add mandarin oranges for even more color.
—*Nancy Johnson, Laverne, OK*

PREP: 20 MIN. + CHILLING • BAKE: 15 MIN. + COOLING • MAKES: 12 SERVINGS

1 pkg. fudge brownie mix (8-in. square pan size)
1 pkg. (8 oz.) cream cheese, softened
⅓ cup sugar
¾ cup pineapple tidbits with juice
1 small firm banana, sliced
1 medium kiwifruit, peeled and sliced
1 cup sliced fresh strawberries
¼ cup chopped pecans
1 oz. semisweet chocolate
1 Tbsp. butter

1. Preheat oven to 375°. Prepare brownie batter according to package directions. Spread onto a greased 12-in. pizza pan. Bake until a toothpick inserted in the center comes out clean, 15-20 minutes. Cool completely.

2. In a large bowl, beat cream cheese and sugar until smooth. Spread over brownie crust. Drain pineapple, reserving juice. Toss banana slices with juice; drain well. Arrange banana, kiwi, strawberries and pineapple over the cream cheese layer; sprinkle with pecans.

3. In a small microwave, melt chocolate and butter; stir until smooth. Drizzle over fruit. Cover and refrigerate for 1 hour.

1 PIECE: 366 cal., 21g fat (7g sat. fat), 38mg chol., 220mg sod., 44g carb. (30g sugars, 2g fiber), 4g pro.

LEMON & LIME STRAWBERRY ICE

My icy fruit dessert is perfect for summer. It's so refreshing after dinner.
—*Marie Rizzio, Interlochen, MI*

PREP: 30 MIN. + FREEZING • MAKES: 6 SERVINGS

1 cup sugar
¾ cup water
1 Tbsp. shredded orange zest
2 tsp. shredded lemon zest
1½ tsp. shredded lime zest
⅓ cup orange juice
3 Tbsp. lemon juice
2 Tbsp. lime juice
4 cups sliced fresh strawberries

1. In a small saucepan, combine the first 5 ingredients. Bring to a boil. Reduce the heat; simmer, uncovered, 5-6 minutes or until slightly thickened. Strain; discard zest. Add juices to the syrup; cool slightly.

2. Place half of the juice mixture and 2 cups strawberries in a blender; cover and pulse until nearly smooth. Pour into a 2-qt. freezer container. Repeat with the remaining juice mixture and berries.

3. Cover and freeze 12 hours or overnight, stirring several times. Ice may be frozen for up to 3 months. Just before serving, break apart with a large spoon.

⅔ CUP: 173 cal., 0 fat (0 sat. fat), 0 chol., 2mg sod., 44g carb. (39g sugars, 3g fiber), 1g pro.

LEMON-LIME BERRY ICE: Reduce strawberries to 2 cups and add 2 cups fresh raspberries.

BAKLAVA

Baklava is a traditional Middle Eastern pastry made with flaky phyllo dough, chopped nuts and sweet honey. This dessert is very rich, so one pan goes a long way!
—*Judy Losecco, Buffalo, NY*

PREP: 30 MIN. • **BAKE:** 40 MIN. • **MAKES:** 4 DOZEN

1½ **lbs. finely chopped walnuts**
½ **cup sugar**
½ **tsp. ground cinnamon**
⅛ **tsp. ground cloves**
1 **lb. butter, melted, divided**
2 **pkg. (16 oz. each, 14x9-in. sheet size) frozen phyllo dough, thawed**

SYRUP
2 **cups sugar**
2 **cups water**
1 **cup honey**
1 **Tbsp. grated lemon or orange zest**

1. In a small bowl, combine the walnuts, sugar, cinnamon and cloves; set aside. Brush a 15x10x1-in. baking pan with some of the butter. Unroll 1 pkg. phyllo dough; cut stack into a 10½x9-in. rectangle. Repeat with remaining phyllo. Discard scraps.

2. Line bottom of prepared pan with 2 sheets of phyllo dough (sheets will overlap slightly). Brush with butter. Repeat layers 14 times. (Keep dough covered with a damp towel until ready to use to prevent sheets from drying out.)

3. Spread with 2 cups walnut mixture. Top with 5 layers of phyllo dough, brushing with butter between each sheet. Spread with the remaining walnut mixture. Top with 1 layer of phyllo dough; brush with butter. Repeat 14 times. Cut into 2½-in. squares; cut each square in half diagonally. Brush the remaining butter over top. Bake at 350° for 40-45 minutes or until golden brown.

4. In a large saucepan, bring syrup ingredients to a boil. Reduce the heat; simmer for 10 minutes. Strain syrup, discarding zest; cool to lukewarm. Pour syrup over warm baklava.

1 BAKLAVA TRIANGLE: 271 cal., 16g fat (5g sat. fat), 21mg chol., 162mg sod., 30g carb. (17g sugars, 1g fiber), 5g pro.

CHOCOLATE BAKLAVA: For the nut mixture, combine 1 lb. finely chopped walnuts, 1 pkg. (12 oz.) miniature semisweet chocolate chips, ¾ cup sugar, 1½ tsp. ground cinnamon and 1 tsp. grated lemon zest. Layer and bake as directed. For syrup, use 1 cup plus 2 Tbsp. orange juice, ¾ cup each sugar, water and honey, and 3 Tbsp. lemon juice. Bring to a boil. Reduce heat; simmer, uncovered, for 20 minutes. Pour over warm baklava. Cool completely on a wire rack.

"I've never written a review for anything, but this was so good that I had to review it. This is by far the best baklava I've ever had. I've been asked to take this many places! Make it exactly as written and you won't be disappointed."
—RODMELIS, TASTEOFHOME.COM

AUTUMN APPLE TORTE

When it's apple season, I always look forward to making this
yummy torte with a cream cheese layer and apples galore.
—*Margaret Wilson, San Bernardino, CA*

PREP: 40 MIN. • **BAKE:** 35 MIN. + COOLING • **MAKES:** 12 SERVINGS

½   **cup butter, softened**
½   **cup sugar, divided**
½   **tsp. vanilla extract**
1   **cup all-purpose flour**
1   **pkg. (8 oz.) cream cheese, softened**
1   **large egg, lightly beaten**
½   **tsp. almond extract**
2   **cups thinly sliced, peeled Granny Smith apples (about 2 medium)**
2   **cups thinly sliced, peeled Cortland apples (about 2 medium)**
¼   **cup cinnamon sugar**
¼   **tsp. ground nutmeg**
½   **cup confectioners' sugar**
2   **Tbsp. 2% milk**
2   **Tbsp. sliced almonds, toasted**

1. Preheat oven to 450°. In a small bowl, cream the butter and ¼ cup sugar until light and fluffy, 5-7 minutes. Beat in vanilla. Gradually beat in flour. Press onto bottom and 1 in. up the side of a greased 9-in. springform pan.

2. In a small bowl, beat the cream cheese and remaining sugar until smooth. Add egg and almond extract; beat on low speed just until blended. Pour into crust.

3. Place apples in a large bowl. Mix cinnamon sugar and nutmeg; add to apples and toss to coat. Arrange over the cream cheese mixture. Bake 5 minutes.

4. Reduce oven setting to 400°. Bake until apples are tender, 30-35 minutes longer. Cool on a wire rack.

5. Remove rim from pan. In a small bowl, mix confectioners' sugar and milk until smooth. Drizzle over torte; sprinkle with almonds. Refrigerate leftovers.

1 PIECE: 270 cal., 15g fat (9g sat. fat), 57mg chol., 136mg sod., 31g carb. (22g sugars, 1g fiber), 3g pro.

GRANDMA'S SECRET

To toast almonds, place them in a dry skillet. Then, cook over low heat until lightly browned, making sure to stir the nuts occasionally.

IVA'S PEACH COBBLER

My mother received this recipe from a friend of hers many years ago, and fortunately she shared it with me. Boise is situated right between two large fruit-producing areas in our state, so peaches are plentiful in the summer.

—Ruby Ewart, Boise, ID

PREP: 15 MIN. • BAKE: 45 MIN. • MAKES: 12 SERVINGS

6 to 8 large ripe peaches, peeled and sliced
2½ Tbsp. cornstarch
¾ to 1 cup sugar

CRUST
1 cup all-purpose flour
1 cup sugar
1 tsp. baking powder

2 large egg yolks, room temperature
¼ cup butter, melted
2 large egg whites, room temperature, stiffly beaten
Vanilla ice cream, optional

Preheat oven to 375°. Combine peaches, cornstarch and sugar; place in a greased 13x9-in. baking dish. For the crust, in a bowl, whisk together flour, sugar and baking powder. Stir in egg yolks and butter. Gently fold in egg whites. Spread over peaches. Bake until fruit is bubbling around edges and the top is golden, about 45 minutes. If desired, serve with ice cream.

½ CUP: 224 cal., 5g fat (3g sat. fat), 46mg chol., 83mg sod., 44g carb. (33g sugars, 1g fiber), 3g pro.

FROM GRANDMA'S KITCHEN: If you're looking to save some time, you don't have to peel the peaches when making peach cobbler. The skins will soften up during baking and also give your cobbler filling a rosy hue.

RECIPE INDEX

NEW

Need home ideas? We've got you covered!

SCAN AND WATCH FREE NOW

Hands-on inspiration for making your house a home, streaming 24/7.